WHERE "SOMETHING CATCHES"

SUNY Series, Identities in the Classroom
Deborah P. Britzman and Janet L. Miller, Editors

WHERE
"SOMETHING CATCHES"

Work, Love, and Identity in Youth

VICTORIA I. MUÑOZ

STATE UNIVERSITY
OF NEW YORK
PRESS

Published by
State University of New York Press, Albany

Production by Susan Geraghty
Marketing by Theresa Abad Swierzowski

Printed in the United States of America

For information, address State University of New York Press,
State University Plaza, Albany, N.Y., 12246

Library of Congress Cataloging-in-Publication Data

Muñoz, Victoria I., 1958–
    Where "something catches" : work, love, and identity in youth /
Victoria I. Muñoz.
        p.   cm.—(SUNY series, identities in the classroom)
    Includes bibliographical references and index.
    ISBN 0–7914–2685–8 (acid-free paper). — ISBN 0–7914–2686–6 (pbk.
: acid-free paper)
    1. Identity (Psychology) in youth—Puerto Rico. 2. Identity
(Psychology) in youth—Puerto Rico—Case studies. 3. Stigma (Social
psychology) 4. Group identity. I. Title. II. Series.
BF724.3.I3M76   1995
155.5'097295—dc20   94-44800
                                                                CIP

10 9 8 7 6 5 4 3 2 1

A Robin, Daniel, y Nicolás
y a la memoria de
Abuela y Abuelo, Mamá, y Julio
con amor

CONTENTS

FOREWORD

I met Victoria Muñoz about eighteen years ago, when she herself was as young as the youths she is giving voice to here in the pages of this book. I remember the day I met her: she was sitting quietly, carefully studying the tapestry patterns of an arm chair, while trying to make sense of life and to contain the passion and commitment that are also expressed here. I remember her incisiveness and ability to critique and analyze reality even back there and then, together with the doubts and confusions that are almost integral to being barely twenty years old. I remember her later, while already a student at Harvard, full of self-determination and giving shape to her passion and commitment to make her work and life an expression of the *opera manum dei* she describes for us in this book. Through the years, I have seen Victoria bloom and develop, her initial shyness disappearing as she found her voice and her work.

That is why I see many layers to this book. It is an inquiry into and a testimonial to the transformation of young people through meaningful work and the love and trust of adults. It is an exploration into the development of identity in the shadow of adversity and questioning. It is also a testimonial to the transformation of one youth into an adult, creative, professional woman, capable of giving voice to others while giving voice to herself. It is an expression of passion and commitment to find meaning in life for self and others. It is the expression of who Victoria has become and where her passion and commitment are taking her. Indeed, work, love, and identity seem to have crystallized in Victoria's life. The meaningful exploration presented in this book we now have in our hands, shows that when "something catches" many different strands are woven together and things fall into place almost unnoticed. This is true for the young people given voice in this book while they are in the process of creating their own life tapestry. It is also true of Victoria herself: a crystallization of her own professional maturity and the purposefulness of her work.

This book is also a tribute to the youth of Puerto Rico, to Victoria's Puerto Rican heritage, and to the adolescent waiting for "something to catch" she once was. Witnessing the transformations in Victoria's life, that she so aptly describes in the introductory pages, helps me imagine the transformations that can be anticipated in the lives of the youths described in this book.

At a time when we are flooded by media messages that tell us that money spent on children and youths of color is wasted money, this book provides testimony to what the dreams of young people could become if given the nurturance, trust, and love they need. It should be self-evident, although regretfully it does not seem to be so for many in positions of leadership, that energy and money invested in youth and children is money invested in our own future. This book gives validity to that awareness and enjoins us to foster the development of youths. It does that, not only because of the young people it describes, but because its existence is a testimony to what youths can do. This book is in a way a proof of the validity of her own study: the fact that Victoria Muñoz is authoring this book today is a demonstration of what the transformation of young people's passion and commitment can accomplish, when they find love for their work, and "something catches."

The content of this book embodies an act of resistance against the devaluing of young people of color. The process of this research also embodies an act of resistance against established practices. Victoria Muñoz's use of stories and photography in the design and execution of this study resists routinized approaches to research. The use of "standard measures" that do not really measure anything of significance and do not listen to what people are really saying about themselves and their lives has hindered many an investigation into human life and development. Luckily, widespread questioning of the value of this empty research is increasing. But to engage in this approach to study human lives still constitutes an act of resistance in the academy. This book is another demonstration of the value of "non-standard" research tools for bringing us closer to people's lives.

The project described in this book is also a vivid demonstration of the value of talking and listening as a liberatory educational practice. I am willing to bet that the youths who participated in this study are a little bit closer to their dreams and goals: Victoria's listening to them has, no doubt, provided them with another bit of adult understanding and encouragement. Her attentive listening to them and their dreams has, no doubt, given them the message that they are worth listening to, that their dreams can become worthwhile realities.

I am touched and honored to have been asked to write the foreword for this book. Writing it, I also become more aware of my role in and commitment to liberatory practice and education. In the measure in which I helped "something catch" for Victoria, years ago, I feel that this book is an expression of my own participation in carrying out *opera manum dei*. For how else can we transform the world except by showing to each generation our love, passion, and commitment to our own work as we live our daily lives? How else will they be able to do their own part in the work of collective liberation but by feeling heard and cherished by those who are walking before them?

Oliva M. Espín
California, 1995

Oliva M. Espín, Ph.D., is Professor in the Department of Women's Studies at San Diego State University, San Diego, California.

ACKNOWLEDGMENTS

This work is a labor of love that has been nourished and guided by many caring and inspiring people. I would like to gratefully thank:

The young men and women who openly shared their lives with me so that I might learn something of use. The directors of programs and agencies who gave me access to the sites and welcomed me warmly.

The three members of my dissertation committee, who each shared their genius. Carol Gilligan has been my advisor and guide through the complexities of voice, psychological theory, and gender: always returning to questions of voice, urging me to return to mine. Sara Lawrence-Lightfoot enabled me to focus carefully on the research questions and through her creativity and vision provided a methodology for writing about the answers. Mel King has known me and my family since I was eighteen; I looked to him for continuity through all the transformations—personal and political—and he was there.

Julio Quirós, friend over the course of the last twenty-five years. During the data collection phase he and I drove together to all the sites. On the way, we would talk about the history, flora, and fauna of that region of the island and on the way back the young people we had met. Julio knew Puerto Rico like the back of his hand, and everywhere we went he knew people. I always felt well accompanied in this journey.

Jack Delano for all he has taught me about photography. Jack's photographs—shot in collaboration with his wife Irene—documenting the struggles and joys of Puertorriqueños in the 1940s and through the decades are a source of inspiration and pride.

María del Carmen Arteta, who would relentlessly call me to ask "¿Como va la tésis?" and help me refocus on the work when I would get to dreaming of planting perennials instead of transcribing.

Deborah Britzman, who has supported my academic yearnings since the days before I had words to express that I had them. Her complex understanding of how education works inspires and challenges me to think further on what I thought was already settled.

I would also like to thank Lorraine Grosslight, Jean Grossholtz, Alberto Sandoval, Mary Ni, Jacki Ramos, Lydia Rackenberg, Laurie Loisel, Sarah Hanson, Andrés Blanco, Ana María García Blanco, Maruca García Padilla, Maruja García Padilla, Nitza Hidalgo, Erick Perez, and Ileana Quintero for their *amistad*; Mildred Martínez for her excellent help transcribing the interviews; Christine Pratt and her Dark Horse Photographics studio in Florence, Massachusetts, for all the time and care she took printing each photograph of the youths; and Eleanor E. Cook for her thorough and precise work.

For all their love and support over the years I want to thank *toda la familia* and especially my grandparents, Luis Muñoz Marín and Inés Maria Mendoza; my mother, Viviana Muñoz Mendoza; my sisters, Teresa, Natalia, and Ana Gabriela; my brother, Andrés; my aunt, Victoria; and my cousins, Belén and Tata, Rebecca and Willie.

Finally, I want to thank Robin Feldman. I am grateful for her loving and patient heart and for her thoughtful reading of and comments on this work.

PANEL 1

Background/Trasfondo

THE WAY THINGS WORK

is by admitting
or opening away.
This is the simplest form
of current: Blue
moving through blue;
blue through purple;
the objects of desire
opening upon themselves
without us;
the objects of faith.
The way things work
is by solution,
resistance lessened or
increased and taken
advantage of.
The way things work
is that we finally believe
they are there,
common and able
to illustrate themselves.
Wheel, kinetic flow,
rising and falling water,
ingots, levers and keys,
I believe in you,
cylinder lock, pully,
lifting tackle and
Crane lift your small head—
I believe in you—
your head is the horizon to
my hand. I believe
forever in the hooks.
The way things work
is that eventually
something catches.

CHAPTER 1

The Catch

Jorie Graham in her poem "The Way Things Work" presents a picture of the mechanics of machines, electrical current that gives movement to parts that open and close, and brings in a belief that things can work: that things *do* work. "The way things work," she writes, "is that eventually something catches." But what catches? And who catches it? How? In what ways?

Graham's image of working is mechanical at first, but underneath that shiny metal surface, attached to that lever, and providing tension in that pully is this line: "I believe in you," repeated several times in various forms. "I believe forever in the hooks," Graham writes, grasping for what she works to catch. For her this may be the struggle to work a poem into its finest form, to catch or be caught by the workings of a poem wanting to take shape, wanting to be admitted or opened. The mechanics of how things work yields to what is not concrete or metal or electrical: "the objects of desire" and "the objects of faith."

For Graham, the way things work is both mechanical and emotional: a relationship between the outer social world and the inner psychological world. For machines can't work without the hand that moves them, and the hand that makes that movement start to go is connected to a heart. The heart believes that the hand can make things work. The believing is the hand's faith and desire. "Your head is the horizon to my hand"; the machine extends the hand to reach as far as eyes can see. The way things work is that eventually something catches the eye and the heart, and the hand reaches to make things work, eventually finding that which makes the heart work best: the objects of desire and faith, love and work.

This is, in poem form, the same concept as Martin Luther's *opera manum dei* (the hands that do the work of God) and what Erik Erikson (1962) calls "that particular combination of work and love which alone verifies our identity and confirms it" (p. 217). A particular combination, the joining of two creative forces

3

that enables us to understand who we are: a human need that is deeply felt especially during adolescence and young adulthood.

To know more about the process of *opera manum dei* or "that particular combination," I asked the following questions: What is the relationship between *opera manum dei* and identity? How are love and work understood and experienced by youth? How are love and work a part of identity development during youth?

These questions led me to interview fifty-six youths in Puerto Rico who were either studying to work at something they felt strongly about, who found work they love, or who left school and fell through the cracks of the system and are trying to find work. Each person tells a story through our conversation in the interview, and each gives a picture of "that particular combination" and how they were "caught."

THE SHAPE OF CONTEXT

These stories in turn led me to question the usefulness of Eurocentric or Anglo interpretations for understanding the journey of identity development for youths in Puerto Rico as well as for youths of color here in the United States. The narratives pushed me to look beyond existing conceptual frameworks in psychology and to attempt to construct a new one out of voices that sound much more like the youths, and like my own. Let me describe the view from here.

Psychology, as a field practiced at the intersection of (white) race, (masculine) gender, (middle) class, and (hetero) sexual privilege, has been slow to grasp human development under oppression and to expose the power relations of institutionalized racism, heterosexism, and classism and their effects on our psychologies in ways that do not blame individuals for lack of food, shelter, health, and schooling. It has been slow to stop the violence of reductive categories which often give rise to guilt and shame: high self-esteem, low self-esteem, no self-esteem; good boundaries, bad boundaries; defensive, pathological, resistant; and on and on. As a field, psychology has supported and propagated an enormous amount of labels in an attempt to explain and predict narrow ranges of individual development with little regard for the social and political context within which psychological life—of the researcher and the studied—occurs. Psychological theory has too often been used as a kind of border patrol (*con todo lo que eso conlleva*) limiting access.[1]

The work of feminist psychologists has over the last twenty years focused on radically transforming understandings of development in relation to gender, sexuality, and race. Still, the field is mined with normative and normalizing labels. For example, pointing to the pull of this normalizing tendency and the potential for "wounding" that psychological labels have supported, Carter Heyward (1993) courageously exposes—through poetry and prose—the trauma she experienced in therapy with a psychiatrist, who was, importantly to Heyward, also a lesbian. The most critical parts of her narrative, for me, are those in which Heyward comes to the knowledge that it is not enough that a healer (she includes psychiatrists, educators, counselors, psychologists, social workers, and professors) be a woman, or a lesbian, or, I would argue further, a person of color. Heyward's journey could not more clearly illustrate how the analytical categories of gender and sexuality, although shared and openly discussed, do not guarantee "right-relationship," friendship, or what Heyward most seeks out because to her it is where God is found: "mutual relation." Her passage of misconnection with a woman with whom she clearly felt that she shared commonalities was fraught with labels and professional roles meant to keep power relations intact and thus theoretically lead to healing, but which ironically and painfully actually broke their relationship apart.

Heyward's experiences, whether one agrees with her interpretations or not, raise critical questions: What constitutes understanding between people who share similarities such as gender, race, and sexuality but who hold different positions of power? What kind of common ground is needed to grasp the meanings of another person's life story, yearnings, and dreams? These questions are central for teachers, psychologists, and researchers interested in understanding youths in ways that refuse subordination.

The hierarchies of professionalism which maintain power are difficult to transform because they give status, grant tenure, rationalize who gets funding, keep fear manageable, keep chaos in order, and give a false sense of safety to individuals, but this, too, often, is at the expense of the majority being kept at risk and at the margins. Gender, race, class, or sexuality as representative "traits" or social categories of imagined, yearned for, or real communities are not in and of themselves enough to forge conceptual or political alliances, and do not guarantee getting rid of reductive categories which violate the complexities and ambiguities of identity. For those *al margen de la vida* this needs to change. What, then, would it mean to name the chaos and the continuity of development in liberating ways? It is at this question and the beginnings of an answer where I want to situate my psychological and educational work.

In this study I draw on several theoretical and methodological strategies. Formulating, integrating, re-searching, and forging a useful analytical framework has occupied most of my time over the last years, and the process is still ongoing; I think of this framework as a coalition of diverse concepts working together for the common good. The approaches included here are the best way I know how to stand in solidarity with the people I love. I want to interrupt as much as I can the many cycles of betrayal that we— and by "we" I mean the youths who shared their stories with me, the women whose poetry I include here, the people whose stories I include here, everyone contained between these pages, and everyone connected to the people in these pages—have endured. And through this I explore *opera manum dei*.

In the following chapters I've attempted to keep the writing accessible and alive. I've been struggling to speak in my own voice while always aware that I was writing in English and not in Spanish. But some words resist translation because to move them from Spanish into English would render the cultural meaning silent. The reader, therefore, will find (has already found) central concepts in the original Spanish throughout the book. Gloria Anzaldúa (1987) writes of this multiplicity of voice: "Ethnic identity is twin skin to linguistic identity—I am my language . . . I will no longer be made to feel ashamed of existing. I will have my voice: Indian, Spanish, white. I will have my serpent's tongue—my woman's voice, my sexual voice, my poet's voice. I will overcome the tradition of silence" (p. 59). Anzaldúa's writings are both narratives and theorizations of the multilayered process of voice and identity for women of color, a process that in itself is the focus of a developing body of thinking and writing which I only briefly point to here but will return to later in the book. Anzaldúa (1990) continues:

> To speak English is to think in that language, to adopt the ideology of the people whose language it is and not to be "inhab-

ited" by their discourses. *Mujeres-de-color* speak and write not just against traditional white ways and texts but against a prevailing mode of being, against a white frame of reference. Those of us who are bilingual, or use working-class English and English in dialects, are under constant pressure to speak and write in standard English . . . Untied, our tongues run away from themselves. (pp. xxii–xxiii)

Toni Morrison (1992), in a series of lectures given at Harvard University and now collected in *Playing in the Dark,* goes to the heart of what standard English comprises. Through a critique of European American writers such as Willa Cather, Poe, Hawthorne, and Melville, Morrison stakes out a literary relationship buried in metaphor, analogy, and symbolism in these texts: the dialectical relationship between freedom and slavery as seen through "the literary imagination." Morrison finds in the language through which the New World's vision of freedom was attained the taking away of freedom: the European man felt "free" in the New World because he now had the power to enslave, something he lacked in the Old World, where he was most likely oppressed. Morrison finds evidence for this in the language, through the use of symbols that contain what she calls an "Africanist presence." Joining this literary tradition, for Morrison, has been a process that requires constant vigilance and critique, a continuing struggle to wrench English words out of an unyielding racist grasp. She writes:

> The principal reason these matters loom large for me is that I do not have quite the same access to the traditionally useful constructs of blackness. Neither blackness nor "people of color" stimulates in me notions of excessive, limitless love, anarchy, or routine dread. I cannot rely on these metaphorical shortcuts because I am a black writer struggling with and through a language that can powerfully evoke and enforce hidden signs of racial superiority, cultural hegemony, and dismissive "othering" of people and language which are by no means marginal or already and completely known and knowable in my work. My vulnerability would lie in romanticizing blackness rather than demonizing it; vilifying whiteness rather than reifying it. The kind of work I have always wanted to do requires me to learn how to maneuver ways to free up the language from its sometimes sinister, frequently lazy, almost always predictable employment of racially informed and determined chains. (pp. x–xi)

Anzaldúa and Morrison both begin their book of essays by stating that free language, writing, and voice are almost impossibly difficult for women of color in this racist society. And yet, they write. And as they write they redefine language by reconstructing metaphors, images, stereotypes, and romantic ideals. The writing of both women has cut a wide path through the thicket of standard English that I try to follow.

Writing, for me, has been a constant struggle for words to express cross-cultural ideas and emotions. I feel what Lorna Dee Cervantes (1981), a Chicana poet, describes throughout her work in *Emplumada* and which is illustrated sharply, as if she wants to cut, in "Visions of Mexico While at a Writing Symposium in Port Townsend":

> there are songs in my head I could sing you
> songs that could drone away
> all the Mariachi bands you thought you ever heard
> songs that could tell you what I know
> or have learned from my people
> but for that   I need words
> simple black nymphs between white sheets of paper
> obedient words   obligatory words   words I steal
> in the dark when no one can hear me
>
> as pain sends seabirds south from the cold
> I come north
> to gather my feathers
> for quills[2]

And like Ben Shahn's (1980) reflections on the process of painting in *The Shape of Content*, writing comes out of the tensions between what is and what can be, what is known and what I want to know. Out of this a content has taken form:

> Form is formulation—the turning of content into a material entity, rendering a content accessible to others, giving it permanence, willing it to the race. Form is as varied as are the accidental meetings of nature. Form in art is as varied as idea itself.
>
> It is the visible shape in all [human] growth; it is the living picture of [a] tribe at its most primitive, and of [a] civilization at its most sophisticated state. Form is the many faces of the legend—bardic, epic, sculptural, musical, pictorial, architectural; it

is the infinite images of religion; it is the expression and the remnant of self. Form is the very shape of content. (p. 53)

A critical part of giving the content a form has been a steady process of trying to articulate multilayered questions and then listen to and analyze interrelated answers, while questioning my assumptions and beliefs. Another important process in forming the content has been the inclusion of poetry—the language of the psyche, association, and symbols—as a connection between experience and psychological theory.

The poets included here confront economic violence, social injustice, hatred, marginalization, and difference, and live identity as a fragmented journey full of ambiguities, contradictions, and struggle, but also full of desire, beauty, and pleasure. These poets give me an antireductive view by opening the big questions and refusing easy answers. This has guided my hand in writing and thinking in new ways about the stories told to me by young Latinas and Latinos. Audre Lorde (1984) in her revolutionary essay *Poetry Is Not a Luxury* has for many years provided a *trasfondo* for this approach. Lorde writes:

> The quality of light by which we scrutinize our lives has direct bearing upon the product which we live, and upon the changes which we hope to bring about through those lives. It is within this light that we form those ideas by which we pursue our magic and make it realized. This is poetry as illumination, for it is through poetry that we give name to those ideas which are— until the poem—nameless and formless, about to be birthed, but already felt. That distillation of experience from which true poetry springs births thought as dream births concept, as feeling births idea, as knowledge births (precedes) understanding . . . I speak here of poetry as a revelatory distillation of experience, not the sterile word play that, too often, the white fathers distorted the word *poetry* to mean—in order to cover a desperate wish for imagination without insight. For women, then, poetry is not a luxury. It is a vital necessity of our existence . . . Poetry is not only dream and vision; it is the skeleton architecture of our lives. It lays the foundations for a future of change, a bridge across our fears of what has never been before. (pp. 36–38)

Maxine Greene (1988), in *The Dialectic of Freedom*, argues for the importance of the arts, and specifically of poetry, in education, democracy, and freedom. She writes how poetry can disrupt and transform what is taken for granted. By making experience defamiliarized . . . critical awareness may be somehow enhanced, as new possibilities open for reflection. Poetry does not offer us empirical or documentary truth, but it enables us to "know" in unique ways. So many poems come to mind, among them W. H. Auden's "Surgical Ward," which may emerge from memory because of the AIDS epidemic, or because of a concern about distancing and lack of care . . . Any one of a hundred others might come to mind: the choice is arbitrary. A writer, like the writer of this book, can only hope to activate the memories of *her* readers, to awaken, to strike sparks. (pp. 131–132)

Like Greene, Adrienne Rich (1993), in *What Is Found There*, writes about the uses of poetry in relation to freedom, democracy, and political life in U.S. society today. Rich sees the openings into the psyche that poetry allows through its drawing forth of emotion in symbols, associations, and memory. Writing from the field of experience, Rich echoes first Lorde and then Greene:

Poetry wrenches around our ideas about our lives as it grows alongside other kinds of human endeavor. But it also recalls us to ourselves—to memory, association, forgotten or forbidden languages. Poetry will not fly across the sea, against storms, to any "new world," any "promised land," and then fold its wings and sing. Poetry is not a resting on the given, but a questing toward what might otherwise be. (p. 234)

In another meditation (she has called this book a collection of meditations) Rich returns to poetry as a bridge between emotion and action, a place where we are called forth to change because what we desire is identified.

A revolutionary poem will not tell you who or when to kill, what and when to burn, or even how to theorize. It reminds you (for you have always known, somehow, all along, maybe lost track) where and when and how you are living and might live—-it is a wick of desire. It may do its work in the language and images of dreams, lists, love letters, prison letters, chants, filmic jump cuts, meditations, cries of pain, documentary fragments, blues, late-night long-distance calls. It is not programmatic: it searches for words amid the jamming of unfree, free-market idiom, for images that will burn true outside the emotional theme parks. A revolutionary poem is written out of one individual's confrontation with her/his own longings (including all that s/he is expected to deny) in the belief that its readers or hearers (in that old, unending sense of *the people*) deserve an art as complex, and open to contradiction as themselves. (p. 241)

In these ways the lines of poems and whole poems that appear throughout this text are not decorations, filling, or additions but are alternative interpretations of the experiences voiced in the narratives. These poems are another way of listening to the youths; like photography, they offer another approach to knowledge, they enable us to cross boundaries, and they bring me closer to understanding the complexities and contradictions of our lives.

There is no easy access route, no direct way, to understand and then explain another's story psychologically. To understand another means to understand oneself in relation to that other: What is mine? What is hers? What is his? Who are "we"? How else do you know that you're not telling your own story through another's mouth? To really listen to another's story has meant to resist labels that foreclose further understanding.

Answers lead to more questions; the story unravels and then recoils. I connect with Leslie Marmon Silko's (1992) reasoning behind why she writes, "I don't know what I know until it comes out in narrative" (p. 10). And once something is written and known, more questions can be raised.

In these ways, what you are about to read is exploratory and open to the world; it is unfinished because the lives of the youths are ongoing, because life is ongoing, and because any study of identity, love, and work in human development is by definition a study of dialectics of change. Unlike onion cells in the biology lab that high school students "fix" and dye, there is no way I can hold the psyche in place: not mine and not theirs. Still, the stories of the youths give clues about psychological development through work and love. My hope is that this work may point to ways of improving education.

OUTLINE OF THE BOOK

The image of a triptych emerged for me while trying to "see" the structure of what I was writing. Each panel, or section, provides a distinct view of the research and is hinged to the other parts. The three panels tell the story from three different views: together they tell a whole story framed by this time.

Panel 1, "Background/*Trasfondo,*" comprises chapter 1, "The Catch," and chapter 2, "Returning to a Question." In chapter 2, I provide a personal history of the development of my interest in exploring further the process of *opera manum dei* and expose the struggle for work that I love. In doing so, I bring my own narrative into dialogue with the narratives of the youths. I attempt to say with my own words what my process has been rather than "use" the stories of the youths to tell my story, or say what I want to say.

Although I'm not comfortable with how revealing this chapter is, I include it because it is not enough to narrowly state that I am a Puertorriqueña from a "broken home" raised by a "single mother," grandparents, and a rarely present "stepfather," also known as "a dysfunctional family." This does not describe my joys, hopes, dilemmas, tensions, and conflicts, or describe those of the youths I spoke with, many of whom happen to share the life conditions encoded by these labels. And so I also include my story as a way of exploring the space beyond and resisting the stereotypes that psychological and educational labels too often nourish.

Panel 2, "That Particular Combination," is the center piece which connects the other two. In chapter 3, "Conceptual Strategies," I begin by reviewing Erik Erikson's ideas on identity, work, and love during youth. I then bring in stories of people who provide insights into the process of *opera manum dei* and raise questions about work and love. Through these stories I gather up a working definition of work and love and the relationships between them and identity. I further explore the concept of "that particular combination" from various conceptual standpoints and discuss theoretical and methodological strategies brought to bear on this study.

Chapter 4, "Methods," is a description and discussion of the methodology employed for data collection and analysis of the narratives.

In chapter 5, "The Youths," I give a brief overview of Puerto Rican history and present-day struggles to situate the study. Then drawing from photographs, observations, notes, and site documents I sketch a portrait of the fifty-six youths I interviewed at six sites, located in diverse regions of Puerto Rico: at the Right to Work Administration, where youths hope to enter three- to six-month job training programs; at the Volunteer Corps of Puerto Rico (in Guanica and Aguadilla), where youths live, study, work, and engage in a special kind of therapy over one to two years; at the Project for Community Education, where youths who were born and raised in the community of Punta Santiago have organized to improve their lives; at the Jesuit Seminary, where youths begin their ten-year journey to become ordained as Jesuit priests; and at the Conservatory of Music, where youths study from two to four years to become professional musicians.

In *Panel 3*, "Profiles of Work and Love," I use the exploratory conceptual and methodological strategies previously laid out to analyze and discuss the *fronteras* of work, love, and identity. Some of the names of the youths profiled are real but others have been changed.

Chapter 6 is titled "Becoming *Hombres* and *Mujeres*: Work, Love, and Constructions of Gender." In this chapter the relationships between masculinity and femininity and choice of work by young people who are poor are profiled.

Chapter 7, "Getting Out of Trouble or Getting What You Want: Work as Independence and Survival for Young *Mujeres*," discusses how work is critical to young women to move out of situations of trauma.

Chapter 8, "Since I Was Three: From Childhood Genius to Adult Work," profiles how young people make the transition from childhood talent to adult work.

Chapter 9, "From Illness and Suicide to the Work of Art," considers how not doing the work that one loves can lead to serious consequences.

Chapter 10, "In Uniform: *Seguridad* as Symbol and Work," discusses the symbolic connection between a uniformed future and psychological security.

Chapter 11, "Peace, Justice, Development: The Complex Workings of Social Change," is the final chapter of emergent themes. This chapter brings together the narratives of youths who are working in what they love.

Chapter 12, "Working Together: Plotting the Coordinates of Work, Love, and Identity," explores meeting places at the *fronteras* or borderlands as a way of conceptualizing identity development and supporting the educative work of nourishing "that particular combination."

CHAPTER 2

Returning to a Question

My interest in work and love began when I was a kid, although I didn't use these words. I just knew I felt good doing things I cared about. When I was a kid I called it having fun or playing—in and out of school. Then during adolescence, playing was no longer a part of the curriculum; instead I was, as were all my friends, required to "grow up." I had some questions: how to grow up without losing the joy and freedom of play; how to translate, transport, and transform child's play into adult work.[1] This was difficult to resolve in high school, where adulthood was described by teachers in ways that seemed to me more like a punishment for having "grown up" than as a welcome goal.

Work was a "career." Love was "marriage." But I didn't dream of marriage and a career. These didn't appeal to me; no, it was more than that—I felt that they were completely irrelevant. To supplement the blandness of the textbook that introduced us to *Psychology Today*, I read feminist manifestos, and wrote to addresses in New York City hoping to receive some "underground" information about life in the margins of what I knew to be the impossible neatness of textbooks. At sixteen, I was aware that my sexuality was lesbian and that this was a messy process. I could tell from the reactions of those around me that my work was going to be, of necessity and out of the desire to form authentic relationships, about liberation. In the last fifteen years I have tried to align work and love in a variety of ways.

In 1985, I became interested in what this process is like for other young people while teaching biology at Lawrence High School. I saw curious faces trying to find and then draw onion cells that they saw through a microscope but distracted or blank looks at testing time. I wrote passes to the bathroom for a pregnant girl who barely fit in the desks made for young people who aren't supposed to grow in that direction. Some of the boys called Rae a dyke, and me a "fucking bitch." Detention never solved this problem. Joe would sit in the front row shining, wanting to know everything about biology until his mother moved them back to Puerto Rico: too cold in winter. Ramon's mother came in to thank me in Spanish; at last she could talk with a science teacher. Robyn would show up when she wanted to. Rita gave me a gold necklace to keep for her because she thought some boys who knew she had it were planning to mug her. Another biology teacher was in tears one day saying she had given everything and still he came in stoned to take the test. She took Valium to calm down.

I was flooded by my memories of "growing up" and confronted by the realization that I was now the teacher, the adult. And I wondered: What were they writing away for? What were they dreaming of? What work did they enjoy? What was it like inside putting all these things together? I was interested in knowing whether they had work they cared about doing and whether school provided a space for this work to be nourished.

I took this with me when I left Lawrence and entered the Harvard Graduate School of Education. The chance to investigate my questions arose in the course "Adolescent Development" taught by Carol Gilligan and while reading Erik Erikson's *Young Man Luther*. There I stumbled upon three words, *opera manum dei*, and Erikson's psychological interpretation of "the hands that do the work of God." I was caught by this. I saw that my process as a youth and then later as a teacher of youths was not just a private and personal one, but a more general developmental one. The process of "that particular combination of work and love which alone verifies our identity and confirms it" felt deeply connected with schooling and "growing up."

I spoke with my friend, Rodney Bowers, who was still teaching at Lawrence. He was interested in collaborating with me on a pilot research project to investigate *opera manum dei*. I made copies of a questionnaire I had designed and set out for his house. After having an accident on the highway, calling him up not knowing from where, and going to the police station, we finally got to his house and discussed *opera manum dei* over a spaghetti dinner he had made. Rodney agreed to hand out the questionnaires to his students, and just about everyone answered the ten questions on work and love.

When the students handed back what they had written, Rodney called me to say he had no idea that students felt this way about work, school, love, and family. He specifically called my attention to a boy who was one of the rough and tough and whom

Rodney considered apathetic. Rodney said, "I never would have thought this student was capable of saying something like 'I love my little brother.'" The youths' answers provided evidence of vibrant life and thoughtfulness underneath the apathy and distraction. Their words provided evidence which pointed to the need for understanding how schools could become places of work and love.[2]

The question, then, was how to provide this space. But as soon as I asked this I realized that all I knew was that a potential for change was there but not how this evolved, grew, or came to be, or even how it could be nourished. What would that space look like? I knew that youths did have work they cared about and loved to do but that this was rarely connected with schoolwork. But I then wanted to know how this came to be and what it meant psychologically in their development. This brought me back, once again, to my adolescence and what my process of aligning work and love was during youth.

POSTCARDS FROM MEMORY

El Barrio, New York City, 1962

I'm five years old and English sounds like gibberish to me. What are people saying? I look around at my nursery school classroom while I chew on graham crackers and sip on apple cider. After several months, I call the teacher over and whisper in her ear, "I can speak English now. Can I go to the bathroom?" To my stepfather, a native of Vermont, who took us to Spanish Harlem so he could work for the Peace Corps and away from my grandparents, I yell, "Shut up!" English is my new language for asking permission and also for anger.

Roosevelt, New Jersey, 1968

Almost ten years old and I start making 8-mm movies with a small camera from my grandparents. The first one is called "Tarzan and the Pygmies." I take days and weeks (minutes and hours) making the costumes, seeing in my imagination what the movie will be like. I script the scenes, seeing everything before it is made to happen, visioning, formulating. This is pure joy for me but I am surrounded by sorrow.

It is 1968, Dr. King is dead and I watch my mother, stepfather, and grandparents look out of windows and weep quietly. Children cry so much louder. It's not the tears but the silence that confuses me. I ask my grandfather what the sadness is and he says, "A great man has been killed." He keeps looking out the window at the trees. He is so tall and big and sad and he has bags under his eyes. All the adults look like this. Their eyes darker than usual. Years earlier I had watched on TV the president's funeral and had been sad for the little boy. I go on making costumes. Through the quiet I keep seeing Tarzan in the woods, shields, and spears, and everything I see on TV gets inside my own head, which has become a viewing screen. This is not the first time that I find my way through tears and sorrow but it is the first time I find my way through seeing another world in my head.

After this, I see two things: what is really in front of me and what my view of that is. It's the same as closing one eye and looking through the other, then closing the other and seeing through the one, blinking back and forth to see how really we are always seeing two different views but the mind smoothes them into one continuous one. We overlook the differences because it is precisely the two views provided by each eye that give us depth of field, allow us to perceive three dimensions. The different views are central to our ability to move around in this world.

Bringing these two perspectives into line, looking for the depth, focusing scenes, will occupy my life and I'll reach for tools (photography, film, video, pastels) to align the two. Aligning these two perspectives becomes the story line. What you see is not what you get: what you get is what you see. The images when caught connect what I see with how I see it. This is my inner world of sight: my psychology of sight, of perspective, points of viewing.

Sight. Riding bicycles (in that same year) side by side I'm holding Chavela's hand and losing my balance. "Let go!" I shout but for some reason she doesn't. My bike swerves to the right, the handlebar jackknifes, and I slam face first into the metal rim of a car tire. I can't stand the pain in my face. I crawl through the front yard to my mother in the house while waving Chavela away to leave me alone. ("If she had just let go! Why didn't she?") Childhood accidents that always happen. The doctor tells my grandmother that I could have lost my right eye. But it will slowly heal, as will my upper lip that is cut almost straight through, and my face will return to its normal proportions. But I will never be able to use it to focus through the camera (not strong enough). My left eye will become my strong eye even though I'm right-handed. My left eye will take in most of the world, and get sore, and my right eye will forever try to catch up. Sight. From then on I protect my eyes, shield them with hands and sunglasses. They are my windows out and I want them open: I want to see.

Roma, Italia, 1970

My mother is divorced, again. We move, again, this time to my mother's childhood dream. I go to Catholic school, St. Francis International, and do very well in math and science. I'm in love with the ruins and marble statues, especially "La Pieta." When a man bludgeons the Virgin Mary's face, breaking the nose off, I feel personally violated. Around the city I take hundreds of snapshots. I never want to leave. I want to return. My grandparents live here with us and I'm happy.

Rio Piedras, Puerto Rico, 1975–1976

"Who's missing from this picture?" I am looking at my family all lined up and posing for the Christmas card in front of the lighted tree. This lineup will become the greeting card that we'll send out—we will send ourselves out smiling—through the mail. I am in high school and in this picture have taken my place among the others after setting the camera up on a tripod, focusing, and pushing the correct buttons advancing the film and doing it several times. This whole thing is my idea. Taking pictures has become for me the best way to send myself out into the world, to take the world in. To connect with what's around, I document what I see. (As a researcher today I'm still at it right now, this very second.) The lens is the eye that cannot be judged right or wrong; it just sees unblinking and records without prejudice. It doesn't know the differences. Years later I learn that even the camera's mechanical eye has a particular gaze but I don't yet know. The camera could see and tell—show and tell—what I was not allowed to and could not say. There is no one missing from this picture. We're all there.

The camera has made us smile and even look happy. Maybe we really were, it's hard to tell and even more difficult to remember that fraction of a second. All photographs are fractions of time (not long wonderful stories that go on and on). With a photograph the story is completed in your mind; you complete it. If there is text that accompanies a picture that fills in the blanks (if there are any). Photography splits time open and makes you look at the details of fragments. Like archeology and Freud's buried city, looking at photographs is like dusting off bits of pottery from Pompeii: a chip of shell from the Taíno burial ground, a dinosaur bone. Unlike, say, a sculpture, one photograph alone tells of only one moment, and although a sculpture captures the moment in, say, marble, a photograph craves and desires another photograph in a way that no other medium does, because time wants to continue. One photograph deserves another one, as one minute wants to become an hour, an hour a day, and days a lifetime.

This is the difficult part. The hardest part is making pictures tell a story. The best part is seeing that story through that particular angle, that particular point in time. It's not that a picture says more than a thousand words. For me it's that a thousand words still will never make a complete picture of what I see. It's the words and text together, interacting, dynamic, filling in sounds and colors; this back and forth tells the story.

In high school I used the camera to answer questions I had about everything; math, sexuality, poetry, friendships . . . everything. I felt that I could participate in what was around me by taking photographs, and I spent hours in the darkroom developing. Photographic development was my passion—my own development hand in hand with the images I was bringing out. Photography gave me a way of talking with adults and teachers, and also gave me a way to see on paper how I was seeing the outside world. I loved working on this. When I trace a line back through the years I can see how photography was one of the strongest ropes for climbing up through youth to adulthood. Participation and sanctuary. Action and reflection. Questions and answers.

Cambridge, Massachusetts, 1990

I have gone through several years of doctoral work and am now finally completing my oral exam. After this I can truly begin on my dissertation research. (Feels like a thousand years passed before I got here.) My committee has asked me to write a difficult memo. I have to write my own narrative, take my own questions to heart and answer them, consider my own answers to the questions I want to ask adolescents and young adults—turn the camera on myself and render a self-portrait in a thousand words. It is a complicated and difficult assignment. I am working at it, on it, but mostly against it. So far I've been writing for over a month because the words don't flow out when I have to write about myself. I don't find myself interesting enough to interview. But self-portraits have always fascinated me.

I wonder if an exhibit of photographs would be a better dissertation: a slim text with many pictures. I keep on trying to write, keep trying to put words to what has been a deeply nonverbal experience for me: finding the work that I love to do, taking pictures, making videos, spreading big sheets of paper over walls and drawing murals (visual journal), making life two-dimensional with the illusion of depth. But it is not just the illusion; I am making depth, yes, out of what is seen as a surface. I love to do this and when I can do this I have great pleasure and joy in my life.

But this work is mostly called "art" and is done by some people called "artists," and neither art or artists are given much support around here. I am an artist who is unemployed. But I am a working artist. I make visual art. No one buys it and I don't sell it (often I give it away to friends). This is work I love to do. I hope to someday soon earn a living (now I am employed part-time at the Media Center) drawing and taking pictures and making videos and producing (bringing forth) my experience of this world.

My experience, represented through my art, is my point of connection between myself and the social world. Art is the bridge I use (I make) to connect with the outer world. To be an unemployed but a working artist means to believe in work I love to do even though it is not valued by the larger society. (But this creates an impasse in connecting with society.)

Teaching has a lot in common with art. Teachers have a lot in common with artists. Teaching for me is also pleasure and work. I love to teach. People say, "Teaching is an art," and I agree.

Trujillo, Puerto Rico, 1990

I come back home to Abuela, my grandmother, who is sitting on the porch in a rocking chair made of *paja* (dried grass), reading a book, listening to old romantic music on the radio. (Oh, how we argue about the volume of the music! I want to hear the birds, she wants to raise her finger in the air and sing along to a Mexican song about impressively strong women!) The cordless phone wants to ring (often does) on the round glass table next to her. All of this is in the intense green of her tropical home in Puerto Rico, my country.

There is no escaping the heat this year. Hurricane Hugo destroyed so many trees. This is Abuela's lament and sorrow. She won't walk with me down behind the porch to the lush garden—tree ferns, coffee, bamboo, hibiscus, lemon, and tangerine—she spent over thirty years of her life planting. It's now caked mud. Tire tracks mark where the construction crew drove recklessly through to remove the "debris" (to think of trees this way broke her heart). Abuela sits on the porch surrounded by the survivors and tells me she would rather remember how it was than go see how it is every time I beg her to walk with me for the exercise. She refuses. I walk alone but talk with her under my breath as if she is walking with me.

I know that every time I come home she will be on the porch waiting for me to tell her about everything that happened in my interviews with young people. She does wait. Her look is intent as she takes her reading glasses off and leans a little forward, then settles back into the rocking chair.

"What can you tell me? ¿Que cuentas? ¿Como te fue?"

This question from her is one I either long for or dread, depending on how my day of research has gone. For Abuela the important thing is that I've done *something* with the day, something tangible, concrete, something that can be held in one's hand and read or looked at or even just carefully thought about. Talking with her about ideas without grounding in experience or careful study is not of interest to her; she regards it lightly. But if I tell her of the young people I've talked with, met, and want to know about she listens with the ear of the teacher she is and always has been. The same is true if I tell her of a good book I've read. Books are like people to her and I can talk with her as if we're talking about someone we both know. We argue about how I sit and write or read and seem to be doing "nothing." I always win the argument. But I can tell this is only because she lets me.

Abuela was a public school teacher who was fired for defending the right of Puertorriqueños to learn in our mother tongue, Spanish. She was a socialist and "independentista" (for the independence of Puerto Rico from the United States) in her youth. She became a teacher at the age of nineteen and worked to support her family. Her father died when she was nine. By all accounts she was a brilliant student from a small rural town, Naguabo, who managed to obtain a scholarship to study at the University of Puerto Rico and then at Columbia University, where she received her teacher's certificate. I've met many of her students, now old themselves, their eyes filled with admiration when speaking of her. By all accounts she was a brilliant teacher who was practicing what's now called "critical pedagogy" long before it had a name and place in the academy. She married a poet who became an important politician, a shaper of Puerto Rico's culture, economy, and vision. Abuelo, my grandfather, was the father I never had, and his steady hand, deep concern for my happiness, and willingness to let me explore is what frees my imagination to consider alternatives. Abuela was my mentor and my teacher, my critic and faultfinder, my relentless supporter.

I don't want to blur the hard edges of our disagreements and confrontations: strong spirits, big voices, high principles, sometimes mistaken, never silenced. I do want to say this work is ours and that I can see in my imagination and feel in my heart Abuelo and Abuela sitting in those *paja* rocking chairs, drenched in green, expectant, wanting to know, willing to listen, forming an opinion, speaking and acting.

Both loved each other and their work. May they rest in peace.

Northampton, Massachusetts, 1991–1992

As I write, I feel alive. I believe in the work I'm doing. I have a relationship with it. I feel love for the youths and the writing. A respect. This is what I want to do.

Mamá calls to tell me that she has finally discovered (*"he descubierto"*) what she loves to do. She tells me that she loves to write poetry, that she is spending all her time writing poems. At the time she tells me this I don't fully grasp the meaning of what Mamá is telling me. In six months, she too will have left this world and joined Abuela and Abuelo. She is very ill and wants to write; it is solace and comfort, evidence, a witness and record of a life. The urgency of her discovery, the full power of it, is not apparent to me.

Rio Piedras, Puerto Rico, January 1992

At the services, the final good-byes, all these tears, friends and family ask grasping for my arm or hand, anxious to know, "You'll

publish her book won't you? It's what she wanted so much."
(*"Ella tenia tanta ilusión con su libro."*) Yes, of course, no doubt
in my mind that her book will survive her, as we are trying to do.
Mama's book is titled *Cantos de Amor y Ausencias* (Songs of Love
and Absences). Love poems.

> *The way things work*
> *is that eventually*
> *something catches.*

PANEL 2

"That Particular Combination"

CHAPTER 3

Conceptual Strategies

In this chapter I lay out the six interconnected theoretical and methodological strategies which I assembled for the gathering and analysis of the narratives. These strategies do not form a conceptual framework in the traditional sense; they are a coalition of concepts and methods which work together as a strategy for this research. The strategy is necessarily interdisciplinary. As I have discussed previously, I needed various points from which to view and interpret what is found in the narratives. Although I had studied liberating theory, liberation theology, and feminism by *mujeres de color* and had these as a base, I put these approaches firmly together with Erikson's observations after completing the transcribing and reading through the narratives.

This occurred because after listening to the youths, then again the youths on audiotape, then "listening" through reading the narratives it became clearer than ever to me that the analytical categories available for interpretation, such as *occupational identity, wholeness, identity crisis*, and even the term *identity* itself, derived from standard models, would, if used exclusively, be silencing. Through this approach I have sought to listen both to the individual voices and to the larger social, historical, and economic context within which we all speak and live.

The work of Erik Erikson begins this strategical approach because his writings first pointed to the developmental tasks of work and love in youth and nourished my interest in these processes.

ERIKSON PROVIDES A COMPASS

Through love and work is a hope for change. It is a human theme that runs throughout our common history/herstory: we humans are a collective of laborers who work every day of our lives for millions of different fruits. Some of us manage to gather enough strength to pass our work along to others and this we do out of love.

Love is not the distorted image of objectification and repression for the sake of someone more seemingly powerful, but that which makes you want to work, and the work makes you want to love. Love includes intimacy, pleasure, generosity, and desire. Love is friendship and community.

Work is not just the nine-to-five or backbreaking stuff for money, although this is necessary work, too. Work is that feeling that you get when you know you are doing something good and want to keep doing it. Freedom work, liberation, understanding work, creative work, listening, and attention can be work, too—work that is making something you love.

Work is Martin Luther's *opera manum dei* (Erikson, 1962), a relationship between work and love that we find throughout history as the source of revolutions of mind and spirit. In *Young Man Luther*, Erikson aligns Luther's theological revolution with psychological development and proposes a path of development which demands "a particular combination of work and love" for supporting identity or "a sense of knowing where one is going" (Erikson, 1959, p. 118). Erikson (1962) writes: "Martin's theological reformations imply a psychological fact, namely, that the ego gains strength *in practice*, and *in affectu* to the degree to which it can accept at the same time the total power of the drives and the total power of conscience—*provided* that it can nourish what Luther called 'opera manum dei,' that particular combination of work and love which alone verifies our identity and confirms it" (p. 217, emphasis Erikson). But what is that particular combination that enables us to know where we are going and who we are? How does this process occur? How is it nourished? Returning to Jorie Graham's poem—*The way things work is that eventually something catches*—similar questions return. But what catches? And who catches it? How? In what ways? How does "a sense of knowing where one is going" develop?

Erikson provides a compass: north and south are work and love, east and west identity and youth; within each individual these points all meet somewhere, somehow. Where they align is a powerful place for human development. Erikson would call it "a crisis" or "a critical step." These moments, and the process leading to them, are what I want to understand, explore, and, ultimately, nourish. Here is the journey.

The opportunity to experience a combination of work and love is, perhaps, nowhere more important than during adolescence and young adulthood, when identity development is felt so acutely and reaches a critical point. Erikson (1964), writing about "Identity and Uprootedness in Our Time" (an area that, as an immigrant and refugee, he knew intimately well) describes the era in the life cycle between childhood and adulthood as a "'natural' period of uprootedness in human life." Erikson explains: "Like a trapeze artist, the young person in the middle of vigorous motion must let go of his safe hold on childhood and reach out for a firm grasp on adulthood, depending for a breathless interval on a relatedness between the past and the future, and on the reliability of those he must let go of, and those who will 'receive' him" (p. 90).

Moving between two developmental points, an adolescent or youth—no longer a child, not yet an adult—searches for the next foothold while at the same time putting his foot down along a certain path. But only in theory can one hold time still and conceive of being in the "middle" or at an "interval": There is no "middle" in an infinite line or in a life not yet completed. For a youth his life is not a time between childhood and adulthood, but life itself. In time and space, a young person is constantly and simultaneously moving, searching out, deciding, moving, moving. "A sense of where one is going" is nourished by work and love in a particular combination. It is a dialectical process, dynamic, complex, charged with change. Erikson continues: "Whatever combination of drives and defenses, of sublimations and capacities has emerged from the individual's childhood must now make sense in view of his concrete opportunities in work and in love; what the individual has learned to see in himself must now coincide with the expectations and recognitions which others bestow on him; whatever values have become meaningful to him must now match some universal significance" (p. 90). Work and love become the climbing ropes from childhood into adulthood.

The youth looking inside herself also looks out at society and tries to find a place to and for herself. She asks if what is outside herself matches what is inside herself. She tests this through work and love. This process of alignment is not just important in a futuristic way, a path to future adulthood; rather, it is critical as a developmental moment in the lives of youths. It is the developmental work at hand (Erikson, 1985).

The strong connection between work and identity during youth is underscored by Erikson (1968) when he writes, "In general it is the inability to settle on an occupational identity which most disturbs young people" (p. 132). Furthermore, he claims that the adolescent mind "is an ideological mind" (1985, p. 263). It seems, then, that work which young people can believe in is especially important: this kind of work can provide young people with a sense of knowing where they are going. At that "breathless interval" it is the hand at the other side: the catch.

And what of this grasping, this reaching and searching for adulthood? The image of hands trying to connect is compelling (the hands that do the work of God, *opera manum dei*, the steady hands of my grandfather, my mother with her pen). Erikson (1968), caught by the image of grasping, returns to it once again to explain the search for identity: "This search is easily misunderstood, and often it is only dimly perceived by the individual himself, because youth, always set to grasp both diversity in principle and principle in diversity, must often test extremes before setting on a considered course" (p. 235). Erikson has another marker for understanding identity; he calls it "wholeness." Wholeness, in adolescence and young adulthood, is composed of "a sense of inner identity" (Erikson, 1964, p. 91):

> Wholeness seems to connote an assembly of parts, even quite diversified parts, that enter into fruitful association and organization. This concept is most strikingly expressed in such terms as wholeheartedness, wholemindedness, wholesomeness, and the like. As a *Gestalt*, then, wholeness emphasizes a sound, organic, progressive mutuality between diversified functions and parts within an entirety, the boundaries of which are open and fluent. (p. 92)

The similarity with Graham's poem is striking here. Erikson describes the mechanics of identity as Graham describes the mechanics of work. They both move between two seemingly opposite points, specific mechanics and fluency of emotion, searching out the dialectic between the two. They both present views of a powerful dynamic between psychological and mechanical parts, as well as belief, faith, wholeheartedness, wholemindedness, and wholesomeness—ways of being that break through mechanics and into a new place, a place where something catches. But this process remains obscure, although the path is pointed out.

Erikson contrasts wholeness with "totality," a part of "normal" psychology especially during times of individual uprootedness and stress. But Erikson finds that if totality is maintained, rather than wholeness, it supports over time a "synthetic identity": the person becomes something other than what she really is. Erikson holds this form of identity, which he terms "totalism," responsible for such social phenomenon as extreme nationalism and racism (p. 93). Clearly, of these two, wholeness is the preferred developmental path. And nowhere else is the choice of paths as wide open as during youth, and at no other time are the decisions as critical.

Following Erikson's markers, I want to explore why it's important, even critical, for young people to experience this kind of work, this kind of love, "this particular combination of work and love which alone verifies our identity and confirms it." Through examples from a diverse group of people, I want to listen to the logic of *opera manum dei*—how it's experienced and understood. I want to know more about the process of including the heart, the hands, the passion, how youths experience and make sense of love and work, how these are negotiated psychologically.

Toward this end I open the door to a few who have, through working on what they love, "made it": some make news suddenly and are on TV, and some are on the best-seller list, in local newspapers, characters in novels who remind us of people we know. They are those folks who ignite imagination. They were once young and had to figure out how to work, how to love, what to grasp, and where to go. Their stories provide views of "a sense of knowing where one is going" and "wholeness." These stories and the questions they raise provide a further backdrop—a *trasfondo*—for understanding the psychological processes voiced in the narratives of the youths I interviewed.

STORIES OF WORK/STORIES OF LOVE

Willy T. Ribbs, the first African American to qualify for the Indianapolis 500, said that since he was a kid driving was the only thing he loved to do. Connie Chung brings this to millions of television viewers on the "Evening News." It's May 24, 1991, and it's news.

Love and struggle drove Willy T. Ribbs to Indy, driving that car so fast to qualify. Bill Cosby sponsors him because "he's good" (*I believe in you*). Nobody else in that fast lane gave Ribbs much. He had a skeleton team of devoted people with mechanical and technical talent. (*Wheel, kinetic flow, rising and falling water, ingots, levers and keys, I believe in you.*) Changing tires, tightening up screws, how fast can we go? Can we win?

Baby Suggs, holy, spiritual leader in Toni Morrison's *Beloved*, "offered up to them her great big heart. She did not tell them to clean up their lives or to go and sin no more. She did not tell them they were the blessed of the earth, its inheriting meek or its glory-bound pure. She told them that the only grace they could have was the grace they could imagine. That if they could not see it, they would not have it" (p. 88).

To see it, to imagine it, to love it, to know you're good, to work with love—Baby Suggs, holy, leads her community inside, deep, where without being seen the heart beats:

> "Here," she said, "in this here place, we flesh; flesh that weeps, laughs; flesh that dances on bare feet in grass. Love it. Love it hard. Yonder they do not love your flesh. They despise it. They don't love your eyes; they'd just as soon pick em out. No more do they love the skin on your back. Yonder they flay it. And O my people they do not love your hands. Those they only use, tie, bind, chop off and leave empty. Love your hands! Love them. Raise them up and kiss them. Touch others with them, pat them together, stroke them on your face 'cause they don't love that either. *You* got to love it, *you*! . . . And all your inside parts that they'd just as soon slop for hogs, you got to love them. The dark, dark liver—love it, love it, and the beat and beating heart, love that too. More than eyes or feet. More than lungs that have yet to draw free air. More than your life-holding womb and your life-giving parts, hear me now, love your heart. For this is the prize." (pp. 88–89)

In another community around the world, Father Zossima, in Fyodor Dostoyevsky's *The Brothers Karamazov*, speaking from his death bed to his beloved spiritual brothers, urges:

> Brothers, be not afraid of men's sins. Love man even in his sin, for that already bears the semblance of divine love and is the highest love on earth. Love all God's creation, the whole of it and every grain of sand. Love every leaf, every ray of God's light! Love the animals, love the plants, love everything. If you

love everything, you will perceive the divine mystery in things. And once you have perceived it, you will begin to comprehend it ceaselessly more and more every day. And you will at last come to love the whole world with an abiding, universal love. (p. 375)

Father Zossima speaks of a "universal love," a love that comes from loving others; animals, plants, men, light, sand, the whole world as a divine mystery. The focus of attention is outside oneself. The hands that do the work of God reach outward toward divine mystery, what cannot be explained, yet can be loved. The Brothers, being men, are included but they themselves are not the starting points for working on love. The reason for loving is to perceive the divine mystery in things and in this way to love God.

Baby Suggs, holy, speaking to the children of African slaves, tells of a love that begins with your own heart, imagination, and vision, with seeing it. "It" is love that begins with oneself: "love your heart. For this is the prize." The prize is "deeply loved flesh." Baby Suggs, holy, speaks about using hands to love: "Raise them up and kiss them. Touch others with them, pat them together, stroke them on your face." People "yonder"—meaning whites—don't want them to love; the ones that have to do it, find grace, are not over there but right here.

Loving your own heart, your own hands, your own eyes—what kind of work does this enable? Or loving the whole world with a universal love—what kind of work does this enable? Paulo Freire (1970), in *Pedagogy of the Oppressed*, in a footnote writes this about love and revolutionary work:

> I am more and more convinced that true revolutionaries must perceive the revolution, because of its creative and liberating nature, as an act of love . . . The distortion imposed on the word "love" by the capitalist world cannot prevent the revolution from being loving in character, nor can it prevent the revolutionaries from affirming their love of life. Guevara (while admitting the "risk of seeming ridiculous") was not afraid to affirm it: "Let me say, with the risk of appearing ridiculous, that the true revolutionary is guided by strong feelings of love. It is impossible to think of an authentic revolutionary without this quality." (p. 77)

More recently, Freire (1993), in a collection of new writing and conversations about his educational *praxis,* returns again to the connections between work, love, and social justice.

My love for reading and writing is directed toward a certain uto-
pia. This involves a certain course, a type of people. It is a love
that has to do with the creation of a society that is less perverse,
less discriminatory, less racist, less *machista* than the society that
we now have. This love seeks to create a more open society, a
society that serves the interests of the always unprotected and
devalued subordinate classes, and not only the interests of the
rich, the fortunate, the so called "well-born." (p. 140)

This quality of love in revolutionary work is illustrated by Alice
Walker (1991) when she writes about the trial of Winnie Mandela
who, in 1988, was charged by the white South African government of kidnapping and beating a teenager. Walker does not
doubt Winnie Mandela's innocence. She explains why:

It is Winnie's work—her care for her children, women, the elderly, the "internal refugees," the homeless—that speaks for her.
Her care for her own daughters, stepchildren, nieces, nephews,
and as a social worker, for the black South African family as a
whole . . . It is in every expression she has made on TV talk
shows, to independent filmmakers who sought her out during
her numerous bannings, and over the bodies of hundreds of slain
children, women, and men above whose coffins she has been
asked to speak. (p. 24)

Walker is reminded of the writer and anthropologist Zora Neale
Hurston who was accused, along with two other adults she had
never seen before, of sodomizing a ten-year-old boy in 1948. The
case was thrown out; Hurston was in Honduras when the crime
was committed. Walker notes that Hurston was, as is Mandela, in
her midfifties. But here the comparison ends, for Hurston died
alone and forgotten, believing her reputation was destroyed by the
accusations, her grave unmarked until Walker herself found the site
and ordered a stone. What is left of Hurston is her great work. Of
this Walker writes: "A person's work is her only signature; we forget this at our peril. It is to the work and life we must turn, especially
in these days of assassination by newsprint" (p. 24).

Writing about her own work in an essay entitled "Duties of
the Black Revolutionary Artist," Alice Walker (1983) says:
"Much lip service has been given the role of the revolutionary
black writer but now the words must be turned into work. For, as
someone said, 'Work is love made visible . . .' I would like to call
myself revolutionary, for I am always changing, and growing, it is

hoped for the good of black people . . . The truest and most enduring impulse I have is to write" (p. 133).

Adrienne Rich (1993) argues that the process of writing poetry is a revolutionary act of love: a love of poetry, transformation, and freedom against brutality. Rich situates poetry as a location for liberatory struggle, a place where the cut-off hands of a young Micmac woman can be remembered. Joy Harjo (1990) in the poem "For Anna Mae Pictou Aquash, Whose Spirit is Present Here and In The Dappled Stars (For We Remember The Story and Must Tell It Again so We May All Live)" does just this. Rich writes of Harjo's work: "What is represented as intolerable—as crushing—becomes the figure of its own transformation, through the beauty of the medium and through the artist's uncompromised love for that medium, a love as deep as the love of freedom. These loves are not in opposition" (p. 249). On the following page, Rich concludes her meditation, "What If?" and her book by gathering what poets love:

> The revolutionary artist, the relayer of possibility, draws on such powers, in opposition to a technocratic society's hatred of multiformity, hatred of the natural world, hatred of the body, hatred of darkness and women, hatred of disobedience. The revolutionary poet loves people, rivers, other creatures, stones, trees inseparably from art, is not ashamed of any of these loves, and for them conjures a language that is public, intimate, inviting, terrifying, and beloved. (p. 250)

Andrea Ayvazian, who is a tax resister, Quaker, and singer, in an Independence Day interview in *The Springfield Advocate* (July 4, 1991, p. 7) discusses the process through which she decided to stop writing out a check to the government every April. "I think there is nothing more moving and nothing that transforms this world more than modeling what we truly believe in and hold dear. It's what has moved me and pushed me toward trying harder to be all I can be." Ayvazian thought about not paying her taxes for years because she objected to how "62 cents of every dollar goes to the military," but didn't actually stop paying until 1982. She gave it a lot of thought and attended a workshop for people interested in taking action against military spending, but she resisted resisting: "I sat there very skeptical, because somebody had once told me that ('When it's right for you, you'll know it') about marriage and I had believed them and was divorced four years later." The following year though, she was "ready." Ayvazian tells that she found herself thinking, "That makes sense. If enough people did that we could actually slow down the war machine. I realized that if it makes sense for *someone* to do, it makes sense for me to do." For Ayvazian, tax resistance is a form of aligning what she believes in with how she lives. It is her practice, her work. As a singer she performs "two kinds of songs, love songs and songs about people's struggles, visions and convictions" with "very welcoming choruses."

Brooks Holmes is the new music teacher, the only new public school teacher hired this year in Easthampton, Massachusetts. Since he was ten years old music was what he loved to do. Holmes is twenty-three now. Rosemary Bonner, the principal, says this about the new teacher: "You can see from his work that he really loves what he's doing" (Julie Ross, p. 14, *Daily Hampshire Gazette*, Dec. 28–29, 1991). Holmes is pictured conducting the school band as if nothing else exists. He says, "Music is a basic part of learning. Students deserve an opportunity to learn. Music is not a frill."

Natalie Goldberg (1990), in her book *Wild Mind*, tells of asking her spiritual teacher a question about why he suggested that she go ahead and become a writer: "I went to Roshi last year and asked him, 'Why did you say so many years ago that I should make writing my practice?' I thought there was some deep esoteric reason. He raised his eyebrows. He thought it was a curious question. 'Because you like to write. That's why.' 'Oh,' I nodded. Huh, that simple" (p. 136). It's the last sentence that strikes me, "Huh, that simple." So what complicated the process for Goldberg? She dedicates two books to answering this question and providing ways to overcome obstacles to writing. But the reason for Roshi's advice to her, to take writing as her life's work, was "simple": she liked it.

The way things work
is that eventually
something catches.

THE GENIUS

Mel King (1989) describes a process of "seeing the genius" in others—the genuine, the magical. *Genius* is from Latin meaning "guardian spirit" what Roshi saw in Natalie Goldberg. The politics of finding the genius has at its core the value that everyone has a talent, a gift, a passion to share. It's rooted in a belief in justice, peace, and a human right to develop to one's fullest potential—a form of freedom. It is also rooted in the desire for peace that is both spiritual and material. King explains:

> It seems to me that there has to be a vision in which you see the **genius** in all the people that you're working with. I'm not just talking about students, because for me education happens anytime we work with people to bring out the best in them, *believing that it exists*. It requires a constant analysis of those things which help and those things which hinder. Because it is important for us to build collectively toward acquiring the techniques and skills to overcome those things which hinder and to improve upon the things which help. (p. 507, emphasis: King, bold; italics, mine)[1]

Where love and work align is a place where genius can be "seen" and a strong point of connection between a person's psychology and society, especially during youth. (*I believe in you—your head is the horizon to my hand.*)

Maxine Greene (1988) connects a politic of genius with a concept of freedom and generates a vision of human being that agrees with what Erikson calls "wholeness." Greene places at the heart of what it means to be free "a capacity to surpass the given and look at things as if they could be otherwise" (p. 3), a position that young people developmentally grow into:

> We might think of freedom as an opening of spaces as well as perspectives, with everything depending on the actions we undertake in the course of our quest, the *praxis* we learn to devise . . . There has to be a surpassing of a constraining or deficient "reality," actually perceived as deficient by a person or persons looking from their particular vantage points on the world. Made conscious of lacks, they may move (in their desire to repair them) toward a "field of possibles," what is possible or realizable for them. Few people, quite obviously, can become virtuoso musicians or advanced physicists or world-renowned statesmen, but far more is possible for individuals than is ordinarily recognized. (p. 5)

Greene notes that not everyone is a "genius" in the traditional way (having an extremely high IQ), but she urges educators to move beyond the limited expectations of tradition and to recognize lacks and constraints, not in order to be bound by them, but in order to break through them. Breaking through into a "field of possibles" is how freedom is made. Creating this "field of possibles" is a process of searching out the genius in all people, the gift, the prize.

Yet, for Greene, this doesn't mean becoming fixed on a goal and then pursuing it and pursuing it. The process is dynamic and open to contingencies; you may change your mind once you get there; accidents happen, new visions arise. Greene proposes a way of being, not a static place to be.

bell hooks (1990), in *Yearning: Race, Gender, and Cultural Politics*, talks about a longing of body, mind, and spirit. She shares with Greene a desire "to surpass the given and look at things as if they could be otherwise," a yearning to transform what is taken for granted and cultivate what hooks calls new "habits of being" (p. 31). hooks brings forth observations that connect freedom and wholeness: the desire to grow, change, the possibility of common ground, points of connection and engagement where something catches:

> I gathered this group of essays under the heading *Yearning* because as I looked for common passions, sentiments shared by folks across race, class, gender, and sexual practice, I was struck by the depths of longing in many of us. Those without money long to find a way to get rid of the endless sense of deprivation. Those with money wonder why so much feels so meaningless and long to find the site of "meaning . . . " The shared space and feeling of "yearning" opens up the possibility of common ground where all these differences might meet and engage one another. It seemed appropriate then to speak this yearning. (pp. 12–13)

hooks herself longs for the "relational love" she felt when growing up in "a segregated small town, living in a marginal space where black people (though contained) exercised power, where we truly felt supportive of one another . . . " She recalls "a beloved black community" (pp. 35–36).

When does this yearning begin? How can the longing be satisfied?

When I think of an education for freedom, justice, and peace I yearn to connect love and work; to transform through this connection an oppressive society; to understand what it takes psychologically to bring forth the genius, the passion, the joy. And I yearn for places where wholeness can develop instead of violence: places of work and love.

Justice, freedom, peace, wholeness, yearning, community—all evoke deep feelings and desires; all encompass huge areas of humanity. Where and how to begin? With oneself or with others? Which one first? Or both? Is it a developmental path that anyone can "decide" to take or is it as it was for Willy T. Ribbs, just something one loves to do since childhood? How can educators join with youths, create places where work and love, and perhaps wholeness, can evolve?

These questions are big and lifelong: the answers to them necessarily change over time because they are contextual, contingent, in relationship with social and psychological life. Like Erikson's image of youths as trapeze artists, so too the process of answering these questions sets them in motion, keeping them moving and open. How do I ground the questions—in order to move forward and investigate and, then, reflect on the answers they yield—without making them static and irrelevant, without arresting their urgency?

The analysis of the stories gathered through this inquiry needs to be grounded and in context; my analysis of the narratives needs to be specific, particular, and resistant to leaps into universality or generalities. My work needs to stand in what hooks calls "sweet solidarity" (p. 77) with the youths and question, search, reveal tensions, contradictions, and ambiguity as well as look for the genius, and if the genius can't be found, ask why not? This investigative process is both psychological and political.

MUJERES DE COLOR:
MAKING *TEORÍAS* AND IDENTITIES

The word *theory* comes from the Greek and means "to view." To reflect on the process of theorizing by returning to its root is to consider how deeply embedded within a worldview, perspective, or standpoint is the work of making *teorías*. "To view" by placing oneself within the world and from this location explain how things work (or don't) in ways that enable social change is critical in the following approaches.

The study and exploration of identity is a central and deeply heartfelt part of the writing published by women of color: who we are within a racist, classist, homophobic, anti-Semitic society has occupied center stage in our writings. You would find it impossible, at this point in time, to find a piece of writing—poetry, essay, novel, or play—which did not directly and explicitly address the issues of growing up and remaining different within U.S. society— a Menominee, a woman of color, a lesbian of color, a working-class lesbian of color, a Puertorriqueña Jew. Identity is lived experience of difference and struggle as well as tradition and continuity within particular communities and also a daily negotiation between these two. For community as a "home" is often problematic when, for example, the woman of color is also a lesbian or the Puertorriqueña is also a Jew.

The interconnections between the many dimensions of our experience transform the notion of a core or essential identity into a conceptualization of *identities*: an ongoing internal plurality forged and changed in and by time and place. The temporal-historical and cultural-geographic process of identities is revealed, shared, given to the world through writing. It is from this writing—these stories of lived and passed-on experience—that women of color make theory that can explain the complexity of "a sense of knowing where one is going" when, for most women of color, to go anywhere at all takes an enormous amount of energy and resources.

What these writers express disrupts traditional models of identity as a unitary process which occurs in neat hierarchical stages. The theorization needed to represent the process of identities for people of color is addressed by Gloria Anzaldúa (1990) in the introduction to a collection of creative and critical perspectives of women of color, *Making Face, Making Soul*:

> What is considered theory in the dominant academic community is not necessarily what counts as theory for women-of-color. Theory produces effects that change people and the way they perceive the world. Thus we need *teorías* that will enable us to interpret what happens in the world, that will explain how and why we relate to certain people in specific ways, that will reflect what goes on between inner, outer and peripheral "I"s within a person and between personal "I"s and the collective "we" of our ethnic communities. *Necesitamos teorías* that will rewrite history using race, class, gender and ethnicity as categories of anal-

ysis, theories that cross borders, that blur boundaries—new kinds of theories with new theorizing methods. (p. *xxv*)

Anzaldúa yearns for *teorías* that will enable women and men of color to understand and then take action against the injustice that oppresses and fragments us: the fragmentation itself becoming a kind of internalized oppression subverting wholeness. Her understanding of the process through which new *teorías* can be articulated is psychological and focused on identity: an investigation of the inner "I," an investigation of the peripheral "I," the outer, the collective "we." Anzaldúa points to a dialectical understanding of identity—identity as an evolving process of negotiation between what is external and what is inside and how this negotiation in turn gives meaning to what we perceive and how we live in the world. Within this framework a social scientific process for investigating *the way things work* is not undertaken to articulate laws, forces, or mechanisms; its purpose is not to control or to predict, but to transform.

It is this process of theory making which makes possible an exploration of identity that can make sense of why Chrystos (1988) sits at a table while being insulted by a woman, who most probably thinks of herself as an ally, in ways that move beyond judgment and self-blame ("I have no self-esteem") while at the same time understanding the effects of internalized oppression. In her book of poems, *Not Vanishing*, Chrystos writes:

> I sit down with my plate to eat
> > You're Indian aren't you?
> > Yes
> > What tribe are you?
> > Menominee
> > What?
> > Me Nom I Nee
> > Is that your name or your tribe?
> > My tribe, Great Lakes region
> > What?
> > Great Lakes region
> > So you're from Wisconsin
> > No, I was born in San Francisco
> > Oh well what are you doing here I mean
> > that's pretty far Do you still live there?

> No, I live in Seattle
> Oh, that's pretty far north
> Yes
> What group are you in?
> The residents who are here to write
>   instead of take classes
> What? Oh So when did you start writing?
> When I was nine
> Oh well then I guess you'd better keep up with it
> Yes
> During this entire conversation my fist clenched at my plate
> polite mask tied firmly to my head with barbed wire
> I sat until I could get up casually
> plate in hand
> seem to move away without intent
> to a bench with no one else
> so as not to insult her
> who had ruined my meal[2]

Why doesn't Chrystos express her rage? Why doesn't she "insult her"? Why does she wait until she can "get up casually," no longer clenching her fist, to move to a bench? Chrystos's fury is in her work, in her writing; she carries not only her own experiences but also those of her father. Like the youths who leave school without any explanations given, so too, Chrystos leaves the table. If I want to know why, if I want to understand, I have to listen to her fury, follow her to where the hurt presses in:

> I was not born on the reservation, but in San Francisco, part of a group called "Urban Indians" by the government. I grew up around Black, Latin, Asian & white people and am shaped by that experience, as well as by what my father taught me. He had been taught to be ashamed & has never spoken our language to me. Much of the fury which erupts from my work is a result of seeing the pain that white culture has caused my father. It continues to give pain to all of us.[3]

To liberate the fury, cut loose that pain, and untie her tongue is Chrystos's work. The writing of women of color has deliberately been to confront and undo the damage of years of oppression which for many have been internalized into self-hate, shame, and silence. This body of knowledge, expressed through metaphors, images, and symbols and peopled with conflicting communities, contains the genius of expression through embattled conditions. In this way, the writing of *mujeres de color* makes possible a framework where identity can be explored as dynamic, changing, emerging, *and* fragmented, constructed, and shattered. Anzaldúa (1987), in her book *Borderlands/La Frontera*, writes:

> The struggle is inner: Chicano, *indio*, American Indian, *mojado*, *mexicano*, immigrant Latino, Anglo in power, working class Anglo, Black, Asian—our psyches resemble the bordertowns and are populated by the same people. The struggle has always been inner, and is played out in the outer terrains. Awareness of our situation must come before inner changes, which in turn come before changes in society. Nothing happens in the "real" world unless it first happens in the images in our heads . . . I will not be ashamed again. Nor will I blame myself. (p. 87)

Anzaldúa's metaphor for the Chicano/a psyche is a bordertown on *la frontera*, the edge or intersection of two cultures where both are constantly being negotiated. This image brings to mind the experiences of youths in Puerto Rico: moving from childhood into adulthood, between U.S. culture and Latin culture, a developed country, a Third World country, postcolonial, not yet a nation, community and bureaucracy, school and the streets, the past and the present. Anzaldúa's metaphor for the psyche can cross the Atlantic and into the Caribbean. The Puerto Rican psyche is also at the borderlands, *la frontera*, at a crossroads in development; youths in Puerto Rico are at a crossroads politically and culturally.

And Aurora Levins Morales does cross the Atlantic, back and forth between Puerto Rico and New York City. The borderlands she speaks of are somewhere between being Puertorriqueña and being invisible, wanting to vanish and wanting to stay. Levins Morales (1980), a Puertorriqueña Jew, in *This Bridge Called My Back*, writes:

> Points of terror. Points of denial. Repeat the story that it was my grandmother who went to look at apartments. Light skinned, fine, black hair: I'm Italian, she would tell them, keeping the dark-skinned husband, keeping the daughters out of sight. I have pretended that pain, that shame, that anger never touched me, does not stain my skin. She could pass for Italian. She kept her family behind her. I can pass for anyone. Behind me stands my grandmother working at the bra and girdle factory, speaking

with an accent, lying to get an apartment in Puertoricanless neighborhoods. (p. 54)

How to understand the terror, denial, pain? How to explain how they press in on who we are, what we feel, what we want? What are the stories we tell to justify, to pacify, to make the past look coherent, to make the present feel coherent? To hold the fragments together?

Alberto Sandoval Sánchez (1993), a gay Puertorriqueño who is a professor of Spanish at Mount Holyoke College and who is living with AIDS, in his first book of poems, *Nueva York Tras Bastidores: New York Backstage,* makes sexuality visibly part of his identity; mirrors which are smashed and fragmented is one of Sandoval's central metaphors. The book is bilingual; each poem appears first in Spanish and then in English. One poem, *"Song of a New York Boy From East 81st.,"* tells of a boy who is looking to his father and mother for gender guidance. In the conversation between the boy and his father the father tells the boy not to be like him because he is profoundly unhappy, but when the boy then says he wants to be like his mother, the father changes his mind:

— Daddy, I want to be like you daddy
   Daddy, I want to be like you daddy
   I want to shave like you daddy
   I want to have hair on my chest,
   your good looks, your suits daddy.

— Oh my son, you don't want to be daddy
   Behind the mirror I am
   Oh, my son, I just smell success,
   9 to 5 and cocktails.
   Oh my son, never be like me:
   a price tag
   a best-seller
   a walking heart attack.

— Daddy, I want to be like Mom daddy
   Daddy, I want to be like Mom daddy
   I want lipstick, wigs and earrings
   high heels, nylons and glamour.

— Oh my God! Oh my son!
   Be the man in the mirror![4]

The father, horrified that his son wants to cross-dress (gender is a kind of bordertown for him), forgets how miserable masculinity has made him and demands that his son be just like his gendered reflection. Through the metaphor of cross-dressing Sandoval's experiences of gender and sexuality are crossed. This experience of gender crossing, being Puertorriqueño, gay, and living in the United States, is described by Sandoval (1990) as that of being a cultural "hybrid," *hibridez cultural*: a crossing of identities, of genders, of cultures, a blending, a mixing, an assimilation particular to being a gay Puertorriqueño in the United States.

This *hibridez*, ambiguously reflected in the mirror, is also expressed by Judith Ortiz Cofer (1990) in *Silent Dancing: A Partial Remembrance of a Puerto Rican Childhood*, a heterosexual Puertorriqueña. Ortiz Cofer uses the metaphor of a mirror and connects herself with Virginia Woolf to express what it is like to be a Puertorriqueña girl becoming a Puertorriqueña woman:

> In her memoir, *Moments of Being*, Virginia Woolf tells of a frightening dream she had as a young girl in which, as she looked at herself in the mirror, she saw something moving in the background: " . . . a horrible face—the face of an animal . . . " over her shoulder. She never forgot that "other face in the glass" perhaps because it was both alien and familiar. It is not unusual for an adolescent to feel disconnected from her body—a stranger to herself and to her new developing needs—but I think that to a person living simultaneously in two cultures this phenomenon is intensified.
>
> Even as I dealt with the trauma of leaving childhood, I saw that "cultural schizophrenia" was undoing many others around me at different stages of their lives. Society gives clues and provides rituals for the adolescent but withholds support. As I entered my freshman year of high school in a parochial school, I was given a new uniform to wear: a skirt and blouse as opposed to the severe blue jumper with the straps, to accommodate for developing breasts, I suppose, although I would have little to accommodate for an excruciatingly long time—being a "skinny bones," as my classmates often called me, with no hips or breasts to speak of. (p. 118)

Ortiz Cofer brings together several fragments; "the trauma of leaving childhood," which meant negotiating gender in new ways, and becoming an adult Latina, which meant negotiating racism and gender in "intensified" ways.

To study identity means to explore *the story of identity*—the narrative of identity—the way we tell ourselves and others who we are, where we came from, where we are going. Stuart Hall (1991) in *Ethnicity: Identity and Difference,* describes identity this way: "Identity is within discourse, within representation. It is constituted in part by representation. Identity is a narrative of the self; it's the story we tell about the self in order to know who we are. We impose a structure on it" (p. 16). A way to "see" or "look at" the structure of identity is to listen to the story of the self being told, and then to look for *moments in identity,* moments where things change. To study the structures we impose means to look for places where, for example, childhood dreams give way to adult work, and then look for the logic of this shift, of this moment.

Anzaldúa, Chrystos, Sandoval, and Ortiz Cofer disrupt traditional notions of identity. Their stories and analyses of their experience reveal images not found in smooth mirrors which reflect a continuity of development, but instead in smashed glass which reveals identity in fragments. Freud's (1933) metaphor of dropping a crystal and observing the fragments brought to the borderlands, *la frontera,* examined at the crossroads.

LIBERATING THEORY: COMPLEMENTARY HOLISM

In *Liberating Theory* (1986), by Albert et al., a group of scholars and activists takes on the critical task of formulating a conceptual framework which makes possible the study of societies in a way that can facilitate social change.

> We tentatively call this new orientation complementary holism. It is rooted in two modern scientific principles: "holism" and "complementarity."*Holism* informs us that reality's many parts always act together to form an entwined whole . . . since all phenomena influence all other phenomena, we should always be very careful about how we abstract any particular aspect of our surroundings from the whole.
>
> *Complementarity,* in the sense we use it, means that the parts which compose wholes interrelate to help define one another, even though each appears often to have an independent and even contrary existence. (p. 12)

Their formulation is dynamic and integrates a variety of elements that are at work at any given time in a society. This framework rejects monolithic theories that explain society by prioritizing a single aspect of social life to the exclusion of other factors, for example, the prioritizing of gender to the point of exclusion of class or race, or the prioritizing of race over gender.

This kind of prioritization, the authors argue, has led to conceptual frameworks which attempt to analyze complex social relations using a single social category. The resulting reductive analysis misses the various interactions between social spheres and how these work within and as part of a whole social system. The central critique of these kinds of theoretical frameworks is outlined by Albert et al. in the following passage:

> Monist approaches fail whenever we need to recognize more than one set of causal factors. For example, black and white and male and female workers don't all have the same interests and mindsets simply because they all belong to the same economic class. Over-simplifying causal factors to include only class relations ignores racial and sexual dynamics that cause women and blacks, among others, to endure different oppressions, not only when pay checks and pink slips are dispersed, but day-in and day-out because of the racist and sexist definitions of their economic tasks. Class concepts cannot alone adequately explain factory life and so, *even to understand the economy*, much less the rest of society, we must go beyond marxism. Similarly, each monist approach exaggerates the influence of its favored sphere, underestimates the influence of other spheres, and largely ignores the crucial fact that every sphere is itself critically influenced by sources of social definition . . . Because they fail to account for multi-faceted defining influences, marxist categories insufficiently explain even the economy, feminist categories insufficiently explain even gender, nationalist categories insufficiently explain even culture, and anarchist categories insufficiently explain even the state. All these foci are certainly necessary, but to use them optimally we need to develop a new orientation that allows us to embody refined versions of each primary framework in *a new whole*. (p. 10)

Complementary holism integrates four "critical spheres of social life" as dynamically interlocking, which together compose a whole society within which individuals interact. Although the focus of complementary holism is on society as a complex social system and not specifically on the psychology of individuals, the conceptualization of social dynamics as "spheres of social life" is an extremely useful formulation. The spheres are especially important for guiding my exploration of individual identity as not only a psychological process but also as a social, economic, and historically based development.

The four spheres comprise economic, political, kinship, and community dynamics. Each sphere is conceptualized as a complex and multilayered rendering of critical social relations. A brief overview of the aspects of each sphere used in this study follows:

- *Economic Sphere*: Includes economic institutions (factories, stores, industries, markets), economic activity (consumption, production, allocation), economic relations (social and technical division of labor, unemployment, competition), and economic classes (workers, professionals/managers, coordinators, capitalists).

- *Political Sphere*: Includes creation of ideology, political activity (lawmaking, controlling information, legitimating), political institutions (state, parties, military, police, courts, bureaucracies, elections), and political allegiances.

- *Kinship Sphere*: Includes kinship activity (courting, loving, sexuality, nurturing, procreating, rearing, socialization, mothering, fathering), kinship institutions (patriarchy, sexism, gender, family, extended family, schools), and kinship roles (heterosexual, bisexual, homosexual).

- *Community Sphere*: Includes community activity (language, spirituality, culture), community institutions (neighborhoods, museums, schools, churches, families, regions), and historical identity or heritage (race, ethnicity, national, religion, geographical proximity).

Putting these spheres in relation to each other, Albert et al. write: "We can think of any social act in terms of four moments related to the four defining types of social interaction." The point at which all four meet is called a "social moment" (p. 73). This concept is particularly useful for considering the economic, political, kinship, and community relations at a particular point for analysis. This to me seems critical to include in a study of identity. I have attempted an adaptation of the "social moment" to use for this study. Each theme is represented by a diagram, "Moment in Identity," which provides a schematic model of the interacting spheres of social life profiled. The amount of overlap in the spheres roughly mirrors the extent of the interaction.

The narratives themselves are within a social moment; that is, they were a social act, generated within social relations of community, economics, kinship, and politics at a particular point in time. The narratives also contain and reveal social moments in the lives of youths. Within these moments are tensions, ambiguities, desires, and contradictions. By making the narrative interpretative process dynamic, I eliminate the need to collapse or reduce what is being said into monolithic categories; rather, the youths' stories can be listened to as complex stories of work, love, and identity through which broader social relations are contested, negotiated, rejected, embraced, and so on.

The interpretative process is dialectical, moving back and forth between, for example, the individual story and the social cultural story, the individual story and the ideal gender story. In addition, the interview itself is understood as a social moment. The position of the researcher, that is, my position, is destabilized as it is exposed as part of a social relation, not an objective position outside of time or history: with the limitations and possibilities that any social relation embodies.

Complementary holism helps to answer questions such as: What underlies statements like "working is just a job" and "a paycheck"? Why is meaningful work not equally available to everyone? Can it be? How? Is a study of work also by definition a study of socioeconomic structures? If this is so, then how do youths develop as unique individuals within a given socioeconomic class? What is in common along class lines? What is different?

How can work, love, and identity be understood and youths' experience be explained? Why is it that when a study of work is put into relationship with a study of love, caring, and meaningfulness, structural accounts lose their grip? Each narrative tells a surprising story of change and development that can't be accounted for by structural theories which predict uniformity of experience, desires, and thoughts along class, race, gender, and sexual lines. Complementary holism, with its focus on "spheres of social life," enables one to articulate the complex ways in which race, class, gender, and sexuality impact upon identity (see Figure 3.1).

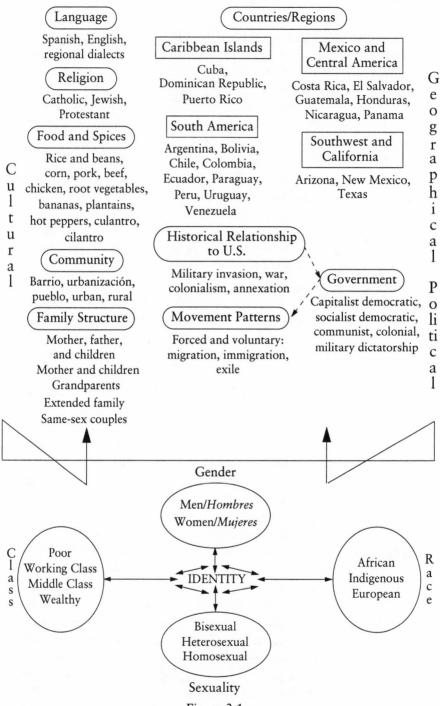

Figure 3.1
Interactive Levels of Analysis in the Category Latina/o

The prioritization of any singular category to explain identity becomes slippery when experience is looked at through a lens where critical experiences that make up identity are constantly negotiating and contesting a hierarchy of labels. Although Juana María, Rafael, and Rosa are poor they are not just poor; although they have left school, they are not "dropouts." This raises the question of what it would mean to not use this label but instead to look beyond the shortcut and travel the longer route of listening to a whole story of why Juana María left school. What are the differences in perspective? What can be learned?

Like a methodological whisper I hear, "Listen to Juana María, Renzo, Rosa, Manuel." Through listening to their stories the categories are made complicated, changing, contingent—development rejoins the world instead of somehow being conceptualized as progressing in spite of it or beyond it. Listening to a narrative of identity that a young person—alive, struggling, learning—tells, I feel a solidarity that comes from shared experience which *is shared* and not denied, forgotten, divided, or made invisible and unknowable by theoretical categories.

TEOLOGÍA DE LA LIBERACIÓN/ LIBERATION THEOLOGY

Two of the sites I visited are Catholic projects which base both the meaning of their work and the actual physical work they do within the framework of liberation theology. I found, therefore, that it was useful to include conceptual underpinnings from liberation theology in my theoretical and methodological strategies to guide me in interpreting the narratives gathered at these two sites.

In addition to this, Christianity has a powerful history in Latin America, and the Catholic and Protestant churches play critical roles in individual and cultural development in Puerto Rico. Thus, liberation theology is also useful as a strategy for placing Puerto Rico within a broader Latin American social and religious context.

Liberation theology[5] comes out of Catholicism and is a movement that defines itself as rooted in community-based action for social justice and for liberation based on faith, love, *la palabra de Dios,* and the life of Jesus. Its members confront both the church and dictatorships. In the more than twenty years since this movement emerged, the Catholic church and liberation theologians in

Latin America have often clashed. In El Salvador priests and nuns have been killed by government assassins for their work with the poor.[6]

But what is especially relevant for this study are two central elements of liberation theology: the purpose and process of making theory and the central belief that community is the context in which change—individual and social—can occur. In this section, I will sketch out the aspects of liberation theology which I have brought into this study as a methodological and theoretical strategy.

In addition to the writings of Latin American men, the writings of Sharon Welch (1985) and Carter Heyward (1982, 1993), two U.S. feminist liberation theologians who keep the lives of women at the center of their theoretical work and daily lives and whose work is deeply connected with Latin American liberation theology, have been especially clarifying and useful in this research.

Welch and Heyward struggle with the given and taken-for-granted methods of their "fields" and institutions—as women, as feminists, as scholars— particularly in their work toward enabling social justice, mutuality, and interrupting violence. Their interpretations of Christianity and their feminist interpretations of liberation theology have been critical to my own thinking about how to engage with the youths and interpret the stories they shared with me.

Liberation theology and feminist liberation theology enable me to view Martin Luther's formulation of *opera manum dei* from the perspective of the possibility of creating justice and peace: the hands that do the work of God are the hands that work for social justice with people who have been marginalized, kept poor, and oppressed in Latin America. The hands that do the work of God are also the hands that through poverty, bad health, and marginalization mend lives and communities, believing that God's work is to love and that "love is justice" (Heyward, 1982, p. 17).

This kind of passion was evident in many of the youths I spoke with, not just because they were "church going," but because they were full of life, desires, hopes, longings, and dreams that seemed to me to be about faith (*the objects of desire opening upon themselves without us; the objects of faith*). How to get close to and connect with this faith, this kind of love, this kind of work?

Carter Heyward (1982, 1993)—a lesbian, priest, and feminist theologian—struggles with questions of relationships in her exploration of what she calls "mutuality." Heyward (1982) writes over several pages in her book *The Redemption of God: A Theology of Mutual Relation* an extraordinary view of the connections between love, friendship, the work of making love, and how this is all drenched[7] in institutionalized and psychologized power:

> Our social order does not encourage mutuality. The possibility of friendship, mutual relation, God's incarnations between us, gives way historically to the perpetuation of an order in which relationships are structured on the basis of greed-for-more-rather-than-equal, and on the fear which feeds the greed. Institutional structures—from multinational corporations to the psychosocial structures of the individual—are sealed fast by a deep and common fear of friendship and love; fear of chaos, anarchy, pain, and loss; fear of power in relation and of what may happen to our "gain" if we take one another more seriously as prospective friends than as potential competitors. (pp. 165–166)

Heyward considers relationships as formed by external and internalized cultural, political, economic, and psychological processes which historically have disrupted a capacity to form friendships or right-relations. Heyward does not believe, however, that individual friendships can right all wrongs; for friendship and mutuality are experienced and formed within a world of power relations which Heyward repeatedly exposes as political:

> This is not to suggest that any one human relationship is, in itself, an agency of social change. For there is no relation "in itself." Every relationship—whether between a person and her friend or between groups of people, nations, religions—is in relation to something else. There is always a "third" something. It may be another person, a group of persons, a topic of interest, a common value, or an otherwise elusive link. The point is that no relation happens in isolation from its social milieu. Thus, no relation is asocial and no act is politically neutral (irrelevant to the dynamics of *power* in social relations). Still, social justice cannot be reduced to the sum of an infinite number of good relationships between friends . . . It is foolish to imagine that even huge numbers of persons could put an end to *all* wars, *all* hunger, *all* crime, *all* injustice—*forever*. (p. 135)

Heyward explores the power *of* and the power *within* relationships as a dialectic and posits this within "something else . . . a 'third' something." This third aspect, the invisible but felt presence at any human gathering, is systemic and institutional and not easily made visible. Yet making these power dynamics visible is crucial to changing them.

Sharon Welch (1982) in her text *Communities of Resistance and Solidarity: A Feminist Theology of Liberation* draws centrally upon the work of Michel Foucault to locate her own developing feminist theology of liberation: "Liberation theology is an insurrection of subjugated knowledges and the manifestation of a new episteme" (p. 35). Bringing Foucault's tools of analysis into conversation with theology (Welch calls this "a genealogy of resistance") allows her to "construct a method of reflection, a strategy in the battle for truth, that reflects my own social location—white, Western, feminist, middle-class" (p. 35).

The recognition of the ambiguities and contradictions of her own identities provides Welch with a theological base. From here she writes at the points of tension, trying to maintain the transitory nature of discourse in ways that get as close as possible to what is happening in the historical moment in which she is writing, because "what we say may not last, and we may not understand its relation to reality, but it does matter. Discourse does, in some complex way, shape our world. The same is true of theology" (p. 29). The same is true of psychological and educational research.

Welch finds that liberation theology provides her with a location from which to contest the dominant theological discourses which have made possible a structuring of "reality" that is brutal and that has left her grasping for a new method to name "reality" in ways that can create social change. Welch writes of her struggle for words, the breakdown of order, and the disruption of normalizing classifications in ways that mirror my own attempts and preoccupations in this study:

> My attempt to develop a feminist theology of liberation is motivated by my experience of the total breakdown of given modes of order and classification when I confront the twentieth century's banal yet deadly entrapment in mass murder and exploitation. It is all too easy to evade the weight of the inhumanity of the twentieth century. The means of evasion are many: a focus on scientific progress; a "mature" recognition of the persistence of human evil; a naive adherence to the ideal of the ultimate triumph of nonviolence and justice . . . My work in liberation theology is born out of this unthinkable horror, out of the shattering of concepts of sin and redemption, concepts of a merciful and loving God, caused by the twentieth century's stark brutality—a brutality that

kills millions and is carried out through active and passive complicity of good Christians and solid citizens . . . What is the rationality of a faith that blinds while using the language of final revelation? What is the meaning of doctrines and symbols that claim to reveal ultimate truth about human life but are in that life the correlates of structures of oppression, exploitation, and terror? What does it mean to believe in a gospel of love, justice, and peace when a Christian head of state, General Rios Montt, was systematically and brutally exterminating the Indian population of his country, Guatemala? (pp. 5–6)

Welsh further explains that "liberation theologians do not analyze the nature of love in itself, but examine concrete social conditions that subvert the possibility of love being expressed." She offers the example of "the impossibility of fulfilling the imperative of love when economic conditions require working in a factory that produces napalm" (p. 64). Theorizing, for Welch, is not a quest for universal laws but is, instead, "more specific, since the challenge is to establish just conditions in reality" (p. 65).

In liberation theology, abstract and universal ideals of love and work give way to personal experience and community-based action for justice. Although concrete experiences of work and love are constrained by economic and sociopolitical realities, acts of transformation hinge on the capacity to imagine that life can be otherwise. The role of theory becomes to explicate what keeps change from happening and name actions which make possible the transformation of oppressive conditions. The theorist is an activist. The potentially critical role of educators is clear. Andrea Ayvazian, Winnie Mandela, Che Guevara, Paolo Freire, Baby Suggs, holy . . .

To investigate "that particular combination" in these terms means to explore how love and work have concretely been experienced by youths: Who has supported you? What are the alternatives available to you? What work do you love to do? What is your story of love and work? This kind of inquiry means including personal examples to illustrate definitions as well as exploring abstract ideals with an eye toward explaining what keeps the genius, the gift, from being lifted up.

An organizing principle of liberation theology, *comunidades de base* (base communities) is key to understanding how youths experience themselves as belonging to a network of people even when they feel pushed out of their family, school, and society. In Puerto Rico, *comunidad, barrio,* and *pueblo* are deeply felt connections of belonging even though these are often concretely lacking in youths' daily lives. In addition, liberation theology offers a way to explore the inclusion of God in the youths' lives. For example, in the interviews the youths mention God and His will as equally important with their own wills and plans. "God willing," "*Si Dios quiere*," is a common saying in Puerto Rico.

To explore "that particular combination," then, requires inquiry into the processes of developing a vision and a history of personal experiences. The "what is" and "what can be" are in relationship with each other. Thought and action come out of their alignment. The relationship between present and future is not oppositional but dialectical. Abstract questions like What is love? What is work? and What would you like to be in the future? reveal what is and what could be and offer a way to view the psychological dimensions of the wanting, the desires, and the yearning that are often hidden or obscured by terms such as, *career, employment, job, dropout, delinquent,* and *HIV positive.*

Setting true north to this, I return to Erikson's compass. An exploration of the psychological processes underlying decisions on work and love by youths and the connections with development becomes an investigation of identity as a dynamically changing and contextually dependent process. The search ceases to be for a core or essence—a static identity or the real self—but, rather, for the patterns of psychological processes in relation to material conditions within particular contexts that lead to statements such as "I am a musician," "I love to cook," "I want to be a Marine," and "You cannot make a mango tree grow apples."

The educative work of nourishing "that particular combination," however, ought not be set on one "stage" of development, namely, youth and the "attainment" of an identity. Identity is an ongoing process, as is human development. Educators are also changing in time and space—in history—with our own identities. Questions on community open this dialogue and search out the texture of what composes nourishing, of what hooks calls "relational love" (p. 35).

I imagine the possibilities of developing in peace instead of violence, in freedom instead of oppression, in learning instead of schooling, in "having a sense of where one is going" instead of dropping out. Could "a whole new poetry beginning here" (Rich, 1978, p. 76) be written?

CHAPTER 4

Methods

To tell a story, or to hear a story told, is not a simple transmission
of information. Something else in the telling is given too, so that,
once hearing, what one has heard becomes part of oneself.
From *A Chorus of Stones: The Private Life of War*,
Susan Griffin (1993, p. 154)

INTERVIEWING: LIVING STORIES

In Puerto Rico, talking on a porch at noon (the heat and humidity!), or in a small rehearsal room with the air conditioning too cold, or in an office with *persiana* windows and the fan on high, or while walking through a garden of tropical flowers and trees (amapola, palma, mango), or in a workshop with motorboat engines waiting to be repaired, the smell of fuel and salt mixed together—the voice speaks the body, spirit, mind, emotion. The story of experience is voiced with details yet also with things left out—forgotten or denied—retrospective but spoken in the present—affected by what's happening now.

Interview questions focus the discussion and organize the narrative which is electronically caught on audiotape for later transcription and interpretation. The story is caught in a moment in time and as such is a particular and specific telling. (What might Mirta and David say next week or next year?) It is limited in this way. I listen to the story as the youth is speaking, then again at home, then again when I reread and search for themes. Over and over, a narrative repeats until I know the story well, anticipate the next sentence, the next moment.

With each rewinding and retelling I am drawn closer to the pauses, syntax, and grammar—the uniqueness of the ways of telling and the commonalities that we share as Puertorriqueñas and Puertorriqueños, Latin Americans, as men and women, as extended family members, sisters and brothers, as people in sexual relationships, as friends, as parents. I also listen for and hear what we do not share in common: *luchas y dificultades* which are not mine, beliefs that I do not hold dear, roles which I cannot embrace, experiences I have never had. Differences are just as important as what we have in common for they disrupt easy agreement and taken-for-granted assumptions; differences put the process of investigating why decisions were made, borders crossed, schools and homes left, drugs bought and sold, in stark relief for the researcher, for me.

THE INTERVIEW

I conducted an open-ended, semiclinical interview composed of eleven core questions in Spanish or a combination of Spanish and English. I interviewed fifty-four youths individually and two youths together who were married, for a total of fifty-six youths.[1] The language used in the interview depended on the preference of the interviewee. Some were more comfortable speaking in English because they grew up in U.S. cities with English as their primary language: others needed to use a few English words, and others spoke exclusively in Spanish. The interview questions were designed to lift up the youths' definitions and experiences of work and love and in this way elicit an articulation of their developmental processes.

The eleven interview questions were grouped into three parts.

- *Part I* was designed to generate a narrative composed of definitions, concepts, and experiences of work and love. This part was created to provide a view of the ideals (what should be) and experiences (what is and has been) of work and love for each youth.
- *Part II* was designed to generate a narrative of the alternatives and support available to each youth, in her or his process of development, at the individual, community, and societal levels. This part was developed to provide a social and historical context for each youth, to give a sense of place and time.
- *Part III* was designed to generate a detailed story of their own development focusing on their processes of aligning work and love. This last part gathers and retraces the two previous ones in the form of a story. The eliciting of a

story, rather than specific answers to questions, was designed to enable each youth to structure his or her account organically, freely, and to give the chance to bring in what may have been left out by the direct questions.

The interview questions are presented in English and Spanish (see Appendix A, "Interview Questions"). In practice, however, I often had to repeat the questions, reword, or expand on what a question meant by using examples. In addition, I asked follow-up questions for the purposes of clarification and for greater detail. The duration of the interviews ranged from fifteen to over ninety minutes. The kinds of responses to each question ranged from a word or two, a sentence or two, to a complex account of personal, political, and philosophical views.

At each site the person in charge of the program I was visiting directed me to a room or area. Generally, the director asked what I needed, how long the interviews would take, and for more information on my study. I would say that I needed electricity, chairs, and quiet. The first two were provided but quiet was scarce. Often there were loud background sounds: cymbals, drums, electric saws, telephones ringing, short wave radios crackling. I explained that the length of the interview varied because it depended on the length of the responses, which depended on the youth, but that the average was twenty five-minutes. When it was an option, I interviewed equal numbers of females and males.

The interviews took place in offices, conference rooms, porches, or classrooms. As a youth would come into the room where I was sitting or getting the equipment ready, I would ask him or her to please have a seat and get comfortable. Sometimes the youth would ask me first, before anything else, what I was doing ("*¿Que es lo que usted esta haciendo?*"), usually in the formal tense of "*usted*" reserved for adults, anyone significantly older than one is, or anyone of higher status. To both the youths that asked and the ones that didn't, I would explain the purpose of the study, and what the interviews were for, and ask if they would be willing to be photographed. I explained that the portraits would be included in the document and also exhibited.

I made it clear that participation was voluntary, that the interview could be terminated at any time for any reason if the youth or director so wished.[2] Everyone agreed to be interviewed.

I would ask if they had any questions. Several youths didn't know what a thesis was and asked. I said that it was a written document that would contain all the information I gathered and what I thought about the things I learned from their interviews. I also said that the document would enable me to graduate. Others asked me why I chose to interview at that particular site. Often the interview process itself was a topic of curiosity and humor.

During the interviewing I saw that many youths were nervous as if they were taking a test with right and wrong answers. This was most noticeable when the interview changed from direct questions (Parts I and II) to the last part, where I would say, "Can you tell me the story of how you arrived at this work?" There would generally be a sigh and a relaxing of the body: telling a story has no right or wrong. Stories have no history of being "wrong," whereas questions asked by adults to youths have a long history, especially in schools, of having correct answers.

When the interview came to what felt like a close, I asked if there were any questions. Some asked me what I was doing, again. Several youths said that the questions made them think. One youth said that she felt that many of the questions brought out what is taken-for-granted about love, work, and school for her. Talking about it made her stop and take another look. She said it was important to stop and think about these things and that in her classes the teachers didn't take the time.

At the sites where I spent the day or visited over several days, after answering their questions, I said that if they had anything they wanted to say or ask later, to feel free to come back. At the sites where this was not possible, I gave extra time at the end to "take a moment" and think about anything that might be missing.

PHOTOGRAPHY:
ANOTHER APPROACH TO KNOWLEDGE

Photographs still what is moving so I can see it without blur: time, place, a glance, posture, details (What does her face express? What do his eyes say? What color is the dress she's wearing? The shirt he's wearing? What kind of material? Does she have earrings on? Do they have wedding rings? What is their hair like? What are their hands like?). All these combine to give a portrait, in black and white, of a person caught at a particular moment in time. And this research, which is based on the lives of young people, ought to include their faces, their bodies, hands, eyes, so that it becomes a place where the marginalized "take up space" in the forbidden country of social science. Photographs provide another approach to knowledge that literally brings me face to face with my questions and their answers. It is not the quality of the portraits in terms of technical, compositional, or artistic "merits," but the faces themselves, the youths themselves, that hold power: their faces telling a story.

I explained to each youth that the photographs were to add another dimension to the study—their faces and what they were doing that day. I said that I wanted to exhibit the photographs in a public place with excerpts from their interviews so that educators, students, and administrators could see and listen to what they said. I emphasized that if this made them uncomfortable that it was absolutely fine not to have their picture taken. I was surprised that not a single youth asked not to be photographed and that they wanted to share themselves in this way.[3]

Portraits of youths working or looking out from two-dimensional space urge me to remember that these narratives are not "data": the stories are alive. Their sweet faces (why are their faces open even after so much hardship?) stilled for just a second enable me to write, to keep talking, to continue the dialogue. They remind me that the point is not to pin down but to observe and interpret a moment in time written into a black and white image— the metamorphosis of living color.

John Berger (1982), in *Another Way of Telling,* put it this way:

A photograph is simpler than most memories, its range more limited. Yet with the invention of photography we acquired a new means of expression more closely associated with memory than any other . . . Both the photograph and the remembered depend upon and equally oppose the passing of time. Both preserve moments, and propose their own form of simultaneity, in which all their images can coexist. Both stimulate, and are stimulated by, the inter-connectedness of events. Both seek instants of revelation, for it is only such instants which give full reason to their own capacity to withstand the flow of time. (p. 280)

In a photograph I took there are two teenage girlfriends making a cake, and they look happy—eyes open and focused, mouths relaxed and smiling, both looking at their teacher—for the moment when the shutter clicked. Their stories are hardship. The happiness and hardship are both true. I don't remember this instant; what I remember about one of the girls was her eagerness to become a cook, and how wide open her eyes were as she spoke.

Photographs show the setting, as well as the perspective of the researcher; every picture shows what I find interesting, what caught my attention. The image presented is limited in this way because what catches the researcher's eye is never the whole picture but only a partial view of reality. Even so, Karl G. Heider (1976) argues that "one of the greatest differences between words and pictures lies in the fact that words are necessarily abstracted generalized representations of reality, while photographs, in contrast to words, and despite the subjective selection in shooting, are in some sense direct, specific representations of reality" (p. 88).

The faces you see are completely real. They are the surface presented to the world, sent out into the world. They are direct representations of a body that houses the mind, spirit, and emotions and that gives rise to voice. To balance "abstracted generalized representations of reality," analytical categories, and emergent themes, photographs give direct versions of a face, body, and hands: they bear a steady witness.

In the silence of two-dimensional space, in black and white, portraits help resist reduction and fragmentation—a whole face, Juana María's face—into abstract parts. They help to remember the whole person—she wears a homemade dress, she is big, her gaze is direct—into an analytical work like this one. Yet they alone are not enough. To understand the psychology which forms the gestures of the face, moves the hands a certain way, positions the shoulders just so, words are necessary too because a portrait does not explain; a photograph can only tell.

And what of this desire to tell? Since I was a child the desire to tell has followed me around like a loyal dog, never leaving my side even when I was not willing to feed it, to nourish it, to help it grow.

Su Braden (1983), in *Committing Photography*, offers an in-depth historical analysis, through photographs and text, of the power of documentary photography to document or distort and the differences between these two positions. Braden argues that "photographs offer information, yet they, especially, are not neutral tools" (p. 1). The photographer's reasons and motives for telling are just as important as what is being told. The agenda of the person behind the lens frames the story in specific ways: photographs can be propaganda or evidence, portraits or masks, or both depending on the context within which they are shown and seen.

Human development is not transparent or invisible—it can be seen. Therefore it can be photographed and put on film. But as Braden and others[4] clearly articulate, the process of documenting development is problematic, particularly when used to represent the ways things ought to be. In psychology, education, and the social sciences generally, photography has been used almost exclusively to represent visually the dominant social order—as visual backups to enforce the borders of what is pathological or abnormal and what is healthy or normal.

Photographs in these textbooks serve two primary interacting functions: to illustrate pathology or abnormality (which pathologizes what is represented) and to show health or normalcy (which normalizes what is represented). As representations of pathology and normalcy the people photographed are reduced to the status of representational subject, voiceless to speak their own story, speaking only through the surrounding accompanying text, which usually signals to the reader which category this visual object ought to occupy—the normal or the pathological.

In the social sciences this representational strategy has maintained the use of photography at a pretheoretical state. There has been, to my knowledge, no reflection or theorizing on the uses of photography *within* the textbooks themselves; rather photographs are presented as uncontested evidence, direct tellings of the real, unbiased documents of a seamless reality where the healthy or normal and pathological or abnormal are clearly delineated. Ironically, the borders are made even more apparent by those who encroach upon their neatness; these individuals who do not quite fit into one or the other are called "borderline personalities."

The youths' portraits contest and disrupt this history of representations of normalcy and pathology because even though they occupy space in this history of viewing (as my voice and this text join a history of social science), they are not speaking within a representational construction of the healthy or normal or pathological or abnormal. In addition, my accompanying text theorizes the use of these photographs as representations—not merely as proof or evidence of the normal or pathological—as portraits that tell about identity. What, then, are the youths telling? Is there a story of identity being told? A story of work? A story of love?

In *Puerto Rico Mio,* Jack Delano's (1990) book of documentary photographs taken—with his wife and *compañera,* Irene—over four decades, Delano, in his autobiographical introduction, "The People, *La gente,*" concludes with an example of what photographs can tell.

> Not long ago I found a letter in my mailbox postmarked El Paso, Texas. The letter was written in pencil on school notebook paper and had many grammatical errors. "Dear Mr. Delano," it began. "I am fourteen years old and when I grow up I want to be a photographer like you . . . " (Well, I decided right then and there, this is a letter I *must* answer.) The boy went on to explain, in two long pages, that he came from a poor family; his mother worked in a shirt factory; that he had started taking pictures but his camera was stolen, and he was saving up for another one; that he found some FSA pictures in books at the library while writing a school paper on the Great Depression; and that he was asking for my autograph because he liked the pictures so much. I am generally a poor correspondent but such flattery was irresistible. I sent him a signed print and a letter with several questions. One of them was, "What is it that you like about FSA pictures?" His next letter was euphoric. He was making a cherry wood frame for the picture to leave for his children and grandchildren. His thanks were effusive, and in answer to my question he wrote, "I like the pictures because they make ordinary people important." (pp. 32–33).

Like the boy moved to write letters to Jack Delano, make a cherry wood frame for an autographed photograph, and save up for another camera, all viewers join a photograph at the point of looking and add a kind of fourth dimension—the meaning made from the image becomes once more a part of the living, acting, moving world in the form of an emotion created in the viewer. Photographs have the potential to move us into action, emotional and intellectual. Indeed, photographs that do engage our emotions and mind are considered "good" and "powerful." And here lies the importance of making critical distinctions between images which document and images which distort and the reasons behind why a photograph was created.

Two particularly powerful and common examples of this process are given by Sandoval Sánchez (1990) and Ortiz Cofer

(1993). Sandoval Sánchez writes of his early experiences in the United States and how he was and is viewed by Anglo-Americans. This view was based on the stereotypes of Puertorriqueñas and Puertorriqueños represented in the movie *West Side Story*.[5]

> Since my arrival in Wisconsin, U.S.A., in 1973, to continue with my university studies, *West Side Story* was imposed on me as the "model of/and for" my ethnic *Boricua* identity. A strange and foreign model to someone recently arrived but not to the Anglo-Americans for whom my presence activated stereotypes of the Other, the Latino. Time and time again to make me feel comfortable in their "family rooms" and to communicate their knowledge of Puerto Ricans to me, they would initiate conversations with *West Side Story*: "Al, we loved *West Side Story*. Have you seen the movie? Did you like it?" On other occasions there would be someone who would in an attempt at parody sing in my ear, "Alberto, I've just met a guy named Alberto," or someone who would at seeing me arrive would quickly begin to stamp and in a shrill voice sing: "I like to be in America! . . . Everything's free in America." Little by little with the passage of time I began to get used to it; I just smiled and ignored the stereotyped image of the Puerto Rican that Hollywood promoted on the screen. (pp. 30–31, translation mine)

Superimposing racist representations from *West Side Story* over Puertorriqueños and Puertorriqueñas is not uncommon. I have my own stories, and so do my sisters, my brother, and friends. It's as if *West Side Story* has been used as a foundational text by Anglo-Americans; it is the one piece of information and visual representation—widely disseminated and viewed, repeated on television at least once a year like *The Wizard of Oz*— which forms the reference point for what being Puerto Rican means. Although *West Side Story* is in no way a documentary, it is used as documentation of Puerto Rican life. Thus *West Side Story*, which is not our story, becomes part of the story of what it means to be Puerto Rican, both for *Boricuas* and for Anglo-Americans.

Ortiz Cofer (1993) describes her own experiences with this dynamic in her book of prose and poetry, *The Latin Deli*. In addition to being what I think of as "Marialized," Ortiz Cofer has been made into "Evita."

> Though rarer, these incidents are still commonplace in my life. It happened to me most recently during a stay at a very classy metropolitan hotel favored by young professional couples for

their weddings. Late one evening after the theater, as I walked toward my room with my new colleague (a woman with whom I was coordinating an arts program), a middle-aged man in a tuxedo, a young girl in satin and lace on his arm, stepped directly into our path. With his champagne glass extended toward me, he exclaimed "Evita!"

Our way blocked, my companion and I listened as the man half-recited, half-bellowed "Don't Cry for Me, Argentina." When he finished, the young girl said: "How about a round of applause for my daddy?" We complied, hoping this would bring this silly spectacle to a close. . . . to him, I was just an Evita or a Maria: merely a character in his cartoon-populated universe. (pp. 151–152)

For the working-class Puertorriqueña whose first language is Spanish and whose English is not as good as Ortiz Cofer's or Sandoval Sánchez's, there is another stereotype: "They make good domestics." Cofer writes:

The myth of the Hispanic menial has been sustained by the same media phenomenon that made 'Mammy' from *Gone With the Wind* America's ideal of the black woman for generations; Maria, the housemaid or counter girl, is now indelibly etched into the national psyche. The big and the little screens have presented us with the picture of the funny Hispanic maid, mispronouncing words and cooking up a spicy storm in a shiny California kitchen. (p. 152)

It seems probable that these racist representations in movies and on Broadway of Puerto Ricans, and of Latinas/os in general, will be actively called forth as long as the stereotypes serve some function for Anglo-American viewers. Like the animation in *Little House of Horrors,* the make-believe characters of Maria and Evita live and are given a body with which to speak and act every time someone references them as a starting point to interact with a Puerto Rican or Latina/o.

This dynamic—corrosive and humiliating—repeated time and time again needs to be disrupted. To interrupt the flow of racist representations means to me that I have to generate portraits which represent us. The photographs of the youths included here are a rewriting of the stories of "María" and "Bernardo," an attempt to change the sound of shrill singing in our ears ("I want to live in America! Everything free in America!") to listening to our own voices.

The dynamics between different aspects of documentary photography beckon to the viewer. Much like someone telling a complex story, a group of photographs strives for cohesion, consistency, and continuity, an overall feeling and tone. Yet, also as in a story, there are conflicts, ambiguities, silences, and missing pieces. Looking at photographs this way, as if listening to a story, offers insights into an understanding of identity as told through images.

Another aspect of photographs that pushes and pulls at their goodness and power is how they are arranged or collected into groups. Photographs exhibited in groups take on meaning that would not necessarily be there if the image were seen alone, say, in someone's home on the wall or as an individual image in an exhibit or in a textbook. Yet one image can also work as a group when it connects with many images already in our minds. Such is the case with the photograph of the Bosnian prisoner on the cover of newspapers in August 1992, that made many call the Balkan war another "holocaust" because the man in the photograph looked as if he was in a concentration camp. Groups of photographs—either formed in our collective memory or displayed on walls—stake out a territory, map a terrain, proclaim an agenda, and are therefore political statements.

Three exhibits illustrate the previous points: *Songs of My People, African Americans: A Self-Portrait, I Dream a World: Portraits of Black Women Who Changed America,* and *Robert Mapplethorpe: The Perfect Moment.*

At the Corcoran Gallery of Art in Washington, D.C., there is a photographic exhibit called *Songs of My People.* I walk around, heart full of something, maybe it's joy, because the beauty, "the song" of each person, is there in each photograph. The black photojournalists caught the story, the song, the genius: a *self-portrait,* finally. It's March, 1992, at a national gallery. I see Willie T. Ribbs getting out of his car. He's there in black and white in the exhibit room entitled "Professions" and I say, "Willie!" almost out loud. I feel connected to this show: a self-portrait, finally. There are a few lines of text next to each photograph, explaining, giving the names and locations. The words place me in specific places: Daufuskie Island, South Carolina; McRoberts, Kentucky; New Orleans, Louisiana; Brooklyn, New York; Los Angeles, Macon, Detroit . . . On the walls are famous faces and an old woman who feeds the neighborhood kittens every morning. Each exhibit room has a theme: "Community," "Professions," "Boyz and Girlz in the Hood," "Spirituality" . . .

And then I want to know, What is behind the camera? Who are the photographers? What is the desire to tell? All are African American, mostly men. One is Gordon Parks (1992), and in the "Introduction" to the book that holds all the photographs, he says this about his work:

> And no other art form has more diligently recorded our painful metamorphosis than the camera. In the proper hands, it burrows deep into feelings of human beings and into the true nature of their conditions.
>
> For these reasons mostly, photography has best served me as a profession. I turned to it with hopes of having a voice that people would have reason to listen to. Because of the frustration that assaulted my early life—prejudice, discrimination and intolerance—I have attempted to show, through my work, the problems of people around me. There was the responsibility to point up the plight of others less fortunate than myself; to communicate the abuse of the underprivileged as well as the insensitivity of those who administer the abuse. Silent watching was not enough. Even verbal condemnation had to give way to commitment. Photography was the most accessible way to put commitment into practice. (p. xi)

As a photographer, I connect with Parks and agree. But there are many faces missing from this group of photographs: Audre Lorde, Alice Walker . . . and I realize that the women of *I Dream a World* are not here. But then again, Audre Lorde is missing from *I Dream a World*. At each level of silence, I see how the desired overall feeling and tone, the correct image, is created. Why is Audre Lorde completely missing? Is it because she is a lesbian? Sexuality, the disruptive identity, is smoothed out through omission. Her missing face buzzes in my ears like a silence heard for too long.

The problematic practice of using only race or only gender as the exclusive point of commonality is further illustrated by the deliberately disruptive work of Robert Mapplethorpe. Mapplethorpe created photographs, censured and closed by the Corcoran Gallery, that told a story of identity, a story about the unspeakable, a story of sexuality, and more specifically the sexuality of gay black and white men. *Stories of My People* did include one powerful image of black and white people together, ironically, a black boy and a white boy on a set of swings holding hands, entitled "Innocence." But my point is not that white men photographers were not included in the exhibit; it is that Mapplethorpe's version of relationship could not have been included because he was not an African American photographer. Similarly, the images of *I Dream a World* could not be included because Brian Lanker is white. Yet Mapplethorpe's work is very much a self-portrait and a portrait of gay black men—a group completely missing from *Stories of My People*.

Viewing images, such as the ones contained in *Songs of My People* and *I Dream A World,* within the complex matrix of race, class, gender, and sexuality, the limitations are bittersweet: the joy, passion, pleasure, and connection of familiar strong wonderful faces and bodies is quickly jolted by the recognition that someone, usually gay or lesbian, is missing. And then again, when viewing the images created by Mapplethorpe, a gay photographer who documented his view of sexuality, the buzzing in my ears is the deep silence of women of color.

The potential for distortion in documentary photographs is not necessarily found in an individual image itself, but in the grouping of images and who the photographer is—the identity of the photographer—and how this affects what story is told, and then whether or not we are able to view it. Just as listening to a story inextricably involves the storyteller, so listening to what the photograph is telling involves the photographer. The limits as well as the range of any collection or group of photographs are always clear; you can literally see who is missing as well as who is there.

Nowhere is who is missing, and who is there, made as painfully clear than by las madres de la Plaza de Mayo in Argentina, who for years, during the mid-1970s and through the 1980s, carried the portraits of their "disappeared" children—young and prodemocracy—to the Plaza de Mayo asking the government and passersby alike, "Where are they?" The mothers—holding up the photographs, glued to poster board, on wooden poles with their children's names, young men and women missing, written on the top of each—push this discussion of photography to its limits. For the mothers of the Plaza de Mayo the photographs are what is left of their children and also who is missing.

Marjorie Agosín (1992), in her beginning essay "The Dancers," reflects on the photographs of Alicia D'Amico and Alicia Sanguinetti of the mothers of the Plaza de Mayo in *Circles of Madness*, a book that combines poems by Agosín in Spanish, then translated into English, with the faces of the mothers. Agosín writes:

Each photograph commemorates *the presence of an absence,* just as does the search that scrutinizes, interrogates, intrigues, and terrifies. Is there anything more somber than some mothers walking together with a poster filled with photographs of their dead relatives? The photographs of Alicia D'Amico and Alicia Sanguinetti postulate an ethic, a way of being, and a presence that does not cry out for only information; the presence of the photographed is already a definite and unadulterated proof of their existence . . . The photographs of Alicia D'Amico and Alicia Sanguinetti *act both as instruments and as an approach to knowledge* that makes us remember that personae go beyond masks. (no page numbers, emphasis mine)

And what of the youths—Juana María, Rosa, Rafael—missing school? And the ones who have stayed in school—where are their faces? And the ones who have returned to programs from the streets? And the ones convinced they can make change? Here they are.

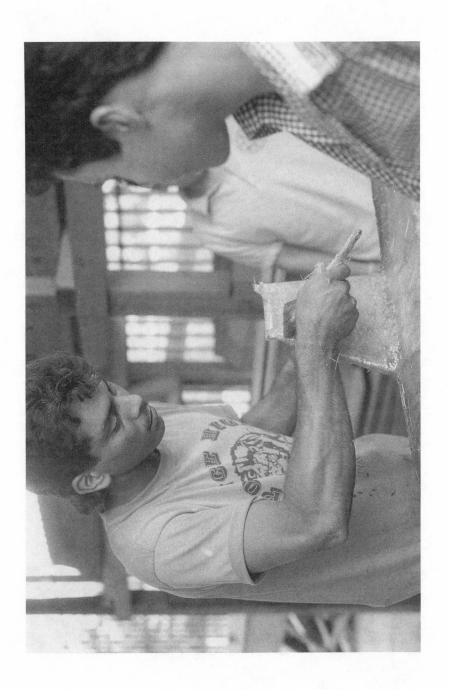

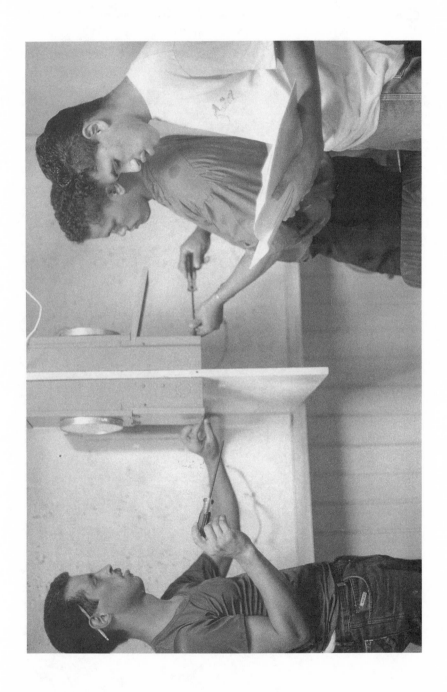

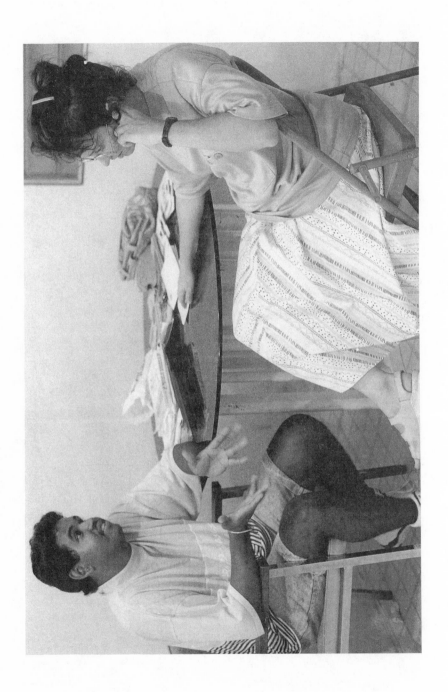

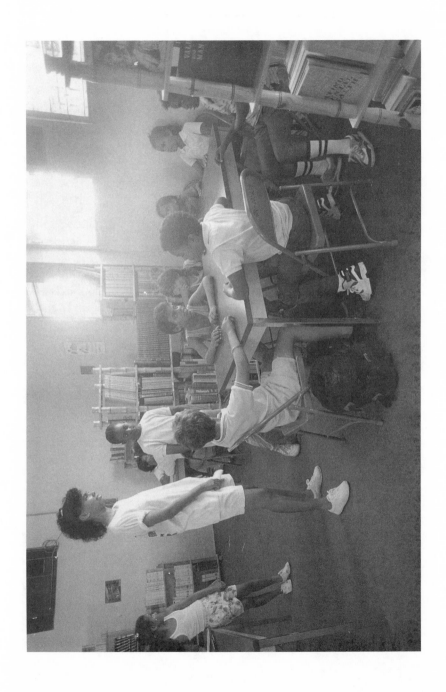

NARRATIVE ANALYSIS

I take direction from Elliot Mishler's (1979, 1986, 1990) approach to and understanding of interview narratives. Mishler considers the social context within which interviews take place and how they are mutually constructed by the interviewer and interviewee: he allows a relationship to grow within the structure of an interview and conceptualizes the process as dialectical. Mishler brings the practice and many of the desires of feminist research specifically into the methodological arena of research interviewing.

In his article "Validation in Inquiry-Guided Research: The Role of Exemplars in Narrative Studies," Mishler (1990) engages the dialectic of narrative and theory making, and then the problems of validity and reliability, asking, Would someone else doing exactly what the researcher did reach the same conclusions? And does the narrative analysis measure what is meant to be measured? His approach to reflecting on these issues is through an analysis of "exemplars" or key examples of narrative research studies—the same approach taken by Sandra Harding (1987) in her analysis of what constitutes feminist research.[6] Mishler argues against a model of scientific inquiry that would throw out studies in which the researcher answered "no" to the above validity and reliability questions and begins to formulate an interpretive framework which is "contextually grounded" (p. 437).

Mishler leaves the laboratory experiment and the search for laws conceptually behind and reframes narrative interpretation not as studies that can be reproduced—a mutually constructed relationship cannot be reproduced by a third party—but as scientific research that can be assessed on its own terms, on its "trustworthiness" (p. 419). Aware of the irony of staking out another canon to replace the experimental model, Mishler gives three tentative guidelines for "trustworthiness" in narrative studies by pointing to what his "exemplars" had in common: "These are: the display of the primary texts; the specification of analytic categories and the distinctions in terms of discernable features of the texts; and, theoretical interpretations focused on structures, that is, on relations among different categories, rather than on variables" (p. 437). In an earlier work, Mishler (1986) explores another aspect of narrative studies, the possibility of empowerment.

The effort to empower respondents and the study of narratives are closely linked. They are connected through the assumption . . . that one of the significant ways through which individuals make sense of and give meaning to their experiences is to organize them in narrative form . . . Through their narratives people may be moved beyond the text to the possibilities of action. That is, to be empowered is not only to speak in one's own voice and to tell one's own story, but to apply the understanding arrived at to action in accord with one's own interests. (p. 119)

Mishler moves both with and beyond the interview into a broader social context: the point at which a person takes action once something has been expressed and understood in a new way. Moving from, or taking action based on, a narrative is a complex psychological and social task.

Mishler's work in this area is "preliminary and exploratory" (p. 118). For more direction, I turn to "complementary holism." I borrow from Albert et al. a model of four "critical spheres of social life," as previously discussed in chapter 3. My analysis and interpretation of the psychological processes housed within the narratives are related and linked to social realities which are made explicit through a consideration of these spheres. This is the basis for my analysis and interpretation of the narratives, which will employ a thematic structure.

Emergent Themes

Spatial metaphors—boundaries, borders, *la frontera* (Anzaldúa's location for identity), territory, mapping, and compass (Erikson provides one)—are central to this work, which travels through narratives and therefore needs a map. They include exploration, new territory, five hundred years of conquest, crossing the ocean, the desire, visions, dreams, as well as the forced immigration, uprootedness, slavery, upheaval of mapping and claiming and being mapped and claimed, surviving and resisting, the hegemony of a colonizer—the blood on the hands—and the daily struggle of the colonized—the blood in the veins—*Latinoamerica*. The metaphorical grounding helps me lay a course through complex psychological and social processes. If I strain the metaphors it is a factor of the newness of the work. Hopefully new metaphors will take their place.

Still, the metaphor of journey for psychological development is a powerful one and difficult to replace, since identity is very much an investigation and movement. And still I wonder how much these spatial metaphors themselves obscure the more simultaneous and chaotic, accidental and contradictory, contextual aspects of identity that follow unseen paths and make sense only in retrospect when the storyteller can put together the fragments in a way that makes sense of the present. These are the two competing metaphorical frames that I hold constant: the spatial—journey, mapping, borders—and the fragments—shattered, broken—the pieces of the story. The emergent themes are quadrants that locate pieces of the narratives.

In the field of identity, what are the parameters of youths thinking and feeling about work and love? What do the youths tell of that "particular combination"? Where are the boundaries that mark movement from one place to another? Through an analysis of emergent themes I will stake out the terrain by plotting the coordinates of work and love that come out of the youths' narratives. The themes are bound by time and place but point to a direction. There are boundaries—social, religious, traditional, gender-based—and there are patterns, common definitions across age, gender, class, and region, but there are also unique views that highlight what is important to each youth in her or his specific context. To cross such a wide field in a useful way it is necessary to stay specific, close to the ground, so as not to get lost in generalities and vague overstatements. The emergent themes organize the journey.

The themes emerged from the careful and deliberate reading of all the narratives and through the use of worksheets for each interview question. The most salient points of each response to each interview question by each youth were highlighted in yellow ink and then written into the corresponding worksheet. Out of this process of reading and then writing I was able to find commonalities among narratives, recurring themes. The development of the categories of emergent themes is based on all the narratives. Each theme, however, is profiled through a selection of narratives. They are not included as definitive or exclusive but as illustrations, examples, of what emerged in the narratives as a whole or within smaller groups of narratives.

The narratives had a wide range of detail; some were extensive and detailed, others short and general. Some narratives were complex and layered, spanning many years; others were caught in the present struggles and not historical. Several times, my interview questions didn't make sense or a youth didn't want to answer. Each theme had within it the complex workings of gender, socioeconomic class, and race. These social categories inform the interpretation of the emergent themes, for the narratives are filled with what I see as the consequences of racism, classism, and heterosexism.

CHAPTER 5

The Youths

With thumbtacks, I've put up portraits of the youths on the wall. Their faces are a few feet away from mine, their eyes looking straight at me or looking at what they're doing with their hands, their music sheets, or dishes they've cooked. The work prints, two-dimensional, come alive.

I'm thousands of miles away from the island, from Puerto Rico, as the Spanish called her, from Borinquen, as the Taíno Indians named her. But in these pictures they are there and I'm there too. Their eyes pull me back to when we sat across from each other and talked about working and loving, and what they're like.

In this chapter, which completes the second Panel, I want to give a feeling for the places I visited and the youths I interviewed through descriptions, observations, and documents that were given to me at each site. I would like to illustrate the complexity of the places that youths move through on their way to something else, call home, visit, or go to seeking help. I find it necessary to also give, even if briefly, an account of the larger context within which these sites are situated. To remove the stories and places, the faces and hands, from the larger social context would be to "blank-out"[1] a critical dimension of life in Puerto Rico: our collective history, our ongoing struggles.

And so the view is broad at the beginning and then becomes focused on individual particulars, laying the road toward understanding their narratives as living stories—dynamic, in movement, composed of daily routines, surrounded by history.

LIVING IN BORINQUEN[2]

Puerto Rico is a developed country which forms a part of the Third World in Latin America in the Caribbean. This single sentence reveals the geopolitical problematics of Puerto Rico.[3] It is a neighbor to Cuba, Haiti, the Dominican Republic, Jamaica, Nicaragua, Panama, and several other nations. As evidence of our past, Puertorriqueños/as still call the island Borinquen, as if to push back the memory of Spanish colonization. And we call ourselves Boricuas although there is no denying that we are descendants of the Spanish. We are also the children of West Africans ripped from several different tribes and enslaved to cultivate sugar. From Africa, Borinquen inherited bananas, plantain, root vegetables that became staple foods, and stories and music. Our particular mother tongue reveals the victory and conquest of the Spanish but also the resistance of the African and Taíno peoples. *Hamaca*: hammock. *Burundanga*: chaos. *Fufu*: a spell . . .

Unlike other European peoples of the "New World," the Spanish *conquistadores* married with Taínos and Africans, usually in the name of Christian conversion and salvation, but like other Europeans they exploited and enslaved. Slavery was not abolished until 1873. Boricuas are a forged blend of conquest and defeat, native people and transposed people; we carry inside the blood of slaves and the slave owners. We have only been Puertorriqueños since the end of the sixteenth century—almost five hundred years—a short history compared with the native peoples of North and South America, Africans, and Jews. We are a relatively new people; as a people we are in our youth.

Today Puertorriqueños share with other Latin Americans the consequences of a military invasion by the United States, the newest imperialist power in the hemisphere. In 1898, as part of their strategy to defeat the Spanish in the Spanish-American War, the marines invaded Cuba and Puerto Rico—never to leave. The United States won the war.[4] After 1898 Puertorriqueños and Puertorriqueñas lived under U.S. military rule for two years and then under governors appointed by the president for fifty years.

We did not regain control of our political process until 1948, when, through struggle, education, and blood, we freely and democratically elected our first Puertorriqueño governor, Luis Muñoz Marín. To not have control over one's own economic, social, political, and educational development in individual terms is problematic and chaotic, but on a mass scale it is an attempt at cultural annihilation. For example, during U.S. rule, teachers were required to teach children in English even though neither the teachers nor the children spoke that foreign language. My grandmother, a teacher who refused to commit this violence, summed up the cultural differences this way: "I was talking with Roger

Baldwin one day and we started comparing words in English and Spanish. I realized why we in Puerto Rico could never be Americans: In the United States the rooster cries 'cuckadoodle doo!,' but in Puerto Rico the rooster cries, 'qui qui ri qui.'"[5]

The historical moment within which Puertorriqueñas and Puertorriqueños are developing today is in profound ways a time of searching out an identity, a "sense of knowing where one is going." We are one people descended from many. Unlike the segregation of whites from people of color in the United States, in Puerto Rico, there has been a blending and crossing of paths. But this doesn't mean that as a people we are exempt from racism or anti-Semitism, homophobia, sexism, or classism. Puerto Ricans have a form of racism inherited from the colonial Spanish: the valuing of light skin over dark skin, European looks over African looks. On the other hand, it is common for people of all shades to marry. This is a social paradox that is alive in the culture.

Puerto Ricans are deeply divided along political party lines first as the United States is divided along racist lines, divided along economic lines so that barbed wire surrounds the houses of the rich and bars surround the bodies of the poor; divided within ourselves with a fragmented history we are at the very beginning, if in fact we are near to it at all, of moving out of a childhood dependence and into a cultural adulthood. To the extent that oppressive relationships change the character of a people, we are still reforming ourselves. We are a new people and, in many ways, strangers to ourselves.

From the United States we've inherited central burdens of imperialism and colonialism, internalized oppression and education for submission. Because of these two conditions the struggles of youths in Puerto Rico are similar to those of young people of color in the United States. But the problems are intensified by a greater lack of economic resources and the small size of the island. And because we are a young people, issues of identity, work, and love are not just individually but also socially difficult to negotiate—there is no pattern that holds steady. Industrialization changed a tradition of agriculture, political divisions changed a tradition of interdependence, and U.S. colonialization subverted education for freedom; the Puerto Rican exodus from the island is a diaspora.

On the political and social agenda are a massive project of public school reform, which has for years now been bogged down in political fighting, in the Senate and House of Representatives, along party lines; a plebescite, held in 1993, that reaffirmed the status quo relationship with the United States but left the ultimate national status of Puerto Rico unresolved; a "dropout" rate that parallels that of U.S. urban schools; declining literacy and increased unemployment; and environmental destruction at all levels. Drugs and crime touch everyone in society, whether it's by way of a push or a gun. Some studies project that by the year 2000 one out of three Puertorriqueños living on the Island (or 1 million) will be HIV positive, giving Puerto Rico the highest proportion of HIV/AIDS of the industrialized nations. The hierarchy of the Catholic church continues to ban the use of contraceptives and condoms.

In 1992, a new governor was elected. Candidate Rosello ran on a strong "anticrime" campaign, similar to the campaign run in New York City by Rudolf Giuliani and others in large cities in the United States. Now Governor Rosello has called out the National Guard, in full camouflage uniform and small armored tanks, to "take over" housing projects. The strategy has three steps: (1) raid at night using small tanks and helicopters, surprise residents, and search all apartments for drugs and guns; (2) build a chain link fence completely around the housing project with only one entrance and exit point; (3) at this "checkpoint" have National Guards ask for identification from all residents who want to enter and leave. It is the young people who are harassed the most and who most frequently have been involved in scuffles with the Guard.

This militarization of the island—small tanks drive up and down main streets—has led to allegations of civil rights violations, and lawyers are filing a class action suit on behalf of residents of low-income housing. Yet some residents agree with the governor and feel safer having the military down the street. The civil rights lawyers are especially concerned that this military approach will lead to more militarism and rights violations and point to, in shock, how in Puerto Rico this kind of military action has never been seen before.

In Puerto Rico what has only been spoken about in the United States as an "anticrime measure" has already occurred. This leads to the question, Is Puerto Rico being used as a testing ground for these kinds of "measures"? After all, Puerto Ricans are U.S. citizens, and surely these "takeovers" would not be tolerated in cities in the States, or would they?

This is the historical moment.

At this time there are several programs aimed toward providing places where young people can study, work, grow, love, support themselves, and rebuild their communities. I visited six places where education is held out as a way of sustaining human development (see Table 5.1 and Figure 5.1). Each description of the site begins with excerpts from the youths' narratives in response to the first interview questions, "For you what is work? How do you define it? What meaning does it have for you?"

Table 5.1
Overview of Sites

	Number	Average Age	Age Range	Female	Male
ADT	18	19.2	17–22	10	8
Volunteer Corps Aguadilla	10	19.6	16–28	5	5
Volunteer Corps Ensenada	10	19.8	16–24	5	5
Jesuits	4	26.3	21–33	0	4
Peces	8	19.4	14–25	4	4
Conservatory	12	22.3	18–26	7	5
Totals	62	21	14–33	31	31

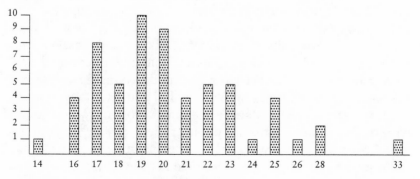

Figure 5.1
Age Distribution, All Sites

Administración del Derecho al Trabajo (ADT)
(The Right to Employment Administration)

> Wow! Okay, let's begin, look, I consider it as all that a person is able to do or produce for the benefit of a company. That is, benefit in the sense that it generates work in itself, that is, that it generates a series of steps to follow, that is, a series of things or, I wouldn't be able to tell you specifically what it is, but from my part, that is, I am who processes and then well, I give it to the business and then the business can obtain its goals or established objectives through that which I produce. [Tomás, twenty-one years old]

> Well, for me work, I believe, that if one doesn't work, where is one going to obtain the money to have one's things, to move forward? Because without money one can sometimes not do anything, you know, like now one has to have *cuarto año*[6] to have everything and just like that if one has a job to, one has to have work, has to go forward. [Marta, twenty years old]

> Well, work, is a way that a person that has studied can make a living after having studied and labored at a university for so many years. It's a way that one can feel satisfied of one's accomplishments. [Papo, seventeen years old]

> *Ay, Dios mio, ay,* I don't know what to tell you. I don't understand, I don't know . . . An occupation, well, an occupation, to work in an occupation that one likes. [Lila, twenty years old]

Juana María is right in front of me: Afro cut short, eyes smiling and gentle, mouth closed, wearing a dress with tassels on the shoulders. The dress looks homemade, the tassels like the decorations on a general. The neckline, cut square, shows a mole on her neck. There's no hesitation in her look. In the background are reflections of fluorescent lights on glass windows of the wall of an office cubicle. She's sitting in the office of the job counselor, who took one look at her, turned to me, and said under her breath and conspirational, moving her hand up and down, as if I would not hesitate to agree, "I don't know what I'm going to do with her." What she sees in Juana María is a young "dropout" who is overweight. But I don't share her point of view. Juana María and I have just talked about what she loves to do and she knows what she wants to do. If the counselor asked her she, too, would know. Juana María loves working with kids, she would like training so that she could be a teacher's aide.

Juana María is seventeen, black, and poor, and she tells me that teachers have told her that she's *"lenta,"* "slow." She says that she and her brother were "born that way, since we were little we are that way." Teachers changed her to special education classes in the third grade. She says she has a hard time reading. Juana María left school at fourteen to take care of her mother, who broke an arm in a fall.

Like many of the other youths I interviewed at ADT, I found that their "problem" was that they had learning difficulties teachers couldn't attend to. They left school never to return, to try to find work, raise children, or take care of family members. Interestingly, they never called themselves "dropouts." In Puerto Rico, young people who leave school before attaining a high school diploma are called *"desertores escolares"* by the Department of Education, which when translated literally means "school deserters." The institutional term for leaving school revealed a conceptual relationship between education and the military. But no youths referred to themselves as *"desertor escolar."* The separation from school was seen as a departure, a leaving, a *getting out*: in their words, *"me di de baja"* or *"me sali."*

Whether the teachers treated them like the job counselor did is not certain, but it seemed very likely. Juana María wants to go back to school not as a student but as a teacher's aide. She knows teachers need help. She knows they couldn't help her. What she knows can be translated into work that reforms education.

ADT, as this government agency is commonly called, was created by the Puerto Rican legislature in 1968 with the Right to Employment Act. The principle behind the act was that unemployment could be eliminated through job training and that positions that were vacant, due to a scarcity of qualified workers, could be filled with freshly trained workers. Further, the act was to provide a way, through training, for workers to exercise their civil right to work. Since, while in training, youths and adults would receive a stipend or a small salary, the act immediately reduced unemployment in that it generated jobs even if only for a short period, the length of the training.

The principle of the act and the reality of its implementation have grown, over the years, further and further apart. ADT itself is now a vast bureaucracy that employs thousands of administrators, counselors, specialists, and so on but provides little work for the population it was intended to serve: the untrained and unemployed. The agency has become a system of violence against youth in its treatment of poor teenagers as "cases," and, if this counselor who sees dozens of youths daily is any example, the agency dehumanizes youths, who are especially powerless at the time they seek help. Many directors of social-educational programs that receive funds for youth training from ADT have repeated this to me in conversation with a blend of rage, frustration, and resignation.

On the days I went to the agency there was a crowd of youths sitting in the lobby of the fifteen-plus-story office building, waiting, waiting, and waiting. They were waiting to see a counselor, waiting to fill out forms, waiting to be told to go home without getting any help. When I described this waiting for nothing to my grandmother, on the porch, we both became angry and saddened, and she told me that this tragedy made her think of the inscription over the "Gate of Hell" in Dante's *Inferno,* where everyone who enters must abandon all their hopes. Most striking to me was the young woman, fifteen years old, who was pregnant and came to ADT for a chance to get work to support her soon-to-be-born child. She was one of thirty-four youths who received letters from the agency to attend an "orientation" meeting for a program on "Youth Competency." This is a six-month program for high school "dropouts" that provides tutoring in academic subjects for three months and job practice for the other three months. The goal is for the youths to be able to take the high school equivalency exam and obtain a diploma. A high school diploma is required for any government job. The government is the single largest employer on the island.

The meeting was directed by the job counselor. It was scheduled for 9:00 A.M. Apparently, more than a few thought they were coming in to receive job assignments, not a general orientation; many asked questions related to where they would be working and when they could start. After waiting for an hour, at 10:05 A.M. the counselor asked all those with high school diplomas to raise their hands. They did. She told them they could all leave because this orientation was for "dropouts." Why did they receive a letter telling them to come? Hope, once again, was told to leave.

The counselor then trained her eyes on a young pregnant woman and asked her when she was expecting her baby. The youth was neatly dressed, her straight brown hair combed back into a ponytail, her face intent on what the counselor was saying. I had watched her slide herself behind the table and into a chair earlier. She looked down at her belly and rubbed it with one hand, and with a smile she said "*en octubre.*" The due date fell within the six months. The counselor asked the youth her age. She said, "fifteen." The counselor said she was too young—the ADT youth programs are for those who are sixteen through twenty-one. The youth said she would be sixteen before the program started. The counselor said she thought she wouldn't "make it" because she was pregnant and told her to come back after she had the baby. Hope, once again, was told to leave.

I saw the young woman's face collapse with her loss of hope for work to support her baby. At fifteen, pregnant, without a high school diploma, she was sent away from an agency created to help her. I wanted to run out after her. I watched her leave, her head down, her shoulders slumping. I did not get a chance to interview her or any of the high school graduates that were told to leave. Where did they go? I felt anger and despair.

The youths I spoke with at ADT were either looking for work or were hired to work within the agency. I interviewed eight youths individually and six youths in a group who were looking for work, and four youths who were working at ADT. Only the ones working at ADT had a high school diploma; the others had left school. The ages of the youths (ten females and eight males) ranged from seventeen through twenty-two.

Cuerpo de Voluntarios al Servicio de Puerto Rico
(Volunteer Corps at the Service of Puerto Rico)

> For me, eh, honesty, eh, that is, sacrifice oneself, for me, that is work for me work is a good thing for me in the future. [Anita, seventeen years old]

> For me work is everything. From the moment one wakes up until one goes to sleep . . . work is what one needs to survive. If one doesn't work, one is nobody, understand, one can't get the magazine, can't get one's car, can't get jewelry, can't get anything. Work is everything for me. [Carlos, twenty-four years old]

> For me work is something that is very important. Above all the education that one has for that work. That is, how one is going to prepare when one has a job. I'm a cashier, I prepared myself, but the important thing is to know what one is doing and truly behave, stay in one's place. That is, work for me is an effort that one does to excel in life. [Linda, sixteen years old]

> Work is truly one of the most important things that human beings count on . . . When one doesn't have work truly it's a little frustrating because we see ourselves desperate. We see ourselves on the verge of doing other things that perhaps will take us to conflicts. [David, twenty-two years old]

The Volunteer Corps is a program that was, like ADT, created by Puerto Rican lawmakers. The program is aimed toward alleviating the suffering and problems caused by unemployment and lack of schooling and toward providing training that enables young people to obtain jobs. Youths eligible for the Volunteer Corps must be at least sixteen but no older than twenty-nine years of age. A stated goal of the program is to know, respect, and love oneself and to be a productive member of one's community. Moral Reconation Therapy[7] is an important and a required part of the program. MRT, as it's called within Volunteer Corps, takes place in a group setting during the first thirty days that a youth enters the program.

The Volunteer Corps has twelve *recintos*[8]—local programs—around the island. At the time of my visit Srta. Rosita Puig was the director of programs at the *recintos* and facilitated my entry into the two sites.[9] Each *recinto* serves a different population—urban, rural, recently arrived from the United States, youth recovering from addiction—and offers a variety of workshops and learning experiences. Each *recinto* has a specialty area: boat making, raising cows, ceramics, agriculture, and so on. There is a local director at each site, although the main offices and executive director are in San Juan. They are residential programs; the youths eat, sleep, learn, and work on the grounds for a period of up to two years. The daily schedule is divided between academic subjects geared toward attaining a high school diploma by taking the equivalency exam, and vocational workshops geared toward developing hands-on skills. The workshop areas are chosen by each youth according to his or her interest after a series of placement tests and vocational counseling sessions.

The youths are paid monthly, through ADT, for participating in the workshops, which are viewed as job training. In the handbook given to youths upon their entrance into the *recinto*, the payment they receive is described this way: "You joined the *Recinto* to learn. You can think of yourself as being employed now; you are employed by the state government and you are earning a salary, your monthly pay. Your work is to learn" (p. 12). The reasons and motives for the creation of the Volunteer Corps are outlined at the beginning of the Legislative Act, which was approved in 1985, and which illustrates the reasoning and perspective of the legislators as well as provides a view of current trends in education, employment, and social conditions affecting youth (see Appendix B, "Introduction to the Volunteer Corps at the Service of Puerto Rico Act").

I visited two different *recintos*: Punta Borinquen, in Aguadilla, and Ensenada, in Guanica. I interviewed twenty youths—ten at each *recinto*—whose thoughts, feelings, and experiences were wide-ranging: drug traffic and addiction, pregnancy in the early teens, motherhood and fatherhood, divorce, families shattered and scattered, homelessness, illness. Ten were young men and ten were young women.

Recinto Punta Borinquen, Aguadilla Punta Borinquen means "the point of Borinquen." It is located in the *municipio*[10] of Aguadilla, the furthest northwestern tip of the island on the Atlantic Ocean. The *recinto* is housed in two large, several storied, concrete buildings that were formerly used as the school for the children of U.S. military personnel stationed at Ramey Base. Across the street from the *recinto* is a military airport which is now used by commercial as well as military planes. As we were driving into the Base, I saw a Federal Express jet parked near a hangar.

Julio Quiros, a close friend who accompanied me traveling around the island, and I arrived at Punta Borinquen sweaty and tired from the over-two-hour drive on roads that were under construction. We were scheduled to arrive at 10:00 A.M. but didn't get there until 10:45 A.M. because of the limited lanes and congestion of traffic. I didn't think this would matter since I expected to be interviewing ten or so youths during the day on a flexible schedule, that is, when it was convenient for them.

Julio and I were both surprised to see, as we got out of the car, a group of about ten youths holding up a cardboard banner that read *"Bienvenida Srta. Victoria Borden Muñoz"* with the flag of Puerto Rico drawn on the bottom left-hand corner. I looked over to Julio and said, *"Ay bendito, y llegamos tarde!"* [11] As we walked over to where they were standing the group began to throw confetti. My head was covered with colorful little round paper cut-outs. I was shocked at the reception, felt completely unprepared, and at the same time felt that the day promised to have more surprises.

The group led us to the director's office, where a man who looked young himself was waiting, sitting behind his desk. We were introduced and shook hands. Sr. Renee Marrero then introduced the teacher who had organized the day's activities, Srta. Elena Perez. I was not taking notes at the time; I was standing across from him not knowing what to expect. This is what I remember him saying: "It's an honor for us to have you visit our *recinto*. We have arranged a schedule for your visit and hope you will feel comfortable here with us. After we have a few snacks we would like you to inaugurate a *sala* that we've newly completed and named Jose de Diego."[12] "Inaugurate a conference room?" I panicked to myself. I had never done anything like that. The day was tightly planned. Looking at the program, which had been typed and copied, I saw that it included quotes and drawings and that the day was to include activities from 10:00 A.M. through 1:00 P.M. with an hour for lunch. After lunch, I was scheduled to begin interviewing for four hours, until 5:00 P.M.

I cut the red ribbon on the new conference room and camera flashes went off. Julio said that all I needed was a hat like the ones my grandmother used to wear and he would have thought she was there. I felt that Sr. Marrero, Srta. Perez, and the youths were honoring the memory of my grandparents. Later, I would hear from Sr. Marrero that he wanted to teach the youths how to welcome and entertain public figures at the *recinto*. I have never before or since had this kind of reception gifted to me.

The lunch was prepared and served by a group of youths learning hotel and restaurant services. There was a buffet of *bacalao, viandas, ensalada,* and *coco,* for dessert—all Boricua dishes. I was hungry and got a little ahead of schedule. I found myself alone on the buffet line. When I turned around I realized they were waiting for me to stop but were too polite to interrupt my dash for the food. They always say a prayer before beginning lunch. I was embarrassed and apologized. Everyone smiled that it was fine. We prayed and ate.

We toured the building as the sky let loose thunder, lightning, wind, and pouring rain. I was taken to see the separate, clean, and orderly dormitories of the males and females. The dorm rooms are organized by similar interests; youths learning the skills of working in security bunk together, youths learning restaurant work bunk together, and so on. The youths showed pride at how well the dorms were kept up. They pointed to everything they had made: their own shelves, curtains, bedcovers, and the painted murals on the walls. I visited every workshop. I was given more beautiful gifts: an upholstered stool to sit on (furniture workshop) and wooden cut-out maps of the island (carpentry workshop). I felt overwhelmed by the kindness and generosity so freely shared.

I interviewed ten youths, in the *sala* Jose de Diego, during the four-hour period. Their ages ranged from sixteen to twenty-four. There were an equal number of males and females.

Recinto Ensenada, Guanica The *municipio* of Guanica is located on the southwestern corner of the island. In the landscape is an economic history of Puerto Rico. Along the Caribbean coast are shut-down petroleum refineries and enormous rusting sugar cane mills. The *recinto* is in a former sugar cane plantation house— Spanish architecture and made of cement—on the edge of a mangrove tree cove close to the ocean. The breeze brings in the smell of salt and boats.

Sr. Julio Morales is the *recinto* director. He and I talk in his office for over an hour when I first arrive. The receptionist, who is Sr. Morales's "right hand," brings us strong black coffee with the sugar already added. He tells me of growing up in U.S. cities and of the racism and neglect he experienced in schools. As an adult, he returned to the island with his wife to, as he put it, "give something back to my country." He is *entregado*—completely dedicated—to his work with youths here. We speak in English and Spanish, mixing up experiences into one culture or another.

Sr. Morales tells me that young women who become pregnant while at the *recinto* are not permitted to stay and that he is involved in trying to wrestle with this because it was rumored that a young woman had become pregnant. He knew that it would be much more difficult for the young woman on the street but said that the *recinto* didn't have the facilities to cope with young mothers. He told me that he was going to have to ask her to leave. My heart sank with the heavy feeling of despair, the same sick feeling I had at ADT when the counselor told the young pregnant woman that she had to leave, too. In two separate programs, both government run, young pregnant women are asked to leave behind services that could help them support themselves and their babies.

Sr. Morales outlines the different programs available for youths in this *recinto*. There are seven workshop areas: Hotel and Restaurant, Electricity, Electronics, Office and Administrative Assistance, Security, Boat Repair and Maintenance, and Building Repair and Maintenance. He tells me I am free to interview whomever I want, if they are willing, and to feel free to visit all the workshops.

After this, we walk around the old plantation house which is now filled with young people taking classes. The dormitories are in newer wooden buildings. Everything is neat and clean, just like Punta Borinquen. The workshops are housed down the street in a smaller building. I interviewed there.

Across the street from where I interviewed is a huge sugar cane mill: buildings, ladders, bins of rusted tin, the grass five feet over-grown, left like this for decades as if no one wants to touch it, as if to take it apart would awaken the misery. It is as if everyone just left one day and no one ever came back. I watched the mill, feeling like there was something caught inside and if I looked hard enough I would see "it." It is a witness to cruelty. It is an unofficial national monument.

I interviewed ten youths, five females and five males, between the ages of sixteen and twenty-eight. After the interviews, I visited every workshop, was briefly introduced to each group by the workshop director, Sr. Balay, and took photographs.

I then returned to Sr. Morales's office to say good-bye and thank him. He asked if I could please stay another half-hour. I did. A car drove up and out came two of the young women I had inter-viewed, a little out of breath, with three red roses that they had bought in the center of Guanica.

Proyecto de Educación Comunal de Entrega y Servicio (PECES) (Community Education Project of Dedication and Service)

> Well, so, it's like a way of helping others and giving of yourself, because for one's well-being and the well-being of everyone else, well, so, it's something for the well-being of oneself and others. [Sara, fourteen years old]

> The work I'm doing now? Well it's a way that one can help other youths, some preadolescents that have many problems at home and I am like a form of support for them. [Wanda, twenty-one years old]

The work I do, well, you truly need a lot of *entrega* in terms of the community and the *niños*, and the adolescents. It's something that truly demands, right, a commitment that is pretty serious because truly one works hard not only with the project but also with the *muchachos*. One sees the need that they have, one lives those needs because I am from here, right, I was born and raised here in Punta Santiago. [Jaime, nineteen years old]

The acronym PECES spells out the word *fish* and alludes to the saying, "If you give someone a fish they will eat for a day, but if you teach someone how to fish they will eat for a lifetime." PECES is a community-based educational project for youths that was conceptualized as a response to increasing problems and then brought into being by Sister Nancy Madden, a Catholic nun from the Midwest of the United States, and concerned residents of the Punta Santiago community in 1985. Punta Santiago is a small *pueblo*. According to the 1980 census it is composed of 6,000 residents. The community is located in a beautiful area, right on the beach in the *municipio* of Humacao, on the eastern coast.

In 1988, I saw and listened to Sister Nancy for the first time at a conference in San Juan for people working in or associated with community-based educational programs. This day-long conference gathered community leaders, educators, program coordinators, youths, and government officials under one roof to discuss the critical issues facing community-based programs and to lay out a plan of action.

There were arguments with and challenges posed to government officials by community leaders; a community leader from Llorens Torres, the largest housing project on the island, spoke about her daily struggles and frustrations; there were professors from the University of Puerto Rico, from the social work department; there were graduate students studying social work. Remembering how I would set up Longfellow Hall with a microphone, I fixed the speaker system, which was crackling and giving feedback, and received a round of applause. The conference was this mix of people from all walks of life trying to make a bridge over government bureaucracy and lack of funding to a network of interrelated and mutually supportive projects.

I remember Sister Nancy clearly because she was the only adult who, after giving an overview of her project, stepped aside so that a youth, from Punta Santiago, could speak about the program from his experience. And speak he did. The project, as described by the youth, caught my imagination. Soon after the conference, I called Sister Nancy, but I kept missing her as she rushed from place to place, meeting to meeting, working for PECES. I left messages and telephone numbers, but her schedule was intense and hectic; finally I had to return to Cambridge. It wasn't until two years later that I was able to meet and sit down to speak with Sister Nancy and the youth who spoke that day, Jose Oquendo, who was then eighteen years old.

Sister Nancy has a U.S. accent in her Spanish; a kind of twang and overpronunciation of vowels that follows North Americans who learn Spanish as adults in Puerto Rico. But she speaks the language fluently and her gestures seem more Puerto Rican than reserved midwestern. We spoke in Spanish in her office. Even though she was congested with a lingering cold, she was warm and open and told me about the short, but intense, history of the project as well as gave me a folder with documents to read: newspaper clippings written on PECES, a history of the project, the funding sources, and so on. Sister Nancy asked several questions about this research study, including how it was that I came to be interested in the topic of work that one loves. I remember her saying, as she listened, "*Es algo muy bonito.*"[13] I did not take notes during our conversation, so the following information is taken from the documents Sister Nancy gave me.

Much like Guanica on the southwest coast, Humacao was in the 1930s and 1940s a thriving economic port. When this port was no longer needed, as roads and highways increased access around the island and economic activity changed, the Punta Santiago community along with other neighboring towns fell into a deep economic depression. Over the decades, what was once an external economic reality has become a psychological one as people have internalized the failures of a capitalist-colonial economy—lack of steady and satisfying work and dependence on government welfare programs—as a personal failure. The lives of the children were, as always, the most severely affected.

PECES is a community response to the following realities affecting the youths who live in the area: teenage pregnancy beginning at thirteen years of age, and a high incidence of alcoholism, drugs, unemployment, vandalism, pollution, poverty, dropping out of school, divorce and separation, family problems, and fighting among neighbors. Sister Nancy points to alcoholism, drugs, and unemployment as being the most critical social problems and then to dropping out, illiteracy, and truancy as the most critical educational problems.

To work toward change, Sister Nancy focuses her energy on four broad areas: community development, social work and individual development, education, and economic development. Specifically, the development of "community leaders" is a central objective and is the focus of the educational part of the project. The leaders are all youths who feel strongly that the future of their community is in their hands.

I interviewed eight youths (four males, four females) in two locations of PECES where youths go to every day after school: at the house where Sister Nancy lives and where many youth activities are held, and at the small library that belongs to PECES where the youth leaders teach elementary-age children. Their ages ranged from fourteen through twenty-five years.

Casa Jesuita
(Jesuit Seminary)

> For me it's any activity that has a specific end, that is personal or communal through which you are seeking to transform or produce something that you need for your different activities or to fulfill the needs of groups or individuals . . . Where you are forming yourself, you're doing something but at the same time you are influencing, all work it seems to me influences who you are. For example, someone who works all their life as a mason doesn't act like someone who has worked all their life making flowers, for example. The work itself has an influence over nature, over the material but at the same time what you are doing has repercussions for your personality and I say that work also is something that forms you in one way or another. [Osvaldo, twenty-six years old]

> Work? For me I would define it, well, where one tries to pursue, to put their abilities, their ability into something that will have fruit not only for oneself but for society. Let's say for the community, community being something very broad. As a matter of fact work should be something that one enjoys from inside oneself, that motivates one to continue forward. [Javier, thirty-three years old]

The Jesuit Seminary is in the rural *pueblo* of Caimito which is in the hills and away from the coast. Intermittently along the curbs of the narrow and curving roads, dumped in the tall grass, are junked cars, parts of household appliances, and twisted metal that I can't shape into known objects. Dead dogs are in the street, a common sight on roads all over Puerto Rico. From San Juan, it takes about twenty minutes to get to the Jesuit Seminary, which is on a road that is, as are many roads on the island, a study in contrasts.

At the end of the road past the Jesuit Seminary is a neighborhood where only the wealthy can afford to live. It is blocked off by a high cement wall and barbed wire. Father Fernando Picó walked with me to the end of the road when I first visited the Jesuit House in July of 1988.

Giving a picture of Father Picó is difficult because he does so much. I have known him since I was in high school. He is a quiet and intense man, a leading historian and professor at the University of Puerto Rico and a central figure of the Jesuit community on the island. He embodies the internal struggles of the Catholic church and the human vulnerability, the fragility, that seems to accompany those who try to live what they believe, not impose their views, live and let live, comfort, give friendship. He is in his fifties, tall; his hair and complexion are fair, and his eyes blend a look that speaks to years of reading and living and working. A prolific writer, he has written in many of the missing chapters of Puerto Rican history from the perspective of the poor and working classes.

On the way to the wall he talked with teenagers who were hanging around on the street. He asked each one how they were and what was going on. He shook hands with them and negotiated various things: to visit someone's friend in jail, to talk with the local police about a problem with driver's licenses. As we walked I asked him if the youths spent the day hanging out. He said to me that when they just hung out it was *"un dia bueno"*— a good day—and that on the *"dias malos"*—bad days—they would commit crimes and get arrested.

In his book *Vivir en Caimito* (Living in Caimito), which is a social commentary, a journal, and a revisioning of Puerto Rico's socioeconomic history, Father Picó (1989) speaks of his neighborhood as a kind of bordertown:

> In a sense, Caimito is the frontier where the city faces the nation. It is the place where institutions and *urbanizaciones*[14] are confronted by the solidarity and the community mentality that has

been able to maintain an identity within a rapid rhythm of economic and social change. Harshly treated and tested by tensions produced by the clash between the two worlds, the community of Caimito could be a valid paradigm for a nation whose population has been rooted out in the last 50 years. (p. 58)

While recognizing that drugs, gangs, and crime are problems (how could he not? the youths he works with are the addicts, the gang members, and the ones arrested), Picó underscores that the most critical problems, the "real social conflicts," are rooted in Puerto Rico's socioeconomic structure (p. 14). Picó argues that changes, to be lasting and real, must affect the structures of economic and social injustice; the cement walls with barbed wire that separate the rich from the poor must fall.

After our walk through the *barrio*, I attended a mass that is celebrated by the fathers and brothers every evening. It was a simple celebration in their chapel, which has a wooden table, candles, flowers, several chairs, and not much else. I recall one of the brothers playing guitar and singing a thanksgiving song of hope from his country. This returns from memory as Julio and I drive up to visit the house again, two years later.

The house is the same: cement, single story in front, two floors in the back because it's on a hill. Behind the house are palm trees, hibiscus bushes, avocado trees, and mango. It is lush green and colorful, and the grass is cut. A Virgin Mary statue, painted white, prays to the sky. It's quiet, but the intensity of the heat keeps me from feeling peaceful. There are also two other houses where the fathers, brothers, and *seminaristas* sleep. The young men who are studying to be priests are first called *seminaristas* because they are still students of theology. After two years, they become brothers, and, if they continue to study and live as Jesuits, they will be ordained as Jesuit priests in six to eight years. A primary function of this small Jesuit community is as a seminary for young men from all over Latin America.

The young men who are studying here live surrounded by two worlds that are intricately intertwined economically but are socially isolated one from the other: the world of the rich and the world of the poor. The location of the house is itself a symbol of the tensions within the Society of Jesus today.

Founded over 450 years ago, the all-male community (with the one exception of Juana D'Austria, a Spanish princess who became a Jesuit in 1554) had the greatest number of members thirty years ago, after World War II. In the last three decades the Jesuits have experienced a drop in numbers and radical change. In the *National Catholic Reporter* (June 15, 1990), Arthur Jones, the editor-at-large, writes of the tensions of what he calls "irreversible change" in his article under the section titled "The Society's Tensions":

> The balance of numbers is shifting rapidly from the First World to the Third World, from the rich world to the poor world, from the old industrial world to the newly developing world, from the north world to the south world, from the marble halls to cinder-block walls. The power, the philosophy, the energy, the theology, the control of the 450 year-old society, have yet to shift from the older men to the younger men, from the institutional model to the social-justice model, from the west and north to east and south. (p. 1)[15]

Jones also writes that "since 1973, 33 Jesuits have 'disappeared' or been murdered." In 1988, in El Salvador, six Jesuit priests, the woman who was the housekeeper, and her daughter were executed by the military for ministering to the poor. (Three years later there is talk by the government of El Salvador of pressing charges against the army officers responsible for this bloodshed, but then a year later they are set free.) The tensions within the society are highlighted by the division among those who believe that the Jesuits brought death upon themselves for being "too political" and those who believe that being a Jesuit means to work and, if necessary, die for justice among the world's poor. Jones, in his own way, asks a developmental question: "Where are the Clerks Regulars of the Society of Jesus, this order approved by Paul III in 1540, headed?" (p. 21).

Father Picó is no longer in Caimito. He was transferred to San Ignacio, a private Jesuit school for mostly well-to-do boys. But he is still there in spirit, among the young men who are studying to become *Sacerdotes Jesuitas*.

This visit I was greeted by Padre Orlando Torres, who has lived at the Caimito *Casa Jesuita* for many years and is now the director. Padre Orlando and I spoke in his office, which is in a small cement house behind the main building tucked away into the side of a hill. We discussed my study and interview schedule as well as the leaking roof in his office. Padre Orlando and I then walked over to the place where I would spend the next several hours listening to stories of work and love.

It was in this climate, thick with moisture and change, that I interviewed four *seminaristas* on the porch of their house. One was from Puerto Rico, another from Panama, another from El Salvador, and the fourth from Mexico. They were the only young people studying there at the time. Their ages ranged from twenty-one through thirty-three years. All were intensely political, and two were activists in their country.

Conservatorio de Música de Puerto Rico
(The Conservatory of Music of Puerto Rico)

> Mostly we're taught to think that it is a way to live, you know. I consider that it's something that I have to, that we have to be very careful about what we work in, you know, because it should be something that one likes . . . So I consider work is a way to live and that it's a very important thing because one should be happy where one works, you know. [Octavio, twenty-two years old]

> Work is something that I do and enjoy and make a living doing it but for me I wouldn't work in something that I didn't enjoy.
> *No?*
> No, definitely, no. [Laura, twenty-three years old]

> It can be two things. It can be something that is imposed on you, you know, that they say, you have to do a certain labor, or something that you do because, as I say, because you studied for that and now you know that your life is on a path towards that . . . You can't live or live dependent on other people. Work is not only something that you have to do for by obligation in life, it's something that you choose to do the best possible, and to live, and continue to do and live to do all things. [Jesus, twenty-two years old]

> It's something I do more because I like it than for the money that they may give me . . . Something that I can learn to do perfectly. Something that helps me to excel in it. Something that I can help with and that I feel, let's say, proud. My work is this and I like it and I defend it, that is work. [Melania, twenty-three years old]

El conservatorio was the first place I conducted interviews. It is a public college that, with and through the University of Puerto Rico in Rio Piedras, confers the bachelor's degree. Usually students transfer from the university or private colleges to *el conservatorio* after two years of taking their core college requirements.

There are also students who enter directly after high school and take classes at the University and *conservatorio* jointly. The conservatory, like all colleges, has entrance requirements, but, in addition to the standards written in the catalogue, there is another one written on the faces of the youths: the students love music.

El conservatorio was created in 1959 by the Puerto Rican legislature and by Pablo Casals, the Spanish cellist who was exiled by General Franco and welcomed by the government of Puerto Rico. Casals developed an extraordinary relationship with Puerto Rico; he adopted the country and its children as his own. He married a young Puertorriqueña who had been his music student, Marta Montañez. He represented Puerto Rico at official ceremonies worldwide. He wanted to make a place for Puerto Ricans to study, compose, play, and enjoy music. *Maestro* Casals believed fully in the human capacity for the good and the need for work which connected people with the world at large. His gift was music; his passport, a cello:

> Music, without equal as a universal language, should be a bond of communication between all people. Once more, I exhort all my brothers and sisters in music all around the whole world to put the purity of their art at the service of humanity so that all the people of the earth can unite. Each one of us ought to contribute, in accord with how we can, to the magnificent and glorious fulfillment of this ideal. (translated, Conservatory Catalogue 1988–90, p. iii)

From these beginnings, the conservatory has grown over the years into the most highly respected school of music on the island. Being accepted into the school was, among other things, a dream come true and a critical step for the students I interviewed.

When I visited the school in the summer of 1990, Julio Garcia Frias, the registrar, provided me with an overview of the school and a place for interviewing. Sr. Frias, a musician himself who left music to become an administrator, told me that classes had ended and that the students that were still around were participating in *El Coro del Conservatorio*. And as if having a conversation with Maxine Greene (1988), Sr. Frias said, "Not everyone will be a virtuoso but many are good musicians that enjoy their work."

The chorus comprises students from all the departments. It is a way to learn music and to perform for the public. *El coro*, as everyone calls it, represents the conservatory at cultural events around the island. During the five days that I interviewed, *el coro* rehearsed four days a week in the mornings until noon. They were getting ready for a performance at *El Viejo Casino*, a popular concert and dance hall in the Condado area of San Juan.

The enormous windowless room where they rehearsed was nicknamed "Siberia" because it was a television studio, and to keep the extremely hot lighting cool, the TV station had installed an extremely cold air-conditioning system. But there were only fluorescent lights in the studio when I was there, metal chairs, music stands with sheets, a piano, and a xylophone. Later in the week they changed to a smaller classroom with student desks, chalkboard, and windows that look out over the parking lot.

The youths are enthusiastic and thoughtful as they rehearse. Their music director, William Rivera, stands in front of the group moving his hands, and the voices take form. Tomorrow is Sr. Rivera's birthday and he has said that he is taking the day off; there will be no rehearsal. But the students want to rehearse. They've made me promise to keep this secret: they will rehearse badly today so that Sr. Rivera is forced to come in tomorrow and the students will be able to celebrate his birthday with him. They will also be able to sing some more. After the rehearsal I ask the director if I should come in to interview tomorrow. He tells me that I can, because they'll have to rehearse again; he doesn't know why but it's as if they have suddenly forgotten everything.

I conducted the interviews in a small percussion practice room. In the mornings I would ask the security guard to unlock the door; then I would turn on the lights and set up the tape recorder, microphone, and chairs. The room had no windows and was crowded, with a drum set and two congas lined up against a wall with a mirror running the full length of it. Surrounded by the tools of the trade, I interviewed twelve youths from *el coro,* seven females and five males, from poor, working- and middle-class backgrounds, between the ages of eighteen and twenty-six.

After completing the interviews I said good-bye to the group, thanking them and wishing them success in their performance. True to their art, they thanked me and wished me well by applauding.

PANEL 3

Profiles of Work and Love

PRAYER FOR REVOLUTIONARY LOVE

That a woman not ask a man to leave meaningful work to
                                        follow her.
That a man not ask a woman to leave meaningful work to
                                        follow him.

That no one try to put Eros in bondage.
But that no one put a cudgel in the hands of Eros.

That our loyalty to one another and our loyalty to our work
not be set in false conflict.

That our love for each other give us love for each other's work.
That our love for each other's work give us love for one another.

That our love for each other's work give us love for one another.
That our love for each other give us love for each other's work.

That our love for each other, if need be,
give way to absence. And the unknown.

That we endure absence, if need be,
without losing our love for each other.
Without closing our doors to the unknown.

CHAPTER 6

Becoming Hombres and Mujeres: Work, Love, and Constructions of Gender

Denise Levertov calls for a restructuring of traditional heterosexual gender roles, that men and women be equally respected and valued in each one's love and each one's work. Her poem is a prayer because what she desires is not yet concretely real in any daily way. It is revolutionary because it calls for a break from the traditions of both work and love for both women and men. Levertov wants love and work to be connected and mutually nourishing—that one inspire and support the other. This prayer ties love and work together in a potentially revolutionary relationship: a kind of relationship which can endure separations, distance, and that which is not at all certain. Levertov is challenging men and women to love and to work in new ways.

The prayer is as pressing today as it was when she first yearned it to paper. What it means to love and to work for young heterosexual men and women is still based on constructions of gender which are divided by the borders of femininity and masculinity.

Traditionally, in Puerto Rico, men have been expected to work outside the home and be providers and women have been expected to work in the home as caretakers. This deeply rooted patriarchal myth which supports the division of labor (economically, morally, educationally) has been slow to change even though the economic reality of Puertorriqueñas who are poor or working class is a long story of leaving home to work in factories.[1] Even with this reality, which continues today, even with the Latina feminist movement throughout Latin America, and even with the harsh economic realities which necessitate that everyone have income to survive, many young men and women still view what it means to be *hombres* and *mujeres* in traditionally gender-bound ways. Trying to live up to a myth or idealized gender role goes to the heart of what it means to be a "good" woman or a "good" man and thus has consequences for identity development which, I will argue, can be traumatic, especially for young people who are poor.

Heterosexual roles—the feminine *mujer*, the masculine *hombre*—are rooted in social norms and the dominant ideology but are lived psychologically as gender rituals and scripts where youths negotiate social expectations with individual desires and economic necessity. This dialectic is central in decisions on work, not only from the perspective of what is "traditional" or "nontraditional" for young men and women but also in terms of what work means to youth, who they feel they are, and who they hope to become. Thus work, love, and gender are a *frontera* which is often edged by conflicting desires and needs.

Identities which are constructed and negotiated on this border meet with class boundaries in particular ways which are experienced and lived differently by *hombres* and *mujeres*. This is a *frontera* where gender is negotiated against economic *barreras* and within what Albert et al. (1986) call "the capitalist economic sphere" (pp. 53–60), the dominant economic sphere in Puerto Rican society. At this *frontera* the individual interacts with the institutionalized economic system in ways that critically impact upon identity. Albert et al. write:

> Because economic institutions define what kinds of economic activity will and will not take place, and because the economic activity we engage in affects our personality, skills, and consciousness, economic institutions profoundly affect society's social and psychological patterns as well as material possibilities. Economic institutions also profoundly affect the needs or preferences people will develop and the productive skills they will learn. (p. 48)

These "social and psychological patterns" are evident through the divisions of labor and the negotiations with gender expressed in the youths' narratives. The youths' stories illustrate how the sphere of economics interacts with the sphere of kinship in ways which create ruptures between what *hombre* or *mujer* have traditionally been—heterosexual, masculine, or feminine, providing or caretaking—and what they actually do as young people living in poverty (see Figure 6.1).

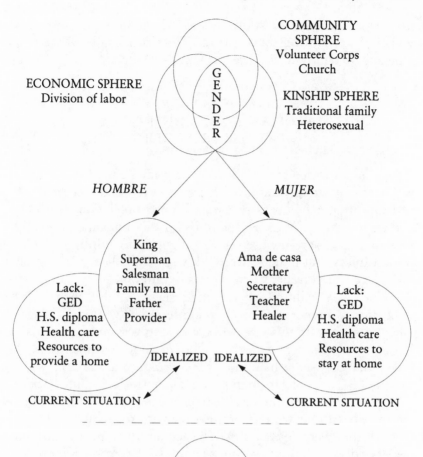

COMMUNITY
SPHERE
Volunteer Corps
Church

ECONOMIC SPHERE
Division of labor

GENDER

KINSHIP SPHERE
Traditional family
Heterosexual

HOMBRE

MUJER

King
Superman
Salesman
Family man
Father
Provider

Ama de casa
Mother
Secretary
Teacher
Healer

Lack:
GED
H.S. diploma
Health care
Resources to
provide a home

Lack:
GED
H.S. diploma
Health care
Resources to
stay at home

IDEALIZED   IDEALIZED

CURRENT SITUATION

CURRENT SITUATION

POLITICAL SPHERE
Lack of connection

Figure 6.1
Moment in Identity: Work and Gender

For the youths included in this chapter (and for many others
that are not), questions about the meaning of work, love, and the
relationships between the two brought to the surface issues of
what is masculine and what is feminine, what it means to be an
hombre or a *mujer*. While reading the narratives I was struck by
how the youths' answers to these interview questions were implic-

itly answering other questions. It's as if I had not asked, What is work? What is love? but instead, What is a man? What is a woman? So tightly woven are work, love, and gender.

WHAT IS *HOMBRE?*
KING, SUPERMAN, SALESMAN, FAMILY MAN, FATHER, PROVIDER

Young men stressed that work was the primary and fundamental way that they would be able to support a family and that the work of supporting a family would entail much obligation, sacrifice, and responsibility. Work tended to be for the young men a gender role that they saw themselves as obligated to fulfill, a gender responsibility that united them with what came before and what the future would bring: work is a male tradition.

Work as a tradition where young men can fulfill their social obligation to support a family was expressed by youths of all ages and across sites. In this way work was seen very much as a male bastion, a place where males needed to develop their identities, to fulfill what they see as manhood, *ser hombre.* As a tradition, work was understood to mean an important avenue to enter into society and participate in it by being able to produce a family and that this was a pattern that would continue on with their own children, whether they were boys or girls. The gender roles of their children were not discussed, but it would be interesting to know if the roles the young men have determined for themselves would carry over into roles for their children, that is, whether the boys would be taught to be boys and the girls taught to be girls.

The importance of work was dictated by its gendered function: if young men could not work they could not be *hombres*, or adult men. This means, then, that work is critical to many young men as a primary identity, and the work itself is secondary to the role of identity definition and social role. Any work is better than no work, but work which allows them to support a family and fulfill this obligation, which they see as their responsibility, is critical to them.

The idealized vision of men being the providers is an outdated one today for obvious reasons; most women work because they want to or need to or both. But the pull of tradition isn't lessened by a changing reality; instead the contradiction that young men who see themselves as providers face is a crisis of purpose which deeply affects who they are as *hombres*.

For young men who were not fathers the role was a future one and based on imagined and traditional male roles. Alvaro, for example, directly connects work with "the responsibility of having a family in the future." Like Alvaro, Mario says that work is "to support the family." Signaling just how compelling this is, the Jesuits, who because of their religious commitments must give up marriage and children, cite the traditional masculine role as not satisfying to them. The use of the role of provider to express why they feel different from other men is interesting in that even young men who definitely have decided against it use it as a symbol of what they decided *not* to do.

Work is a source of identity for young men because it provides them with a means by which they can fulfill their proscribed social roles. In the absence of work, a sense of knowing where one is going breaks apart. The fragmentation that emerges from the disjunction between what an *hombre* should be and what the young men see themselves as being can be devastating.

MANUEL

Manuel is nineteen and dressed in the Volunteer Corps' army green security guard uniform, a beret, and black lace up boots. His ID pin has a different name than the one he gives me and so I ask him which one is his real name. Manuel tells me that the one on the pin is wrong, that the Volunteer Corps didn't have an ID pin with his correct last name inscribed.

I wonder to myself if he minds being called by a last name that is not his own and recall when my mother remarried how I had to learn to spell a new name. Sitting at my desk I'd glance behind me at the foreign surname, written on the tab of a manila file and tucked into my shelf at the back of the third-grade classroom. I was embarrassed that I didn't know how to spell my own name. I didn't question the new spelling. I answered to it and it became a reluctant part of me. Several years ago I changed my name again, dropping the foreign one and returning to my mother's family name, after I discussed it with her.

Manuel's mother died when he was twelve, leaving him and a sister with their father. He had to go to work because his father "didn't really care much about us because he was worrying about getting married again." Manuel's relationship with his father finally broke apart when he was sixteen:

> I didn't know if he really loves me or not because we got into this religion, Pentecostal religion, and for two and a half years I liked it but then everything started collapsing. I started seeing things completely different because I wanted to go out. I wanted to go and see other people, know other people, just go to different places and my father he didn't want that, he said that it was bad to go out because the devil was out there and all this and so we couldn't go. And he restricted me of many things that youth want, understand?

Manuel has been back and forth between the United States and Puerto Rico. At the time of the interview Manuel had been in Puerto Rico for only three months and had been living with an aunt. Before that he was living in South Carolina:

> I was working as a salesman and met a woman who was twenty-one years old, she lived in South Carolina. I went to live in South Carolina, went to live with her for three weeks. I went to live with her for three weeks and then I found out that she wasn't good for me. She wasn't nothing, you know, so I went to live outside for two weeks I lived out in the streets. I slept in alley-ways, I slept in corners, I slept in buses, I slept everywhere, you know, just to keep myself warm. I didn't have anything, actually I had all my bags with me, everything with me. And um, that was stolen, too, all that it was taken away. It was like you don't you shouldn't have any of this so I was left with nothing. And a little bit at a time I found the Salvation Army and I worked there and I stayed there for about three months and they helped me with my clothes and they helped me with everything. And I met another girl, another twenty-three-year-old girl, and at that time I was only eighteen years old so it was kind of a wow, and so I stayed with her for about two weeks, decided she wasn't good enough, left, slept on the streets for about four more weeks, about a month. During that time I was just suffering I wasn't I just didn't like it, you know, I was the days would go by without me eating, things that make you feel bad, that hurt you, understand? I cried, you know, from the pain I cried.

Manuel ties the difficulties of his life to the women he has lived with. Manuel left an aunt he was living with, too. The reason for being out on the street is his realization that they were "not good enough." The relationships are strikingly similar. Following the contradictory masculine script of finding the perfect "girl," Manuel ironically calls himself "an expert in love." But this script is a painful one to follow. It is full of loss, disappointment, and deception. Masculinity becomes a story of broken relationships where the women are never good enough. Fittingly, Manuel describes how he didn't know what was really going on in his relationships:

> Love! I'm an expert in love . . . Love that is sincere I think that love is defined when a person, you feel something profound towards a person, understand? You are sincere with a person, understand? You love that person so much that you open yourself completely to her, understand? For example, a man and a woman. For a woman if a man feels true love for her, then he loves her, he respects her, understand? he has trust in her, understand? I have been through many cases of love, quote unquote love, understand? that I have had to learn how to truly define love, understand? because I have found myself in situations that I have been with women that they have not been sincere with me since the beginning, what they've done is play with my mind, with my feelings, understand. And I was thinking that they truly loved me because we were together day and night. Well I thought that but it was the contrary.

Manuel is talkative but speaks deliberately as if thinking through every word and switches back and forth from English to Spanish. As the interview continues Manuel speaks mostly in English, which I begin to realize is the language he feels most comfortable with because he spent most of his life in the United States. Manuel often says, "*¿entiendes?*" which means "understand?" or "you know?" and is also a manner of speaking in Puerto Rico. When he switches to English he says "you know" instead. (These switches are reflected in the transcription.)

The language switching—like all the dramatic, if not traumatic, changes Manuel has been through—underscores how much is constantly changing for him. In both the work he is engaged in and the relationships he says he knows so much about there is a duality: two stories told at the same time. One story is about how Manuel sees himself ideally. The other is the story of what has actually happened. These two are not aligned but are instead disjointed and only meet in one place: the work that Manuel loves. But it's not that simple or settled.

Manuel defines work mostly through a discussion of his current work as a security guard:

> I think that my work is important, that is, very important because what I am doing is bringing to do, is trying that the vigilance that is done in the *recinto* is correct and that all the *muchachos* are, like they say, are safe. That nothing happens to them, strange things in the *recinto*, things that are going to harm the *recinto*, understand? And I think that a security guard, well, one should maintain the correct line and everything correct, and give an example because that's what the security course is there for, understand? To maintain the *recinto* up high. I think that one should feel proud of being in the security course because it's a course that's worthwhile . . . In security I like it because how can I say? I can show people that they need to learn more about the laws, how they should respect the law, the security, you understand, how they should understand that we do it for their good, for their sake and not for ours. We're risking our lives, we're risking everything of ours, for their safety and they should learn that. That's how come I like it. You understand? Because it shows good.

But it becomes clear that this is not the work he would like to be doing, that being in the security course is only temporary:

> I would like to go back to what I was before, as a salesman, understand, and I would like to, I would like to study more about business, I would like to, you know just go up to that, understand, and just be what I wanted to be, you know, a long time ago, understand. I could also be a security guard, that's no problem, I could be a policeman but I don't know I just don't feel sometimes I just don't feel comfortable with it so I would just like to sometimes I just want to go back to that, you know, to being a salesman, you know. Dressing up nice everyday, working like that. Even though, maybe you won't get paid as much but I enjoyed it very much I really do. I don't know now if it could be possible for me to go back to what I wanted to do because of where I'm at now but I would like to go back there . . . I want to be a salesman. I would like to work in those big stores, I'd like to be a manager. I'd like to have my own store. I know, I know I'm asking a lot, I know I'm probably asking too much, but that's what I've always wanted to do and that's what I've always wanted to be, you know . . . Make a life for myself, you know, make something for myself. I don't want to worry about what's going to happen to me the following day, you

know, that's how come here I try to do my best, you know, I try
to follow the rules, rules and regulations, always try, you always
have to follow the norms, everything.

Unlike the young men and women who want to continue to work
for the police or the military after leaving the Volunteer Corps,
Manuel sees the security course as a way to get back on track. Following the norms, teaching others about the law, keeping people
and property out of harm's way, no longer on the street and at the
mercy of strangers, Manuel is mapping his own course back to
what makes him feel good about himself. But rules and norms
have gotten him in trouble before when he began to disagree with
them, when he "started seeing things completely different."

The line he is walking is tenuous. The order he is enforcing is
within a small community he feels comfortable in, and the security
is transitory. Manuel does not feel connected to a larger society,
although when he worked in sales he did:

> I don't participate much in the society. Society would be the out-
> side world, right? Society, okay, it could include the *cuerpo de
> voluntarios*, see but we don't go out much. I don't do much out-
> side, you know, and so society is everything that goes around in
> the outside and so I don't feel part of a society but part of a com-
> munity. A community is just one small area, a society is a big
> area. I don't feel a part of a society. I would like to be part of a
> society, I used to be part of a society.

The lack of connection between society and the Volunteer Corps
for Manuel may arise from two places. First, he has moved around
a great deal and just recently arrived in Puerto Rico. Second, the
Volunteer Corps as outlined in the previous chapter follows a mil-
itaristic model which sets it apart (by design) from society as a way
of providing youths with structure and discipline. Indeed, Manuel
enjoys the authority of being a security guard, and it makes him
feel good and important to protect others and to protect himself,
but he is also ambivalent about continuing on this course once he
leaves the Volunteer Corps.

Manuel is caught at the *frontera* of becoming an *hombre*
within a small ordered community, away from the chaos he's
experienced in society ("the outside world, right?"). It will be a
difficult crossing for Manuel to make. Manuel will have to translate what he's learned about norms into working in big stores, into
working as a salesman, into living in a world where strange things

do happen, where harm can't always be regulated, where the messy rules of relationships and love need to be negotiated, not enforced.

ANTONIO

Antonio is twenty-two and at the Volunteer Corps program in Aguadilla. Like Manuel in Ensenada, Antonio is currently learning the skills of a security guard and then wants to move on. His goal is to work as an emergency medical technician in an agency that devotes itself to rescuing lives. Antonio envisions himself playing a role in updating the emergency response system in Puerto Rico.

Antonio's definitions of work and love are closely linked with the masculine roles of provider and family man, with feelings of obligation, and the pain of broken relationships which seem impossible to put back together:

> One has to work to make money. For example, to support a family, to have a car, to have x or y thing, this means working for it. One sees oneself obligated, for me, work is an obligation that one has to exercise because if you don't you will be living off a story . . . I have been divorced for nine months and three days, I have a boy who is two years old in the town of Jayuya. Love for me was, boy! it was hard, it is hard, you cry, you laugh, you struggle, you make sacrifices, sometimes so that your partner is alright . . . The boy who is two years old it's a rare thing that I see him because of the distance from that town . . . Love for me right now doesn't exist. It doesn't exist. It doesn't exist, it was three and a half years of war, hard, but I'm here to better myself.

Antonio's interest in the area of medical emergency began when he was eleven years old and his mother suffered a heart attack from which she thankfully recovered: "One time we were at home, just everyone together and *Mami* got a strong pain in her chest and man, she got to the hospital and that and I always saw when the medics jumped on top of her and put her on the stretcher, and started to give her CPR and they kept on top of it all the time and I said, *caramba*, I would like to learn that." It was also at this time that Antonio watched a lot of television shows such as *Emergency 51, Code Red, MASH* and became fascinated by what he saw. As a child he was "always crazy about" the *Emergency 51* show, which was about fire fighters. Within his family, Antonio's uncle was the director of civil defense in his hometown of Aguada and would to talk with him about planning for the future and became his mentor:

> Then at eleven, that was when my uncle went into the Civil Defense. Then he would break out and talk to me; you're a little kid still but learn, and then I started getting involved with the Red Cross. I soaked in training, like I say, I couldn't get certified but I was present in that class [CPR], but I was soaking it in. I was a sponge . . . and although I didn't have anything to do with that class, I would ask questions until I turned sixteen years old and I could enter the Rescue Academy . . . and later it was that, at home again, my *Abuelo* got another one [heart attack] and I was the one that dealt with him, and I was the one that saved his life, me and a cousin. I gave him resuscitation and my cousin compression, and we brought him back to the world, we saved him and that's why I have always liked the emergency. I have always liked them, working in emergency rescue units and all that I have always liked it, always, always, always, always.

Antonio also names the Coast Guard, Fire Department, and Police SWAT as the other "units" that deal with rescuing and "tactical operations" that are of interest to him. His father, Antonio tells me, wanted him to go into the army: "He always wanted me to be a military man . . . because I was the only son." His mother, on the other hand, wanted Antonio to become a priest. Although Antonio says he wanted to become neither, it seems he has instead found a way to become both.

Throughout the interview Antonio expresses a single-minded commitment to "saving lives and property." There isn't a sentence in his narrative that doesn't directly relate to his goal. When I ask Antonio if the work that he is doing at the *recinto* is helping him move toward his future goal, he tells me that it is, especially because of the month-long group therapy (MRT) which is required at the Volunteer Corps:

> Especially here they give a course to prepare you, MRT, that helps a lot . . . That opens one's mind and takes one towards finding oneself, who one is, towards where one is going, what one wants, what one is looking for. And I arrived here very confused, yes, arrived very confused about myself and here I am. They call me the philosopher, the *muchachos*. The psychologist,

too, the *muchachos* call me . . . I get them involved. And the *muchachos* tell me and the director too, tells me, "You have incredible leadership that's why we have to exploit you" and we're into that. But I can do it, my commitment is with Puerto Rico.

Antonio credits the MRT process for giving him a sense of "where one is going," echoing Erikson's words about identity. No longer feeling confused about what he wants or who he is, Antonio tightly grasps work which commits him to helping Puerto Rican society. But Antonio remains disconnected from his son and from relationships which are not abstract and philosophical but are, as he says, "hard, you cry, you laugh, you struggle . . . Love for me right now doesn't exist." Antonio loves his *pueblo* enough to risk his life to save strangers, yet can't make it to Jayuya to see his son. It is Antonio's ex-wife who loves his son specifically, concretely, with the hands-on work of child rearing.

To love in the abstract and save in the abstract is a central part of Antonio's masculinity, encouraged and nurtured by his uncle and the Volunteer Corps director. The process of clarifying this has given him a sense of what he wants and what he is looking for. Settling masculinity in this way has provided Antonio with the direction he clearly needed. But how is it that Antonio's logic places his ex-partner and child outside of the *pueblo* of Puerto Rico and that this does not confuse him?

Antonio voices again and again how deeply he feels connected to Puerto Rico as a *pueblo*—as a people—in addition to his hometown community and the Volunteer Corps community of Aguadilla. When Antonio uses the plural *we*, he is referring to all Puertorriqueños and Puertorriqueñas. Antonio also sees himself within a global context—*mundial*—although the United States is his primary geographical focus when speaking about "the world," reflecting the deeply embedded colonial view:

I am from Aguada. I know I am part of the *pueblo* of Puerto Rico because we are who represent our country, even though where we are is just another little corner of the world but wherever we go, the example we give, that's how they will categorize our *pueblo*. That's why we have to be aware of what we're doing, it's not going to fall on us, but instead on the others that are part of our *pueblo*, understand? One can go to the United States, do whatever stupid thing over there and they'll say, "Look at that Puerto Rican, that's how they all are." Yes because there are many prejudices, and good people go and new people and they are going to be treated like that one because that's the way that is. One always has to be aware of what one does, says, in what one gets involved at those places outside one's *pueblo* and I feel *mundial*.

On the one hand it's odd that Antonio can be enormously committed to his work of saving lives and just as hugely estranged from those whom he loves. But then, this is typical of how masculinity constructs identity. Central to becoming an *hombre* is this contradictory process of disconnecting from the personal as a way of committing to work which connects with society and the world.

GILBERTO

Gilberto is twenty-four years old. He talks quickly and what he says in Spanish is often a translation from English because he's spent most of his life in the United States. He begins to define work with this brief statement: "Work is working." But this gives way to a complicated interview in which he reveals the tremendous struggle it has been to survive and to change his life. Gilberto continues:

> The way one can support a family, what one has to do to get to a place, a goal . . . when one sweats, where one makes the effort with the body, one has to have responsibility with one's things, whatever presents itself at that moment that one's in whether young, married, and are in other words I have the name of work as something that makes one responsible . . . be awake at all hours . . . I'm a kind of person that has gotten up with the sun many times there *afuera*.[2]

Gilberto began working when he was nine years old cleaning out basements in New York City. He has also worked "replacing glass in the city of Manhattan also worked in washing machines for a year, worked in a cable electrical factory for two years and the other job I worked was cutting trees. Then I learned to do things with construction, the last job I worked was here in Moca." He tells me that he enjoys hard physical labor—construction, paving sidewalks, excavation, operating heavy equipment—because "I have the body for that" and it "puts my mind to work." When I ask him how working hard with heavy equipment feels, he gives a sigh of relief and says: "Inside, ah, free. I feel free, open, taking in the fresh air, I don't feel trapped, nothing bothers me. I feel really comfortable." On the other hand, what Gilberto calls "easy work" makes him bored and puts him in a bad mood. I ask Gilberto how it was that he began working cleaning basements at nine:

> That was a job I would go look for, it was something that my *Abuelo* left for me as a memory before his time passed. He taught me how it is that a young *muchacho* can find the beans, how to make a dollar, his daily bread and not to have to do the crime and robbery things, you know. Take what is not one's, to get into problems, to look for getting into jail. He also taught me that sometimes it's much better to ask than to lie . . . I am allergic to rats and allergic to dust and I would go into those basements and come out sneezing, fatigued, but I'd do it . . . I can get a basement that's really a mess, the max and I can get it, I will get it like a nickel because I've done that a lot and that's why I can get it like a nickel. I'll take out the last bit of dust, even in the corners, and at the end of that work I had gotten twenty basement jobs just because of one job I did. I cleaned it well and people kept hiring me.

Even though Gilberto's *Abuelo* taught him to stay out of trouble, he was not able to do so. Before Gilberto found his way to the Volunteer Corps in Aguadilla he was a drug dealer in Miami, Florida, Brooklyn, New York, and Puerto Rico. Like Manuel, Gilberto lived on the streets for months with little to eat and in hiding from the bigger traffickers. He lost everything he had after a gang war that almost left him dead. He tells two stories. A friend's mother and father and the friend were shot and killed in front of their house at 1:00 in the morning. The other story is that Gilberto was tied and stuffed in a closet with two others for six days, without water, and given daily beatings. He was beaten on the head and face and had ribs broken. Somehow he and the others managed to jump out a window after six days. Gilberto and one other escaped with broken bones; the other one, who would not jump down the three stories, was killed. After that Gilberto spent three months on the street.

Looking back at his experiences of dealing drugs, Gilberto points to the ways in which drugs and the money they provide enabled him to fulfill the role of family man. But the contradiction of being a provider through the use of violence eventually became clear to him when he realized he was hurting other people, after he himself had been severely hurt. Tragically this realization almost cost him his life:

> I thought it was fantastic at that time. Drugs for me was a tremendous thing. First rate. There was nothing else, it was incredible. You felt like you were a Superman, you felt like you were a man that was regular and then in a moment you grow muscles, that whoever comes at you you'll knock him down and traveling a lot free and I had a great quantity of money. I didn't know that I was harming other people, other countries, children, my trafficking in drugs and I also hurt twelve people really badly and I really regret it now. Because I had a lot of guns, a lot of weapons, and I thought I was a tremendous person with a weapon. I saw myself as big, showing off, but really I wasn't what I thought I was.

The violence that Gilberto inflicted on twelve people and the violence that was inflicted on him was enabled by the disconnections between himself and others and the rupture between his image of himself and who he felt he was, a "regular" man. Drugs and money made him "grow muscles" and made him feel invulnerable: "Whoever comes at you you'll knock him down." This is the violent side of masculinity, supported by drugs and money and patriarchal tradition. This is a place where being a regular *hombre* is not enough, a *frontera* where becoming a man can be fatal.

Gilberto offers a further view of the deeply contradictory process of identity for young men because they do have personal (not just *mundial*) needs and the desire for mutual respect (not just dominance) in relationships. But to express needs and desires necessarily involves a kind of vulnerability and emotional risk, which had not been part of Gilberto's masculine script as a boy. On the contrary, he felt he had to be violent. He had to learn later, after his first relationships broke apart, because he felt that his world had crashed around him. Gilberto describes how he began to watch how his family argued and then how they got back together and became happy, how older people tried to get along. He illustrates a process of having to learn how to have mutuality in relationships against the masculine myth of the *hombre* as "king:"

> Well, love I didn't understand it. For me it was like confused . . . and then, now, at this age, well I, love for me, is a tremendous thing . . . I have a girl who is one year and six months and one that has not been born yet. She'll be born this week. After Friday

I hope to have a new son or daughter. Whatever God gives me . . . I've been married two years with my woman. She is from *afuera* too. She had less capacity than I did. I made her understand what I base love on, that it is not something that I wanted to be higher than her or for her to be higher than me. It's something that can be shared. Everything that happens in marriage can be part of both. That it's not more for me or more for her. I have understood that in love one can't maintain oneself like the king of that place, because we both need each other. So now love for me is also about what the woman can do for the man. There are lots of things that the man can't do for the woman, I used to think the man was the king, I believed the man was the one who could do everything, that the woman was there only to love you.

Gilberto wants to return to his wife and children, who are in Brooklyn. He would like to drive interstate trucks for a living and hopes the experience working with heavy equipment will serve him well. He no longer sees himself as a "Superman." He sees the work at the Volunteer Corps as preparing him to go back to the United States because, as he puts it, "My wife and I are used to English, so we need that environment. I could get used to being here but she couldn't and for me to make a family, so that it doesn't break, and that there aren't any problems, well I want to do that. Do the most I can."

RAFAEL

Rafael is nineteen years old and married to Rosa, who is twenty. They both walk into the office where I'm interviewing at ADT. When I ask if they would like to be interviewed at the same time or separately, Rosa tells me that at the same time would be good. At the large round table, they sit together closely, to my left. After taking a few minutes to arrange the microphone, figure out the logistics of how I'm going to ask the same question twice, who will go first, and hoping that this will yield a useful interview, we begin. Rosa answers first. (Her profile is included in the next section on *mujeres*).

Rafael's answers are very brief, mostly one or two sentences, not more than three short ones. This interview begins to feel to me like a great methodological failure and I'm regretting my lack of ability to elicit longer answers because I truly want to know more.

But after transcribing and reading the narratives over, what I had perceived as Rafael's lack of words and my lack of ability no longer looks like a "methods problem" or "a lack of," but instead a complicated representation of the relationship between a researcher (who has thought a lot about the interview questions) and a youth (who hasn't given these questions much thought). But there's more to this.

Rafael's answers are facilitated by Rosa. The interview which at first felt to me like "not enough data" is a nuanced moment of relationship, a moment which at one and the same time tells a story of support for each other and the enormous *barreras* of class and gender while also illustrating the relational process of interviewing:

> I ask, "How do you know that you are working in something that is important to you?"
>
> Rosa answers first and then Rafael says, "Well, I feel good for that work that I'm doing."
>
> This answers my question and I pause before asking the next one. Perhaps sensing that I would like a fuller answer Rosa rephrases the question and asks Rafael, "In other words what she means to say is that for what work do you, out of so many that there are, carpentry, janitor, which one is the one you like the best?"
>
> I can't make out his answer. Rosa asks him, "Cutting grass? What other work do you like?"
>
> Rafael answers, "Lots. Cutting grass, garbage pickup."
>
> I ask him, "Is this work that you have done?"
>
> Rafael, "I was working over by Carolina [Puerto Rico] picking up trees and that and picking up trees by the roads and all that, the garbage."
>
> I ask, "And that is what you liked?"
>
> "Yes, I liked that, all of that."
>
> Rosa, "*Chacho.*"[3]

Rafael's views on work are strikingly grounded in religion and devastating in their implications: "God sent man so he could work to support his family so it's that way one is sent to work." What is devastating is that he has few skills and little formal education (they left high school together), and he has difficulty making himself clear even with his wife encouraging him to speak out; by the second half of the interview only she is answering the questions and I am asking the questions in plural instead of addressing each one separately. "God sent man to work," but when I ask him what work he loves to do, the question itself makes no sense. Rafael says: "Well, work because I have to work to support my wife from whatever comes my way." Any work will do; it is the God-given mandate to support his wife that carries primary importance. Rafael tells that he can work at the following: cutting tall grass, garbage collecting, and picking up fallen trees. Underscoring their class and gender locations and their views of what is possible, Rosa presents a narrow range of alternatives to him (carpentry, janitorial) while simultaneously saying that there are so many different kinds of work. But these kinds of work will not allow him to fulfill God's will as he has defined it. What will change or give way? If Rafael gets work at Public Works, which he would like, this will still not be enough to support his wife and the family they plan to make together.

As with the young men who say their role is to support a family and yet they don't, to resolve this apparent contradiction into categories of hypocrisy, blame, values, or morality wouldn't shed any light on how a young man with these convictions squares the reality of unemployment. He is very involved in his church and at ADT wants to get the *cuarto año* because he says that without it "one can't do anything." Education becomes the way to align God's will with what he can do.

The stakes are extraordinarily high and the expectations difficult to meet in a state-run agency. ADT as an agency will most probably fail him. Rafael is, like the other young men who saw themselves as providers, at a *frontera* of meaning and purpose which, without any intervention, if Antonio and Manuel are guides, will become a crisis of meaning and purpose.

These young men are caught in a place that is fraught with contradiction and complicated by masculine myths that bear little resemblance to their own lives. Their resources are extremely limited; they are poor, have little schooling, and being *hombres*—masculine, heterosexual—are expected to provide. Their relationships are either at risk or fragmented and torn apart. Manuel ends up on the street after his two relationships break up, Antonio ends up in another town, and Gilberto is in another country. For Antonio and Manuel their previous partners either "don't exist," were at "war," or are "nothing" and "no good." Their inability to meet an impossible masculine role brings with it a corresponding annihilation of their relationships: if they can't be *hombres* then the women can't exist, can't be somebody, can't be *mujeres* either.

Gilberto is trying to maintain his relationship with his partner and children but is an ocean away, a four-hour flight away, an expensive ticket away—any way one looks at the distance, he is separated by time and space. He is also at risk because of his previous involvement in the traffic of drugs. But his primary reason for staying in and getting through the Volunteer Corps is to make good this time on his responsibility of being a man.

For young men like Manuel, Antonio, Gilberto, and Rafael work is both a means of self-support and survival as well as a place where they can be *hombres,* a place where they can be "something," a place where there is no "war," where they can better themselves to be able to then better provide. All view work as the ticket to manhood, to being *hombres,* and in this way are moving counter to what most young women view as the purposes and roles of work in their lives. This crisis of meaning and purpose, then, is also that young women whom young men might hope to provide for don't want to be provided for but, instead, want to gain independence through working.

The effect of not having work for young men who tie their masculinity with the traditional gender role of *hombre* is no small matter. Work is a place where young men can go about constructing what masculinity has traditionally been. This is a socioeconomic and psychological bind which pits work and masculinity against each other and contributes to putting poor young men at high risk of homelessness, violence, and drugs, and correspondingly puts young women who are their partners and their children at risk.

Work is a place where the complexities of developing masculinity—whether through a God-given mandate or a culturally dictated one—and the contradictions of gender construction for poor young men are played out, practiced, and rehearsed. The daily problematics of being an *hombre* coexist with the myth of provider. These two hold hands, but have the unintended yet corresponding effect of damaging—or worse, destroying—relationships.

WHAT IS *MUJER?*
AMA DE CASA, MOTHER, SECRETARY, TEACHER, NURSE, DOCTOR

Nowhere are the interconnections between work, love, and gender made as painfully clear as by young women living in poverty whose desires for themselves and their families are routinely sub-jugated by class, race, and sexual oppression. In the face of this daily denial and marginalization they struggle for meager progress in areas that most light-skinned middle-class young women would take for granted as basic rights of equality and freedom, of democracy: access to education, health care, and equal employment.

The monumental effort involved in taking steps outside the home to work is pushed back by an adherence to traditional gender roles which keep these women constantly checking their movements against a mythic norm of gender, of being a *mujer*, an internalized norm of femininity, of caring for others selflessly, willingly. The message that comes at them from within and without is that to be a *mujer* means to care for children, to be a mother, to be a caretaker, an *ama de casa*—a housewife. The image of mother described by youths in the interviews is traditional and based on ideals of self-sacrifice and selfless giving: mother love is glorified.

When young *mujeres* reach out past the private work of women in the home, they reach out toward the traditional work of women outside the home—working to help others. When they place themselves in traditionally female jobs, work is a place where their femininity is not endangered. It is a balancing act between economic, cultural and religious necessity. Caught at this *frontera* of economics and gender, their choice of work is also defined by institutionalized divisions of labor which push *mujeres* into historically female and low-paying professions.

These young women view work from a different perspective than the young men. They enter the workplace through a back door that is open to them because it is work traditionally done by women: nursing, clerical, secretarial, teaching elementary school. In this way the young women who see themselves in traditionally feminine ways, as *mujeres*—mothers, caretakers, housekeepers—seek out work that extends their gendered role into the work sphere. They move from home to work along traditional lines as if by doing this they will not endanger their relationships. Entering the workplace is a risky balance which entails redefining themselves but not enough to question their traditional gendered role of *mujer* and negotiating the ambivalence of simultaneously reaching out to find work that will give them economic resources while feeling that their primary place is at home.

Like the young men who draw on traditional gender scripts to situate themselves in the world of work and use work to situate themselves in the world of *hombres*, young women also draw on traditional gender-scripts to situate themselves in particular work-places but, unlike the young men, find themselves betwixt and between. If work is the world of *hombres*, how can they work and be *mujeres*? How can they keep their femininity in a masculine place? This is a difficult situation which locates many young *mujeres* in contradictory and ambivalent places: *mujeres* have to take care of others and also take care of themselves; they have to do what's good for themselves and also what's good for others; they have to pursue their own interests while watching out for the interests of others. These are the *fronteras* of the traditional gender roles for young women who view work both reluctantly and hopefully.

ROSA

Rosa, Rafael's wife, wants to be a nurse, and she also says she loves being a housewife. Rosa is one of several young women living in poverty who see their primary work as traditionally feminine, as wives and caretakers, but also want to pursue a profession working outside the home. Rosa crosses the *frontera* of public work and private work throughout the interview:

> Work, well, I define it as something God sent man to do, right? He had to work to be able to get his sustenance in life and work, well, is what everyone has to look for because, well, it's through work that one has experience, that one associates with other *compañeros* at work, you have experiences and little by little one acquires capacity and it's a form of making a living, of sustenance for nourishment and the basic needs that one has.

Rosa then goes on to say that her first line of duty is to be a housewife: "For me the first work that I have, right, is to be an *ama de casa* that is work that, imagine! that is for me my first work. You see, it's because of being an *ama de casa* . . ." Her answer is interrupted by a coughing attack and she has a hard time talking; she gestures to her congested chest and doesn't say anything else. Rosa was sick during the interview. She said that she had a cough for several weeks; she said she had left school because of an accident. The accident has left her chronically ill and she had to leave school. Rosa is twenty years old. I pursued what her illness was but she said that it was just a cough. To me her cough sounded like some sort of bronchial asthma. I thought it could be tuberculosis, which is coming back. She didn't want to make much of her illness and accident.

Rosa explains what she enjoys about working as an *ama de casa* and how she sees her role of wife:

> Well, because, well, because I get along fine doing the work of *ama de casa*, whether it's well, picking up the house, cleaning it, sometimes I even clean the outside yard, plant flowers, well, I feel love for that work . . . Loving another person, sharing with them, being with them in the circumstances of life . . . through good and bad. Never say no instead, right, help the other person. Well, that is how I am with my husband, well, I am with him.

Rosa has come to ADT to enter a job training program and receive her GED, which in Puerto Rico is referred to as *cuarto año*, meaning "fourth year" of high school:

> Let's see if with this I can reach *cuarto año* because I wanted to take it because I also went there to the high school to see if they'd give me *cuarto año* and then I was there, but later, you know, they didn't pass me, you know, they didn't give me the *cuarto año*, you know, take it then, well, I left. And then, well, I came here to apply for work but since they said there isn't any then there's this opportunity to take the *cuarto año*. I want to take it so that then, if God helps me, right, get into a job training so that later if I take nursing because that too after *ama de casa*, I like it, but always my hope was to be able, you know, to reach *cuarto año* and then take other studies and reach being a nurse. This work, you know, of nurse.

Rosa says that a neighbor encouraged them to come to ADT and gave them a ride to the agency. The neighbor's urging, Rosa tells, was "Look you have to take advantage of that you're young and you have to keep on going forward and you have to take advantage now because right now you're alone and later when you start having children . . ."

The problems of health and education of young people living in poverty were nowhere made clearer to me than by the young women I interviewed at ADT. The tyranny of gender roles is perhaps most damaging to the poor, and especially poor women, who lack education and skills. How can Rosa be a housewife, pursue her GED and then a course of study to become a nurse while chronically ill, and also have children? For Rosa the contradictions, rooted in socioeconomic *barreras*—I want to write *violence*, not *barriers*—may become internalized into feelings of failure. For the chances are that ADT will fail her as did her high school. Her religious source of support comes from her church, which she and her husband participate in as part of the "ladies and gentlemen" group, and each have duties that they perform for the pastor. Rafael is her primary source of emotional support.

Rosa lacks skills, health, and support, and wants to work as well as to sustain a traditional gender role. The work which she loves, housework, and the work which she has hoped to be able to reach, nursing, stake out her *frontera*. Her genius may be nursing and I want to know if part of her desire to nurse is to take care, even cure, herself. Through her wretched cough her desire and hopes of becoming a nurse are expressed, as are her expected traditional roles. Nursing is a historically female-dominated profession; she could join a traditional script. And one can see how this is easier for her, how taking care of the house and others is what she knows best. But the chronic cough points to a tragedy in the making which is not unique to her: her own health is at risk, she is the one that needs taking care of, she needs a nurse, and she isn't getting one.

JUANA MARÍA

Juana María is seventeen years old and the young woman who the job counselor didn't want to deal with at ADT. Apparently, Juana María is used to people not being able to help her or not wanting to. She said that several public schools wouldn't accept her and that teachers repeatedly told her that she is a slow learner. Juana María explains why: "because I couldn't read and write so fast they put me in special education since third grade. My brother and I are slow, we were born that way, since we were little we're like this." Yet Juana María, in her sweet and soft-spoken voice, defines work this way:

> Well for me work is well it's an experience and well, I the only work I've had is summer jobs and I've liked that since I was fourteen years old I've been working and I've always liked it and I'm planning to keep working. The people have treated me very *chévere*[4] and the place where I work is really good.

What have you worked in during the summers?

Well the first time that I worked in summer was at an elderly center in Cupey Alto, my mother also worked there and everyone was really good there and they know me. The second time was in the *municipio* of Hato Rey, at Hato Rey they are also good and almost everybody knows my family, well, the third was at Los Lirios picking up what was there with the other *muchachos* and it was with my cousin and also everything was good and I've always liked working in the summer. If now I have an opportunity to work and not only in summer but all the time then I'll do it with pleasure because I like to work.

Juana María also shows this same willingness and openness to other people when she tells me what she defines as love, although at first she says she's doesn't know anything about it:

Ah, about that I don't know because I don't have a boyfriend yet. I have friends yes, that I like for me it's very *chévere*, I don't know, for me love it isn't love like you being with the *muchachos* doing things that you shouldn't be doing but instead sharing, telling each other your problems, being trusted, and not only with the *muchachos* but also with the mother and father, loved ones, and I'm one of those persons that loves people a lot. I get along well with everybody, wherever I am I have friends, I'm always alright with the *muchachos* and *muchachas*, I don't have problems with that.

Out of school now, she is her mother's caretaker:

In '88 when I jumped for, I don't remember, I was going into the second year of high school, well, and I had already stopped working, studying there, I couldn't I had other problems in other schools and they never wanted to accept me and I left and in January I began to take *cuarto año* free but I still haven't finished because my mother fell and so has a broken arm and I can't finish until she recuperates totally. But I think about finishing and now I'm here to see about work, study three months and work three months since I see that here the people are very *chévere* and so I think about working and studying here for the three months.

When I ask Juana María what work she likes, she talks about four kinds of work. She sees herself working as a teacher of children with special needs and disabilities or taking care of babies. She says she would also like to be a doctor and a secretary. The only one she's "experimented" with is secretarial work by writing letters at home to her family and letters to television stations for free passes to movies and activities on a typewriter. She has aunts who have been secretaries and worked in government agencies and they have encouraged her to use the typewriter. Juana María also says she likes working with computers.

Juana María is supposed to help her mother and herself. Her mother can't take care of herself and Juana María has been bounced around from home to home. At one point she lived with an aunt who didn't enroll her in school. In the face of this she still maintains an open and sharing stance toward the world. She is overweight. She is poor. She is female. She is of African descent. Since third grade she's been told she's slow.

These are all identity markers; like sign posts, they have guided Juana María. She expresses a desire to be a doctor, a healer, perhaps to take care of her mother better, to heal her mother's arm. The signs and guides are contradictory and give rise to a great deal of ambivalence which is expressed through a series of professions that are related to each other symbolically but lack relation in any practical educational way. Being a secretary symbolizes the achievement of reading and writing skills, being a doctor, having the capacity to be healing, but these can't be reconciled in the context Juana María is in now.

At this *frontera* where young *mujeres* collide against institutionalized racism, classism, and sexism, Juana María sits waiting for the job counselor, who without having spoken a word to her already finds her hopeless, to help her enter a six-month job training program and attempt to get her GED. Her sweetness in accepting the brutal judgments and conditions of others haunts me more than anything else in the entire study.

SUSANA

At nineteen, light-skinned with hazel eyes and long sandy hair, Susana is what's called in Puerto Rico a *rubia*, a blond.[5] Susana is lively and speaks quickly. When we spoke she had been working as a secretary for two and a half months as part of ADT's summer jobs for youths program. Susana was hoping that her summer position would be renewed so that she could continue to work at ADT, but if not she'll go to night school and work part-time. She would like to study for work related to the travel industry, and she mentions two possibilities: travel agent or working for an airline company. Susana graduated from high school and went on to earn an associate's degree in computers. Since she was a child Susana has been talking about how secretarial work has dominated her choices:

> Since I was little, I don't know since I was little, I always said that I was going to be a secretary, so in *cuarto año* one takes a commercial [vocational] or general [academic] course and well, I took the commercial, then when I would take the computer classes, well they taught one typewriting and that and since it was something I always liked well, I took advantage and almost all the jobs I've had have been in that.

> *When you were little did a teacher say are you interested in being a secretary or let's see how we can help you to do this?*

> It was almost always well, almost all my aunts, my aunts and the people that were close to me were secretaries and so I would see them and always since I was little I believed well, that this career I had this on my mind and always well, I would say that I was going to be a secretary well, and always was going to work in that.

> *And your mother?*

> No, my mother is an *ama de casa*.

> *And your father?*

> He works but in construction and like that.

Susana's narrative points to how divisions of labor along traditional gender lines interact with kinship relations to reinforce decisions on choice of work without providing alternative views. Caught at the place where economic and kinship relations intersect with gender, Susana doesn't explore alternatives to what she has been seeing around her since she was a child.

I was curious whether school played a role in Susana's choice of work.

> *In school were you helped to be a secretary, in elementary or middle school?*

> No.

> *Was it in high school?*

> Yes, it was just simply in middle school that they always ask you, "What do you want, think about doing in the future?" I

would always say, "Secretary." Always, every time that they asked me. So in high school I took the commercial course the three years, 10, 11, and 12 and after that I took the associate in computers degree that also has typewriting, well, that is what I have taken.

I can't help but wonder what might be different if Susana were a boy. What if a boy always responded that he wanted to be a secretary? Posing this question makes it clear that gender has consistently guided Susana's hands over the keyboard, the typewriter. It also exposes what is called into question when boys assert they want to go into "women's work," and what is not called into question when girls reaffirm traditional choices. Choices of work at this *frontera* enact sexual roles as well as gendered and religious ones. In fact, no young *hombre* said that he had ever thought of or engaged in nontraditional work for men. It is only the young *mujeres* who at least verbally venture past these gendered borders.

Like Rafael and Rosa, Susana's definition of love reinforces the rules of relationships as made up of religious mandates but also hints at her lack of experience with the messiness of relationships: "Well, love for me I define it that it has to be something very beautiful and has to be something united between two people because that is how God created it so that love could be a beautiful thing like they say, rose colored, I define it that way." Susana describes work as a psychological relief because work provides a place for her to use what she has studied. By providing her with a measure of economic independence to have her things, work also provides Susana with an opportunity to explore what she likes and enjoys having: "Well, for me work is like a therapy, too, you know, that the person to have their things, to have like I say, that the person has to have work because if not well, they won't have anything and it's something that one studies for and what one takes advantage of is a job in life, you know, it's something very important and good."

Even though Susana has known what she wanted to do since she was a child, I have not placed her profile within the chapter entitled "From Childhood Genius to Adult Work" because being a secretary is not what Susana wants to be. Over and over again, Susana tells me that she wants to "get outside" and "keep moving," expressing her desire to change the work which has gone unquestioned for so long. She is restless and grasping for something new when discussing the work she does now and what she would like to do in the future:

> Well, for me I like to deal with people and go on trips to places and in terms of my job take calls and things like that. What I like the best is to visit places and that and take proposals and things like that, that's what I like the most . . . I like to have a job that's fast-paced. To be outside the office, like they say, I like that a lot . . . I have worked in very different things than secretarial . . . I worked at a printing press doing well, general printing and like designing a plate or something like that to enlarge it, lot's of things that have to do with printing, that is very different from secretarial. Well, things like that. Almost everything I've worked at has been the work of secretary . . . Well, I don't know, well, I'd like to, I've always liked, well, like I said, getting involved in things that aren't in the office, what do I like? Well, I'd like to get involved in dealing with work that is about getting *afuera* for trips for things like that, that's what I really like a lot . . . But I don't know because also, well, it's kind of like the one of secretary, not specifically like the name it's called but also a promoter, to promote an orchestra or something that one has to that one has to go to an interview here and there and like that and appointments and those things, look for places, locations, that too. That is I like more or less something like that. To go outside and be moving all the time, like I say.

Wanting her summer contract to be extended at ADT but also wanting "to go outside" and have the opportunity of "getting *afuera*" the secretarial lines which have been so clearly drawn for her, Susana is grappling with issues which could have been attended to years earlier when she was in school. Rather than accept her constant answer, teachers ought to have encouraged her to reflect upon her choice in relation to what she had seen in her family and what was expected of *mujeres*. Instead, school reinforced gendered roles and divisions of labor without providing any sort of critical or even alternative view.

Susana's new alternatives—travel agent, working for an airline, promotor—are more aligned with her desire to get out and see new things, travel, and be in a fast-paced environment. Each one involves a getting away or planning a new show, as if symbolically Susana could move past the places she has seen herself cornered into occupying and plan a different kind of occupation.

MERCEDITA

Mercedita is seventeen years old and the mother of two young girls, ages one and two. She says that her oldest daughter has "a condition" which she describes as a combination of having "attacks" and being in the hospital for a month with pneumonia and measles. At the time of the interview she was in the Volunteer Corps at Ensenada.

Work for Mercedita is "a very big responsibility, well, it contains a lot of study." Mercedita tells me that she loves *comercio*, literally business or commerce, but Mercedita means secretarial. She likes the idea of being a secretary because it would enable her to "meet more people and have conversations with, well, quite a few people." Much like Susana looks to work to enable her to get out, Mercedita looks to work to make connections. Like Susana, Mercedita also holds a definition of relationships which is idealized: "*Ay*, love is something very pretty. Above all, if there is someone who can attend to one and well, for me love is something beautiful."

Later in the interview when I ask Mercedita what alternatives she's considered she says she would like to study nursing and then adds that she would like to be a doctor and that she likes pediatrics. Mercedita says that she would like "to have a doctorate" to be able to in the future take care of her oldest daughter. She left school at the middle school level. Her children were taken away from her but she doesn't say why except that it was because of her oldest daughter's "condition." She is divorced and the father has the girls. Mercedita explains why she is at the Volunteer Corps:

> I didn't used to do nothing . . . I was always hanging out with my sister . . . When we divorced, well, the father, the father, told me to go study, well, if I wanted to get them back. I said to myself, I didn't know where because the middle school wasn't going to take me because I already have two girls and at night I didn't like it and during the day what am I going to do? So I was like that for four months, but I couldn't go on like that, you know, never, I never thought of anything.

At the Volunteer Corps she feels that she is getting her life together and hopes to get her *cuarto año;* she is studying *hostelería*. It will be a very long road for Mercedita to become a doctor. It will also be a long road to continue being a caretaker to her girls.

This is another *frontera*, the borderland between the personal desire to cure your own family and the *barreras* to making that vision concrete through work. For young women like Mercedita, Juana María, and Rosa, there is a rupture between work and love that is brutal in its dismantlement of their dreams. Love holds out a promise of beauty, but the psychology of systemic *barreras*/violence is one of rupture, of roads leading out that you can't take, of a future that is entered without a map, without trustworthy signs. For Juana María there is the added social *barreras* put up against Puertorriqueñas and Puertorriqueños of African descent: racism.

NELIDA

Nelida is sixteen years old. She is not married, isn't living at home, and doesn't have a house to keep. She is in the Volunteer Corps program in Aguadilla. She left school before getting her *cuarto año*, in eleventh grade, because she says she "didn't care about anything." Nelida defines work as "something that one has to do, because sometimes, many times one is the one who, that is, like if one didn't have a job, you'd get bored and I don't know." As was the case with the other young *mujeres* profiled, Nelida's view of love is "something very pretty, one suffers, one is happy, that is, something very beautiful . . . Love is when you are sharing with an *amigo*, a boyfriend, and with your husband, with the mothers, the fathers, the brothers and sisters, etc." And like Rosa, Nelida feels love for working at home:

> For cleaning the house . . . It fascinates me . . . I don't know why, I just don't like to see so much of a mess. I see a big mess and I get like a thing, and I turn on the radio and begin to clean the house and it's as if I was doing something for myself too . . . Because sometimes like from all the things that one is doing there always has to be something that calls your attention and I don't know why but my attention is called by cleaning the house. I don't know but it fascinates me to clean it . . . Inside myself I feel good. I feel happy for what I am doing and sometimes I get to thinking that if I don't do it, who is going to?

Asked if there is any other work that she enjoys, she says, "*Diantre*, no" and laughs. But later she tells me that she would like to be a secretary, work in a sewing factory or at a retail store that sells beach clothing, or be a dancer. Nelida says that sometimes while housecleaning she'll start dancing with the broom. Dancing with a broom is good-natured custom in Puerto Rico when you don't have a partner for a song at a party. At the Volunteer Corps Nelida has performed for the youths in a "talent show and party." But her responses take a while to articulate and it seems difficult for Nelida to even think of work she would like to do outside the home. She has never had a job; housework is the only work she has ever done.

The connection between choice of work and traditional views of gender runs deep both psychologically and socially for young women like Rosa, Juana María, Mercedita, and Nelida. There is a strong connection between the process of gender construction, of being a *mujer*—being feminine, caring, attentive to others, never saying no—and the process of choosing work. This process of choice, if that is even a good word for it, walks hand in hand with gender in ways that are not easily disentangled.

The stories they tell give a picture of identity as being formed by the layered demands of what they are told to do as *mujeres* and what they would like to do as human beings, what they can do as *mujeres* and what they dream of doing as human beings. There is a critical intersection of work, love, and gender that young women who are poor will find extraordinarily dangerous to cross so that they can reach the side they set out to reach. These young women point to a complex interlocking, a multilayered concept, of identity that takes into account social myths, scripts, and norms and the internal negotiations that take place against a backdrop of bone-grinding poverty and oppression.

CROSSING GENDER:
EMMA, ELECTRICIAN AND MOTHER

Emma was married at sixteen, had five children and was a traditional wife for eleven years. Then she felt "oppressed" and was "suffering," and she began to change at the age of twenty-six. Her changing began when she saw herself "sinking lower and lower." Today, Emma is twenty-eight years old and is an electrician. Being an electrician is the only work she has ever done outside the home. Emma received her training through the Volunteer Corps at Ensenada. The director is very proud of her and wanted me to interview her: Emma is a success story.

Emma talked about her views on work: "Well, for me work is a form of making money and also a way of being able to express myself in the form of work." When asked what work she feels love for she says "for the one I am presently doing," being an electrician. She doesn't know any other women electricians but this doesn't bother her because she is proud of her work and wants to have her own business and be one of the women who succeeds in the trade: "Because it's the first job that I have in my life. I'm twenty-eight years old and it's the first work that I've accomplished in my life. And I've had many new experiences and I like the work that I'm doing and I feel proud that even though I am a woman, well, accomplish a job that is almost always done by men. For me it has been a beautiful experience and I feel proud to be an electrician among the men." Before turning her attention to the study of electricity, Emma had tried to find work in factories and department stores, but found herself feeling "inferior":

> Before I came to study I would go to look for work at different places like factories, well, department stores and I don't know if it's because I feel a little, I look at myself and like I feel more inferior to other people even though I have the same capacity as everyone else, no, but because I was a married woman and I have children and well, I said to myself maybe it's that I'm ugly. I said maybe the department stores won't take me for work because, well, because I don't have blond hair, I don't have green eyes, well, I found myself really needing work and I decided to study and I said, I have a brother who is an electrician and he is always finding work. I said, *caramba*, why don't I try that line of work, too, and progress even though it's men's work.

Emma is the mother of five children ages eleven, nine, five, four, and three and says that she has the problem of finding good child care for them when she is working. Her "goal is to have her business, raise her five children, and that they are also men and women who progress in the future." The person who has given her the most support in pursuing her talent is her mother and her teacher. Emma's brother, who is also an electrician, tried to persuade her not to study that trade:

> He would tell me that this was work for men. Since he already had experience doing jobs he said that the work was too tough for a woman, that it looked ugly, a woman working among so many men. On the other hand my mother supported me. She

said that no, don't listen to your brother, look for work, look for the best way to stabilize yourself, that I couldn't continue in the situation I was in, that's to say, like a suffering woman and that not let anyone tell me what to do. I also received support from my teacher. He said to me "no, you go on, if you want to be an electrician I'll help you," and thank God, right now I have my apprentice license that with it I can do whatever electrical job that doesn't need a certified electrician. But I can do any electrical work.

Ironically, Emma felt "ugly" in the more traditionally feminine place of department stores and her brother said that it would look "ugly" to be a woman alone working among men: what Emma did wasn't fitting into what a *mujer* should be. Caught at the *frontera* of femininity and work, Emma's story is the story of a *mujer* who has battled the oppression of gender bias and lack of schooling and against the odds is getting on with a life that she now wants to lead, that she feels in control of. But it wasn't always that way. Emma tells the story of a *mujer* who married a young *hombre* and how things broke apart:

> I married young. I married when I was sixteen years old . . . I had five children. I went through stages in my marital life that are not very pleasant. I confronted many problems in the marriage, with regard to alcohol on the part of my husband and I had to struggle a lot to have what I have now. I suffered a lot and even though I didn't have enough schooling when I got married, I had only completed my junior year of high school, I am a person that is strong in character and when I say I want to do something, I do it even if everyone tells me not to . . . In part it was my personal problems in my house, in my home, that led me to have the life I have now, to exercise this profession.

What Emma calls "character" is a trait that is also called upon by many of the young women who view work as a road to economic independence and emotional freedom. The ability to say "no" to what is destructive and struggle against other people saying "no" to you was critical to Emma. This "character" was earned through daily struggle and risking an established sense of right and wrong, of what is correct, of what is feminine.

For Emma, the struggle for changing her life began when she was twenty-six, two years before the interview, when she decided to separate from her husband even though her marriage from the outside "looked beautiful but for me it wasn't." Emma tells what brought her to make a decision that for many years she was opposed to, divorce:

> I did it mostly for my children because I saw that they, the necessity of having one strong person in the home, one head of the household, that even though I was married for eleven years we didn't have that. Even though my husband was there, but he wasn't a responsible person to maintain a home, and a home with five children needs responsibility and more so the head of the family is the most responsible to take on the head, the battle. I saw myself so oppressed in that situation that I decided to end my marriage, to separate from that beautiful family picture, because it looked beautiful but it wasn't. I don't know, I was one of those people who didn't believe in divorce or anything like that.

Today she describes a completely different picture of work and family life:

> In my house I'm the boss, I'm what you'd call, the *hombre* and the *mujer*. I'm a mother from the evening hours to dawn with my children, during the day I'm the father, the person who works and brings sustenance to the house, and I feel proud that's to say, of my children, they also help me in this. How I have been until recently, I don't know, that has strengthened me to be able to be in the position I am now.

Emma calls herself both the *hombre* and the *mujer* and both the mother and father. She holds traditional definitions of what masculine and feminine roles are—the man/father provides through working and the women/mother is the caretaker—but she has to negotiate between them, blend them into something that works for her. During the day she is an *hombre* and at night she is a *mujer*. Work is a masculine place and even more so because she works among men and so becomes one of them.

The process of negotiating gender is an ongoing one. The balancing of caretaking and providing move back and forth every day. Some days the balance tips more toward the demands of family, and other days toward the demands of work. As an electrician, Emma sometimes has to leave the house at dawn, which creates a problem of child care. She's working hard to be an electrician and a mother. Emma calls it being both a woman and a man and says people are "amazed" when they see her coming to do an electrical job: "'A *mujer* electrician! It can't be!' People look at me and say, ' I just can't wrap my mind around a *mujer* electrician, it just can't be!'" This is an unheard-of combination in Puerto Rico. Yet there she is, bearing witness to the possibilities of change.

There is a great deal of independence, expression, and growth for Emma that has come out of her experience of crossing gender lines, experience which she shares with girls. She tells girls that she sees on the street to not get married young, to go to school, to have a job, to study for something they want and not get caught up in marriage just because it looks like a beautiful thing, or the boy has a good body. "Even though one is a *mujer* that has nothing to do with being able to do whatever work because just as an *hombre* can do it, one can do it. We are all human."

Emma, when speaking to younger women, moves away from speaking about *mujeres* and *hombres* as defining roles. Instead, she follows a logic of a larger concept that can encompass both her masculine and feminine roles; Emma invokes being human. By crossing the borders of traditional gender roles, Emma has been able to get a divorce and work for the first time in her life. By getting the support she needed from both a family member (her mother) and a teacher (a man), she was able to study and learn a trade.

Emma's narrative charts the *frontera* of femininity, masculinity, and identity, to what is needed for young women to make changes that make possible the rearrangement of oppressive conditions: an awareness that their situation is in fact oppressive and not simply natural, that there are options even if they are decisions one has disagreed with previously, that support in the family as well as support in an educational setting is critical, and that working within a profession or trade is crucial because economic independence supports a process of change.

THE JOURNEY

One day you finally knew
what you had to do, and began,
though the voices around you
kept shouting
their bad advice—
though the whole house
began to tremble
and you felt the old tug
at your ankles.
"Mend my life!"
each voice cried.
But you didn't stop.
You knew what you had to do,
though the wind pried
with its stiff fingers
at the very foundations—
though their melancholy
was terrible.
It was already late
enough, and a wild night,
and the road full of fallen
branches and stones.
But little by little,
as you left their voices behind,
the stars began to burn
through the sheets of clouds,
and there was a new voice,
which you slowly
recognized as your own,
that kept you company
as you strode deeper and deeper
into the world,
determined to do
the only thing you could do—
determined to save
the only life you could save.

CHAPTER 7

Getting out of Trouble or Getting What You Want: Work as Independence and Survival for Young Mujeres

The following narratives are illustrative of young women who view work as an escape route away from abuse, violence, neglect, and dependence on unreliable caretakers. They are also narratives of trauma which, to my surprise while interviewing, erupted out of their responses to questions about work and love.[1] I would like to, therefore, briefly sketch out several elements of Judith Lewis Herman's (1992) research which I found useful as a *trasfondo* for the interpretive process with these narratives. But I am mindful that trauma, abuse, neglect, and sexual harassment are all enormously complex experiences which have been studied from diverse perspectives. My attempt here is to provide a discussion of trauma as a way to broadly sketch the outlines of the issues raised in the narratives, and my hope is that this discussion will give voice to what has been silenced.

Herman in her ground-breaking text, *Trauma and Recovery*, explores the psychological impact of events which are public and readily recognized as traumatic—natural disasters and atrocities of war—but she also investigates how what is private and seemingly "normal" can also be traumatic. By considering how normalcy can have common attendant—possibly even necessary—traumatic elements, Herman argues for a reformulation of post-traumatic stress disorder which includes the "private" experiences of women.

Herman's definition of psychological trauma is purposefully broad but at its center holds the view that traumatic events are defined by how powerless one is to stop them: "Psychological trauma is an affliction of the powerless. At the moment of trauma, the victim is rendered helpless by overwhelming force. When the force is that of nature, we speak of disasters. When the force is that of other human beings, we speak of atrocities. Traumatic events overwhelm the ordinary systems of care that give people a sense of control, connection, and meaning" (p. 33). Herman conceptualizes these events as occurring within two interlocked spheres: the public and the private. These spheres are gendered spaces where men occupy the public sphere (war and politics) and where women occupy the private sphere (domestic life). Herman finds "that the traumas of one are the traumas of the other":

> Fifty years ago, Virginia Woolf wrote that "the public and private worlds are inseparably connected . . . the tyrannies and servilities of one are the tyrannies and servilities of the other." It is now apparent also that the traumas of one are the traumas of the other. The hysteria of women and the combat neurosis of men are one. Recognizing the commonality of affliction may even make it possible at times to transcend the immense gulf that separates the public sphere of war and politics—the world of men—and the private sphere of domestic life—the world of women. (p. 32)

By connecting the public violence of men at war with the "hidden violence" of rape, incest, battery, and abuse of women and children, Herman shows how it is never just men who go to war.[2]

Herman also explores the private realm of daily violence where normalcy—as an ideology composed of gender roles, economic class, and laws to hold these all in their "normal" place—masks and silences the existence of private traumatic events. For this, Herman offers a new social and political theorization of psychological trauma:

> A single traumatic event can occur almost anywhere. Prolonged, repeated trauma, by contrast, occurs only in circumstances of captivity . . . Political captivity is generally recognized, whereas the domestic captivity of women and children is often unseen. A man's home is his castle; rarely is it understood that the same home may be a prison for women and children. In domestic captivity, physical barriers to escape are rare. In most homes, even the most oppressive, there are no bars on the windows, no barbed wire fences. Women and children are not ordinarily chained, though even this occurs more often than one might think. The barriers to escape are generally invisible. They are nonetheless extremely powerful. Children are rendered captive by their condition of dependency. Women are rendered captive by economic, social, psychological, and legal subordination, as well as by physical force. (p. 74)

Herman argues that the unspeakable must be voiced: the action of speech is critical and necessary to begin to move out of traumatic conditions and heal. But the story is not easily told; dependency, terror, and captivity are especially difficult for women and children to contest. To speak out against abuses in one's private home is to disrupt the foundations of what has become—or has been all along—acceptable and normal. The process of creating a narrative about trauma is fraught with fear, guilt, and shame. Herman states that "the conflict between the will to deny horrible events and the will to proclaim them aloud is the central dialectic of psychological trauma" (p. 1).

Sonia, Rocío, and Ana each told a story of a traumatic event when telling their stories of work and love. In each story the relation between the public sphere (work) and private sphere (domestic and family life) is traumatic for these young *mujeres* in specifically gendered ways. Each story had its silences, places where speech was not yet possible or desired. Each illustrates how work can be a place, a *frontera*, where these women try to rebuild what has been destroyed and move away from what has tried to destroy them. In this way, work is necessary for both physical and psychological survival (see Figure 7.1).

I'll return to parts of Herman's work which focus on recovery later, but now here are the stories that were told.

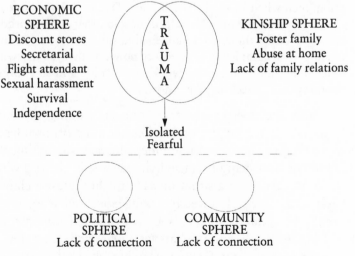

Figure 7.1
Moment in Identity: Work, Independence, and Trauma

SONIA

Sonia is twenty years old and working within ADT as a secretary. Right away in her first response Sonia links work with her psychological well-being: "Work for me is something very important, well, it's a help, it's a pleasure when one does something that develops one mentally, is busy with other things if you have worries or something well, then work helps you a great deal, you know, you learn other things and it's very good, that is, if every day you develop new things. I don't know, for me work is very important." Like Emma, this is her first job, but unlike Emma, Sonia doesn't like working at ADT. Sonia feels like it's make work and not something she is interested in; she would like to be a flight attendant but lacks English language skills. She graduated from public high school and, as all public school students are required to do, took four years of English, but she shrugs off what she learned in school as useless. From the time of her graduation to when she began working at ADT Sonia was also going through tough personal times:

> Lots of times I've felt really bad and in my opinion, I'm just going to tell you straight out, I've felt really bad, really bad and before starting to work here in ADT I had the kind of problem that's really personal, that's to say, since I didn't work I was at home all the time and I had my mind all the time on that same thing, then when I found the work at ADT, well, I was able to be independent and also it's helped me a lot, that is, I've forgotten many of the things that happened in the past and I'm a different person completely . . . because now I'm always busy with other things and I'm always working, working and so I forget the things that affect me, you know.

Even though she doesn't like the work she's doing, working at ADT has helped her feel better. It takes her mind off problems she has had and gives her economic independence, something that is critical to her well-being because living at home, clearly, was bad for her. Sonia points to a situation at home but doesn't elaborate.

I felt uncomfortable directly asking Sonia what exactly was the "really personal" problem and so I didn't. I hoped that she would feel safe to talk about whatever it was as the interview went on. When I ask her what love meant to her, she said: "For me love is that people get along well, that there isn't hypocrisy things like that, if we need something well, that we help each other, without hypocrisy because here there is a lot of hypocrisy, and so there are very few people who are really sincere, that give you lots of kisses, lots of hugs, lots of little things like that, details, and really sincere." Later she did tell her story, which was filled with instances of neglect and abandonment and of having to play the role of wife to a foster care father. Sonia grew up as a foster child, moving from one family to another. Sonia tells the story of her childhood this way:

> Look, my mother gave me up when I was three years old and my sister too was two years old. Then a family took us, very particular, you know, very particular, people that are foster family. I was there for ten years and from there my mother wanted us back again. She lived in public housing, then we went to her house but we couldn't be together, her problems, she drank and stuff like that. Then we went from family to family, without knowing the family, you know, we would go visit and like that because it was the first time that we saw them and like that we went from many houses to houses until I got to the Home for Girls with my sister. We were always together until we were separated at an aunt's house and she stayed there and I went on alone. What happened for her then I don't know but I presently I relate to her and like that, but she's younger than I am and she has a child too, there are many things. The blows I've received, that's to say, if I start to explain every detail I'll never finish, that's to say, we'll be here all afternoon talking because my story is sad.

Sonia feels that she is getting her life together now and wants to "give an example" to her family of what a person can do and doesn't want to be "like them." Sonia has left her family this time, instead of the other way around. She moved out of an oppressive situation and into a life that she has more control over. This has given her independence, but the cost of this for her has been huge; the personal "blows" have taken their toll. Her distrust of people runs deep, and her fear of the violence waiting for her outside her door is enormous. Although at the beginning of the interview she said that work helped her forget, the years filled with personal betrayals can't all be set aside by the act of keeping busy:

> I live alone now, but like I told you now I don't depend on anyone, I depend on my salary from here, on the people, on the few people that I relate to, my boyfriend, my girlfriends, very few

and also no one visits me at home, because I don't allow anyone to, because many people have failed me, you understand, and those small blows have hurt me and I go through one or two but at the third one I stop trying. No, then well no, and I am terrified of the street, a terrible fear of the street, it's a rare thing for me to go out. It's been a month since I went to the movies. I'm here at work then when I leave I'm tired and I'll go to the park to walk or something and from there I go home to eat something and go to sleep. I do that every day. The weekend I take to be at home and be calm, rest, clean or something I have to do and there goes my weekend flying by or I take a little drive and I don't get out because of how bad things are and when you least expect it things happen to you and so I try to avoid all those things and so that's why I tell you that I'm here but I don't like it, you understand, I'm here because I need to be here.

Sonia is at ADT because she needs to be there to continue on her path of becoming independent. She has the goal of studying English and becoming a flight attendant because she loves to travel. As a young girl of ten or eleven she would watch airplanes fly by and want to go with them. At first she wanted to be a doctor, but then after she took a trip to Orlando she decided that she wanted to be a flight attendant. I ask her if she told any of her teachers that she wanted to be a flight attendant when she was ten or eleven years old. Sonia says no because "I didn't used to talk. I was very shy, I didn't talk about any of my things for anything. If I had talked maybe that would have helped me, you see, maybe they would have oriented me, they would have told me to study English then, and things like that starting before and who knows if I'd be there already." Sonia points to the critical educational piece of choosing work that Emma spoke of too: the hand at the other side of the school desk, the hand of the teacher. For Sonia that hand was not there, perhaps because she couldn't speak and ask, and perhaps because no one ever asked her either. As a ten-year-old girl she knew what she wanted to do but couldn't express it. The work that she wished for would give her the ultimate form of mobility, flight. She could go anywhere, and, maybe more importantly, she could leave and go far away.

Sonia's story offers a view of the anxiety and mistrust of a ten-year-old girl even though she was a quiet and undemanding student, a shy girl. Much of her development was negotiated in purposeful silence—not speaking up—about her experiences and her thoughts and dreams of her future: afraid to want, afraid to tell. Now that she is working and has economic independence she is able to express this and move toward her goal.

ROCÍO

Rocío is twenty-two years old. Before the interview starts, Rocío shows me a piece of paper that she received from ADT and tells me that she has always had very good grades and that she completed fifth grade. Rocío is one of the youths who thought that I was a job counselor at ADT. I tell her that I'm not part of the agency but that she can go downstairs after the interview and that they can help her there, instructions I gleaned from the real job counselor.

There is no work that she cares deeply about but says that she does like "honest work." What might this mean, I wonder, not selling drugs, avoiding prostitution? I don't ask and in this way collude in her not telling me this part of her story. I miss an opportunity to listen further, to encourage her to tell.

Rocío does begin to talk about what love means to her but abruptly stops and says she doesn't want to go into any more detail. The following was the interaction we had. When I ask her what work means to her, Rocío responds:

> Well, for me it means a lot because, well, there I, you know, always have my mind occupied and I'm not thinking about bad things like drugs and all those things and I'm entertained and I have always bought my clothes, my shoes, since I've always liked to have my things in order, well, work for me means a lot because it's through it that one can buy those things because things are really bad and no one gives anyone anything now, right, and for me it means a lot because I've worked and I would like to work again.
>
> *Where have you worked?*
>
> I worked here in ADT and for the moment I haven't worked anymore but I find a little job I'll work.
>
> *For you, what is love?*
>
> Well, now that's already a completely different thing, you see. Well, it's beautiful and I don't want to get into details of that.

Okay, and for what work do you feel love?

I don't feel that for any work but look I like honest work.

Like Sonia, Rocío also feels apart from her family. She talks about how she thinks about herself and tries to help the family with advice when they need it. Her narrative contains the undercurrent of what being a *mujer* is, but she tries to move away from it, while still remaining helpful, and assert her own needs. It is a difficult negotiation:

> I have a family but my mother is a person who is always busy and my brothers are also always busy but I always think, you know, think about everyone but also I have to think for myself and so when I've thought about myself, well, I also think about them and if I have to give them advice I give it but since I'm twenty-two years old already and well I always do what I think is good for me, you understand. When I want something well I try to get it and if I don't get it then fine, you know, I feel a little bad because I didn't get it but I'm calm . . . I have always shared with everyone around me, see, I don't like to get into trouble or anything with anyone, instead I'm calm and if you go to my house and you need something and I have it well I'll give it to you because I can't deny you it, if I don't have it well I'll tell you, look, I don't have it.

Work for Rocío is important because it allows her to buy what she needs and wants. But it is also important to her because working allows her to think about herself and her own needs and make decisions about what she wants. Unlike Sonia, though, she hasn't been able to find work since working in a summer job training program through ADT. When I ask her who has helped her and supported her she says that she is doing it alone, that she is the only one that gives herself support. When I ask her about why she left school in fifth grade, Rocío responds: "Well because my mother had a friend and she lived in public housing well I wanted to go with her and so I wanted to stay with her and then well she told me to leave school and that she was going to put me in the school near where she lived and it just so happens that I completely forgot about it and I forgot school."

Rocío would like to work in banks because she has liked what she has seen. Banks are symbols of prosperity: banks are where the money is, the stuff of which economic independence is made. For Rocío to get to work at a bank will be a long road. Like Sonia, work allows Rocío to think for herself, to buy her things. Her family has not helped her; on the contrary, her mother sent her to live with a friend, and it was at this point that she left school and never went back. And like Sonia, she wants to work at something that symbolizes what she lacks. For Rocío it is money; for Sonia it is the ability to leave.

ANA

Ana is nineteen, married since she was fifteen, and working on and off as a cashier in "discount stores" for the last four years. She asks me, "You know what discount is, right?" I answer her that I do. When she was fourteen she "fell in love" and left school in Brooklyn to come to Puerto Rico. She hasn't been back to school. Now she is trying to get her GED and find work through ADT. She left her most recent job because she said she had trouble with her boss, whom she describes as a "strong-willed character that treated us badly in front of other people and friends of mine and I didn't like that and I left." She also left another cashier job because her boss made advances toward her sister when her sister was applying for work. Later, as a kind of revenge against her sister for refusing his unwanted attention, he started to act disrespectfully toward her. She felt she had to leave that job, too. She views work this way: "Well, work for me is a responsibility. I have to work to obtain what I want. Without work I can't obtain what I want." Like Rocío, Ana won't say what love means to her, and our interaction with that question is brief:

Wow! *Ay*, I don't know! I know but [she laughs].

Should we move on?

Yes.

Ana does know work that she cares about, that she truly enjoys, working as a cashier: "Well, the work that I enjoy is dealing with computers, dealing with like since always what I've worked as has been a cashier, that is, because I tend to look for that kind of work because I like it. And I work happily let's just say because I like it." Ana hopes to learn to be a secretary through ADT because she also likes writing on the typewriter:

I like secretarial because I know how to work with typewriters, that is, I like that kind of thing. Look they lent me a typewriter, an *amiga* of mine lent me a typewriter and I spent all my time writing letters, and I wrote to my *amigas*, to my mother that is *afuera* and to my sister and now that I don't have a typewriter I haven't written her in five months and with the typewriter I spent the time writing and I'd make up songs. Writing like that I like it. The songs that they play on the radio that I know, well, I'd write them, yes the ones I like.

When I ask her if she feels that she is a part of a community, if she feels a part of the people she lives with, Ana, like Sonia, speaks of her isolation at home but as making friends and finding support at a workplace:

No, you see, I'm a person that I don't even go out. I'm always inside the house and I'm a person that's friendly because wherever I go, I came here and made a lot of friends, wherever I go . . . I made friends with the two security guards here, an older man downstairs, I don't know if you know him, and another one and they advised me to go take the exam for *cuarto año* and I went and took the steps because, you know, it motivated me, it motivated me and I went to do those errands to take the exam for *cuarto año*.

Two men, one older, security guards; Ana says speaking with them was the connection that motivated her to do the paperwork needed to sign up for a program at ADT. But for the most part Ana has had to be her own support, although she does say that her husband has also helped her. If the kindness and attention of adult strangers can motivate her, imagine what the kindness and attention of interested educators could do.

Sonia, Rocío, and Ana illustrate the struggles for young women who want and need to work to gain independence, whether it's the independence to make their own decisions, live alone, or buy what they want. For Sonia, work is a place to keep busy and get out of her house. For Rocío, work is the freedom to think about herself and make her own decisions on what it is she needs. For Ana the workplace itself has both been problematic and given her independence.

But even though work promises the hope of buying power, independence from abuse and neglect, and a way out of a bad family situation, because these women have few skills in the kind of work they want and little formal education, their needs hang in a precarious balance. Their vision of themselves as doing something different in the future is vulnerable to other people's actions, which have been largely beyond their control. In addition to the economic and educational *barreras*, the youths are struggling with psychological distress: Sonia's fear is of the danger embodied in other people, and Rocío's and Ana's refusal or inability to give answers to what love is for them signals ruptures or losses in relationships.

These youths need psychological safety. They need to feel secure in their own ability to survive and to recover from violence and its traumatic consequences, to move out of isolation toward trusting other people and being able to love, to form relationships, and to regain control of their lives. Herman documents how disempowerment and disconnection form the central characteristic of psychological trauma and finds that "the first principle of recovery is the empowerment of the survivor. She must be the author and arbiter of her own recovery." "Recovery can take place only within the context of relationships; it cannot occur in isolation" (p. 133). Herman outlines what negotiating this *frontera* involves:

> Recovery unfolds in three stages. The central task of the first stage is the establishment of safety. The central task of the second stage is remembrance and mourning. The central task of the third stage is reconnection with ordinary life. Like any abstract concept, these stages of recovery are convenient fiction, not to be taken too literally. They are an attempt to impose simplicity and order upon a process that is inherently turbulent and complex . . . One therapist describes the progression through the stages of recovery as a spiral, in which earlier issues are continually revisited on a higher level of integration. (p. 155)

A metaphor that Herman uses to represent the "stage" of remembrance and mourning is visual: still snapshots, a silent movie. The "second stage of recovery" hinges on "reconstructing the trauma story": telling and feeling what happened in as much detail as possible—as if watching a movie—which causes a reliving of the traumatic event and explains further why the story is difficult to tell (p. 177).

In the interview Sonia says that if she tells me everything we would be there all afternoon. All afternoon is exactly what is needed and more afternoons, too. Sonia has changed from being a child that doesn't talk to a young woman who wants to tell her story. Rocío and Ana are not yet speaking about what has happened in any detail. For these young *mujeres,* finding work, even if they love it, isn't enough.

> *The way things work*
> *is by solution,*
> *resistance lessened or*
> *increased and taken*
> *advantage of.*

CHAPTER 8

Since I Was Three:
From Childhood Genius to Adult Work

> "I feel that 13-year-olds are not mature enough to make a decision about what career path they want to follow," School Committee member Mary Ann Phoenix said, applauding the administration for cutting back the number of students who will attend the vocational school.
>
> Reported by J. Danko, *Daily Hampshire Gazette*,
> Tuesday, June 30, 1992, p. 8

When we were children living in *El Barrio* our grandparents would take us to the Museum of Natural History. I loved to walk around looking up and around at all these "stuffed" creatures. I also enjoyed the slices of life displays where we could see the tunnels of rodents on the bottom half through the large sheet of glass and the plants and stuffed animals on the top half. It reminded me of being just at the surface of water but in enough to see a bit of what was under water too.

Near the cafeteria was a display that illustrated a more abstract part of natural history. It was a large circular hands-on model which was meant to teach about color and the spectrum of light. If I rotated one of the gels, say yellow, over another, say blue, this made a third color, green. Though these filters were demonstrating color absorption, I had no idea of this at the time. What absolutely fascinated me was how two distinctly different colors could combine into a third which was neither fully one nor the other, or even more like one than the other; it was something different from what composed it, a blending.

It's impossible for me now to recreate the sheer joy of this experience, but there was something of this when I listened to the youths' stories profiled here. In these narratives there is a kind of joy from aligning two distinct and too often divided parts of our lives—genius or talent and love—and making a third entity from these: making work which gives joy. I think, too, that I was reminded of the color wheel because these youths went back to childhood when seeking out an answer to how it was that they arrived at what they were doing.

There were fifteen youths who expressed that they had known what they "wanted to do" since childhood. I was surprised by how many young people knew at any early age, anywhere from three to twelve, what they wanted to do, what they were good at, what their genius was. These youths were trying to reach their goals through academic or religious study, job training, or working: seven were studying at the conservatory; four were in the Volunteer Corps at Ensenada; two were in the Volunteer Corps at Aguadilla; one was at the Jesuit Seminary; and one was working at ADT.

I was especially surprised by two aspects that emerged from the narratives. First, the traditional notion of high school as the place to seriously begin to think and plan the future as an adult—college, vocational training, work—is misleading. These youths had been thinking and having feelings about work since they were young children. Second, cultural traditions in concert with popular views of psychology in subtle ways support the belief that adolescence is the "stage" that marks the beginning of a kind of emotional maturity that is required to enter the adult world of work. These narratives, however, underscore the need to consider that children's notions of "want to be when they grow up" is potentially a deeply rooted vision that they grasp tightly, albeit with small hands.

Both young men and women told stories of having participated as children and youngsters in activities that changed them forever, that somehow told them that this is "what I want to do." Some of the youths who have had these experiences as children have not been able to make the transition from childhood genius to adult work: for example, Sonia, who has always wanted to be a flight attendant, and Juana María, who has always liked secretarial.

What does it take?

At this place gendered divisions of labor, family expectations, and fears about economic survival meet with childhood desires and dreams to form *barreras* against youths pursuing what they feel is right for them. Yet these narratives are illustrative of the struggles of youths who have persisted. The following stories profile the *frontera* of childhood genius and adult work (see Figure 8.1).

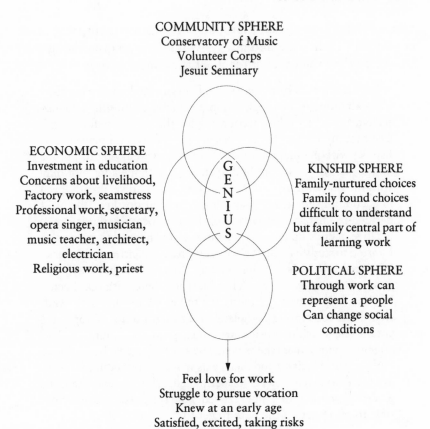

COMMUNITY SPHERE
Conservatory of Music
Volunteer Corps
Jesuit Seminary

ECONOMIC SPHERE
Investment in education
Concerns about livelihood,
Factory work, seamstress
Professional work, secretary,
opera singer, musician,
music teacher, architect,
electrician
Religious work, priest

GENIUS

KINSHIP SPHERE
Family-nurtured choices
Family found choices
difficult to understand
but family central part of
learning work

POLITICAL SPHERE
Through work can
represent a people
Can change social
conditions

Feel love for work
Struggle to pursue vocation
Knew at an early age
Satisfied, excited, taking risks

Figure 8.1
Moment in Identity: Work and Genius

JUDY

Judy is twenty-six years old, married, and studying for her bachelor's degree in music at the conservatory. At the age of three she was singing in the church choir. Like Sonia, she knew at an early age what it was that she enjoyed and wanted to do, but, unlike Sonia, she had a music teacher in her father, who played guitar, and a music teacher at her public school. But Judy didn't find out until her twenties that one could study for a degree in music and major in an instrument, even though she was in the high school chorus and says she "never missed a class." Judy says that she is "a secretary" and has three years of training in accounting but that something happened that made her change paths, that made her return to what she had always wanted to do even though she was older than the other students at the conservatory:

> When I graduated from high school I began studying accounting. I had already finished high school business, accounting and also secretarial . . . I studied accounting for three years before I realized that my vocation was music and in fact when I realized this I spoke with people, with professors that were trying to put me on the path of music but had to struggle with me a lot, not only with me but with my parents, my family, "You've already been in accounting for three years, how can you do this?" before I decided to change. But when you have a vocation and it's real, it's love, it ends up dominating you. And I changed to music and I started to study a bachelor's in art with a concentration in music. I finished it but it's not the same as a bachelor's that's why I'm here at the Conservatory. What I learned there with that bachelor's has helped me as a foundation to be able to enter here. And, well, I left accounting completely forgotten I did a minor and I got the bachelor's in musical arts and a minor in accounting. And after graduation from there, well, I was at Mayagüez, I didn't have much musical activity and then I was working for about two years as a secretary. I had been given permanence, but imagine that isn't precisely what fills me, that I moved, I did the possible, the impossible to try to get on the path to get to that and with all the permanence that I could have stayed there in that job for life.

At the age of twenty or twenty-one Judy had her first voice professor. He told her that in all his fifteen years of experience teaching voice he had not found many voices that were good enough to be able to study for a bachelor's in singing. Judy said she "didn't know any of that and so I didn't know what he was talking about." It was this professor who convinced her that anyone could do a bachelor's in accounting, secretarial, nursing, teaching—interestingly, work that is done mostly by women—or computers but that only a few could study music and that she was one of the few, that she had "talent." He kept at it, telling her to study music and to change from accounting: the professor saw in her this gift, the genius, and sought to support her in her move from tradition and what was expected of her to what she loved.

Changing from accounting to music was risky for Judy because her family didn't understand it and thought she was wasting the years she had already put into accounting: the three years studying accounting were also an economic investment. But she did change with the support of a professor, keeping accounting as a minor but making music her major. Then after graduating she married and started working as a secretary, her excitement with the possibility of music subsumed by class and gender. After two years working as a secretary Judy was given "permanence," which means that she was more or less guaranteed the position for life. But she felt deeply dissatisfied with what she was doing.

Her decision to continue her study of music was reaffirmed for her at an audition by a professor from Juilliard who was on the jury. The experience of being valued by this professor was a critical one for Judy and added to her previous experience of affirmation by her voice teacher:

> She wrote me a note in English and since I didn't know English I thought she said something different. I thought she had written me something like, well, I congratulate you and advise you to keep taking classes if you're not taking them and if you are taking them then keep taking voice lessons because you have a voice with a wide register and this and that and at the end she wrote that there weren't many voices like mine "out there." That was it, "out there." And I thought that she meant in the United States there aren't many voices like mine. And then when I took the note to my voice teacher who was American he told me that when she said "out there" she didn't just mean in the United States but that there aren't many voices like mine in the music world, in opera. And I said she's a doctor of voice from Juilliard, so that's two people now. And that was my fate and well one keeps growing roots as they say. Because this is a career that one keeps developing confidence. Self-confidence is, well, it's something that one almost never has from childhood because one begins with twenty thousand insecurities. One wishes that the children didn't have to go through that, *caramba*. That they wouldn't have to go through the odyssey I went through to find their vocation if they have it.

Caught at the border of parental expectations, fear, and economic *barreras,* it took Judy over a decade to feel secure enough to pursue her vocation. At twenty-six, studying at the conservatory, Judy feels that she is firmly on the path to work that she loves—singing opera. She sees herself as combining opera with set design or teaching music. Judy wishes that children could have an easier time of it, of finding their vocation, their genius, that they wouldn't have to endure her "odyssey." The years of studying accounting must indeed have been difficult for Judy; opera is so different, so expressive and big, dramatic, so unlike sitting at a desk crunching numbers.

Judy has found her voice. Now she views music as a profession that is needed not only by her but by society because it is work which is "just as necessary or more to maintain the arts of the people, of a country, well represented." This reminded me of a kind of bearing witness—an accounting—which Irena Klepfisz (1982), writing on her role as a Jewish poet, explores in *Keeper of Accounts*.

CARLOS

Carlos is twenty-three. He grew up in a family where what he was supposed to be when he grew up was clear: he was to be an electrician just like his father and all of his brothers. But it didn't turn out that way. The symbolism in his choice of career is striking; before he finally decided to study music he picked a field related to electricity, called *instrumentación*, instrumentation, which is a branch of engineering that, he said, "specializes in the chemical processes in industry." What could be closer symbolically to an instrument than *instrumentación*? Carlos tells this story of the twists and turns and how it was that he finally made it to the conservatory to study music:

> I studied in high school in my high school I studied at vocational school and I studied electricity. Studying electricity because it was due to the influence of my father. But really it wasn't my decision, you understand? So then, see what happened is that all of my brothers have been electricians and they've been good and so it was a field that even though it's dangerous it has a lot of benefits, economic and fringe. So then one's father well, my father perhaps thinking about what was best for me influenced me to study that but at the end after finishing vocational school I didn't want to continue studying electricity because I was afraid of electricity, I was afraid of it. I didn't know how to get into it, you know, I was too passive a person to do work that's so rough and dangerous, you understand? So then I said since I'm here with this knowledge about electricity well then I'm going to switch to something that is related, so I decided to study instrumentation. At first I found it interesting but then when I was almost finished with my studies I started thinking that I really hadn't gotten anything out of them, that I hadn't taken

good advantage of my studies, that is, I believed that I could
have learned more than I did and I came to the conclusion that
it was because I didn't really think it was important, you know,
I wasn't dedicated because I didn't have any love for what I was
studying. So then since before I had knowledge of instruments
and I had played drums in a marching band with baton twirlers
and that kind of thing that motivated me to study music and I
prepared myself alone at home. I prepared myself alone and then
entered the Inter American University at San German where I
studied to get ready to enter here. Now thank God I've been here
two years and it's going well and I like it and I do what I do.

When I asked Carlos who supported his decision, he said his parents didn't but that he had a friend who did. His friend, Angel, is
also at the conservatory. Carlos explains:

> I supported myself. I saw that I was good at that and that I liked
> it and had a big attraction for it. So I also had the support of a
> friend who also studies here and is also singing in the chorus. He
> also had a similar case as mine that he was studying something
> else and so then since he had the talent since he was little he
> played piano he also stayed to study music. I did it all without
> consulting with my parents because really I knew that if I asked
> them to support me they wouldn't, you understand? So it's that
> the ideas between my parents and me are very antagonistic but
> really it was me who helped myself and him.

Carlos made the decision to study music at twenty and had doubts
about whether it was too late to be beginning. Carlos's doubts
echo a theme among the musicians I interviewed who said that it's
a myth that you can only be a good adult musician if you're a child
prodigy or take classes since you're very young but, aware of the
powerful pull of this idea, still worried about being too old. He
says he has "advanced very quickly in the short time I've been
here" and points to his achievements: he has high grades, has composed musical arrangements (one of was picked up by a well-
known band and played on the radio), has been in two bands, and
gets calls to play free-lance for holidays and celebrations. But his
successes are a continuation of what he wanted when he was a boy
of ten or eleven but couldn't directly pursue because his father had
set out a course for him that he was required to follow:

> It's just that since I was little I think I used to listen to a lot of
> music. And then, I don't know, I think it's a natural talent that

I have, I have a natural talent. Because when I was ten or eleven years old I was already playing regularly in a marching band, I was playing regularly. Still that passed and I kept studying my normal classes, middle school and high school, but after high school when I went on to study the technology and that stuff then I said, *contra* if I think I can develop this more, I can take it to the maximum. And then I decided to study music.

He says that playing in the marching band "passed," and it's as if he just watched it go, as if it was a favorite childhood toy that he had to grow out of. He then had to continue with what was "normal" for boys in his family, electricity, even though he was "afraid of it" and saw himself as "too passive" for such "dangerous" work. It's difficult to know what he means precisely by "passive" from his narrative, and I wish that I had asked him directly. Yet it's clear that he sees himself as creative and contemplative, someone who needs time to compose and play and that this can't be aligned with electricity.

As a child in a marching band he was happy and comfortable with music expressing his talent, having fun, and learning about music through what he heard, what he listened for. As a child in middle school he was also expected to take "normal" classes and then went to vocational school to take technical classes. What happened to the child in the marching band? Where was he all those years? Is it the worry about economic survival that doesn't allow a father to see the joy in a child's face?

Carlos is also interested in becoming a music teacher but is concerned that teacher openings, especially in the arts, are scarce. In any case, whether in a group playing percussion or piano, composing, making arrangements, or teaching, Carlos sees his future as a continuation of what he is doing now. When I interviewed Carlos I was struck by how comfortable he was in a room full of drums, congas, and cymbals, and as he told me of how every male member of his family is an electrician and how he is terrified of electricity I thought how wonderful that he has made it. And then I thought, there ought to be an easier way across this *frontera*.

CARMEN

Carmen is nineteen, and loves to sew and make clothes. She wants to be a seamstress or a supervisor at a sewing factory. Carmen first began sewing on a battery-powered machine when she was nine years old. At that age she "pinched" herself a lot, but she was "fascinated" and completely enjoyed it: "I have fun when I sew." She says that since that early age she knew "that was for me" and "What I like the best is the sewing machine." As she speaks I'm pulled into a world of sewing and tailoring that I had never given much thought to. I don't know much more than how to sew a button back on. Her enthusiasm draws me in to her world of sewing machines. And it is a world because Carmen doesn't just sew; she creates stories:

> I imagine sometimes I'm sewing, I'm sewing a pair of pants and I quickly start to sew and *coño* I'm sewing my wedding dress. Or I start to think, look, I'm sewing a tablecloth for the governor, you know, things like that get into my head. Things like that, and then I say, I'm going to sew this for the governor, I do it with more pleasure, like I feel that I do it with more pleasure, as long as it's sewing, forget it. I'm crazy about sewing.

I ask her how she feels when she is creating her stories and sewing:

> When I'm in front of the sewing machine I feel good. I feel secure in what I'm doing because I know I can do it, even though sometimes I get angry because sometimes a needle breaks or something, but I feel that it's something that I like, well, I do it with pleasure. It's something that, I don't know, from inside me says "sew, sew." Sometimes I go to a house of a friend and I see a machine and oh! how beautiful! And what kind is it? I'm fascinated by sewing.

Carmen says that it's "thanks to Elena," the sewing teacher at the Volunteer Corps, that she has been able to pursue what she has wanted to do since childhood. Carmen says that she wants to leave the Volunteer Corps with a seamstress diploma and feels that "once I have that, well, I'll be sure of myself and move onward"; the diploma will secure for her an official validation of her talent and permit her access to adult work in a factory.

Carmen talks about how when she was growing up everyone in her house sewed and it caught her attention. When she asked if she could sew, she was shown and then given her own battery-powered machine. Carmen is from a large family, nine sisters and four brothers. She tells how she would watch her older sisters sewing, creating pieces of clothing, and was fascinated. She took to sewing right away, although she says that it was partly due to the fact that she was a "failure in the kitchen" and sewing was a place she could shine.

Carmen also made sewing her own secret place. When her family would ask her if she wanted to sew she would say "no" but then "there were times when I would hide and find something and start to sew on the machine real quietly. I started with doll clothes." Her sisters taught her to sew when she showed an interest, but once she knew how to she didn't do it openly but instead would sew in hiding. In a big family, sewing became the place that was her very own, where she could do what she wanted, make her own world.

At nineteen, lacking money but having great skill, Carmen makes most of her own clothes. First she goes to the stores and studies carefully what she likes, buys some material, and then goes home and writes the details down on paper. "Sometimes I make dresses that cost 40 or 45 dollars I make them for 2 and a half dollars." Carmen, no longer hiding, describes how she remembers what she saw at the store and how she goes about getting help for making a dress: "Sometimes I make it up in my memory. I get home and I start to draw and I say this is how I want the dress. I tell my sisters and they help me cut the material or if not I go to the *tecnica*, that's Elena, and I say, "Elena, I liked this dress. I saw it in Marianne or Kress." "Oh, how pretty let's make it, let's make it." At the time of the interview Carmen was waiting to hear if she had passed her GED exam:

> I'm waiting for the results because I took it on the sixth of September and I'm missing the results. I think I'll get them in three months, that's what they told me.
>
> *Did it go well? Do you feel that . . .*
>
> Well, to be sincere, the science part was a little, really bad for me. The English part was easy for me because I know English.

At this point in the interview Carmen begins to talk about her family in a different way. The sisters sewing together and helping each other becomes part of a much more complicated story. Carmen was born in New York City and lived there until she was eleven years old but then had to move to Puerto Rico. It was in the eleventh grade that she left school for good. Previously she had been cutting classes and skipping a lot of school. Carmen tells why:

I was missing one year. I left in eleventh in April. What I was missing was to finish May and take twelfth. I left because it's just that I was tired already of school. You see I had a lot of problems because I would go back and forth, and every time they would hold me back a grade. They would drop me a grade. Well, I was going back and forth for about five years from the United States. I would be here a month, and then go back to the United States. Well, first it was because my grandmother died. After that my mother died. When my mother died is when I had to come here to Puerto Rico. Then I lived with my aunt. They were the ones that adopted me when I was eleven because I didn't have any place to go. So then I came here to Puerto Rico with my sister. I was fourteen years old and it was something that I wouldn't want anyone to go through what I went through. She died of cancer, you know, and unfortunately I never knew my father. I lived with my mother and my stepfather. But for me, the stepfather is not like my father. Even though he raised me but sometimes they treat you badly, you know, and I don't like it.

Carmen frequently traveled across the Puerto Rico–U.S. air bridge, but her life began to dramatically change with the death of her grandmother and then changed completely from living in New York City to living in rural Puerto Rico with the death of her mother, with whom she lived. Carmen took the bridge back indefinitely when she was fourteen and has been here for five years, but she had been back and forth for four years before that.

Carmen doesn't elaborate on what she means when she says that her stepfather treated her "badly" and that a stepfather is not a father. In fact, at that point in the interview she quickly changes the subject and talks about how much she is enjoying the Volunteer Corps and how she tries to recruit friends from her *barrio* to study there: piecing together the story, turning it this way, turning it toward a comfortable direction.

Although Carmen doesn't say, I suspect that she has suffered similar abuses as those suffered by Sonia, Rocío, and Ana. Carmen's story can be added to that of the three young women and underlines for me how silence, changing the subject, or not fully telling what has happened to them is a sign that something indeed did happen to them and that it was traumatic. These are signs that I have learned to look for through the course of this study. It's clear that Carmen doesn't want to discuss her stepfather further and she wouldn't want anyone to go through what she went through. This is a strong statement that gives a different perspective on the happier scenes of sisters sewing together and perhaps sheds light on why Carmen would hide and make up her own secret worlds.

Carmen went back and forth across the Atlantic and also between the two worlds that existed in her home, her own secret world of sewing and the world where her mother had cancer and her stepfather treated her badly. Carmen feels happy at the Volunteer Corps because she is finally able to continue what she began as a child, sewing. She is also mending her life, sewing it back together.

Carmen's narrative illustrates critical aspects of how children who are in difficult circumstances grasp something they enjoy and make that their childhood gift, genius, and talent. Their genius is enabled both by the difficult situation going on around the child, because it forces the child to look for a safe place, and by access to materials which can nourish it. This combination of creating a world within a family with whatever materials are available is typical of this group of youths. For Carmen, sewing was a place where she could have control over what she wanted to do and where she could fantasize a different world.

Fantasy and imagination have remained with Carmen and are the places where she creates relationships. Carmen still makes up stories about what she is sewing and for whom she is making a piece of clothing. As when she was making clothes for her dolls, she is still making clothes for people whom she connects with through her imagination.

In these ways Carmen has much in common with Judy and Carlos. Both Judy and Carlos spoke of how they imagined audiences, as did many of the youths at the conservatory. For these youths, creating, whether it's a piece of clothing or a piece of music, involves the ability to imagine an audience that wants what they are making. Part of making the transition from childhood dreams to adult work may be the ability to envision and believe there is an audience, that there are people who want what they are able to create, who believe in what they are doing—and that they can make something of value in both senses of the word: that their contributions will be valued and that this will make economic survival possible.

In a recent letter Carmen tells me that she is "working hard but mostly studying very much." Carmen is studying secretarial and working in a bra factory. She writes that although it pays very little, she can make a living that feels comfortable. Carmen signs her letter, "Your *amiga de siempre*."

PEDRO

Pedro is twenty-one years old and studying to be a Jesuit priest. His father is an art teacher and a painter. Pedro talked some about how he felt his father had to let go of his true passion, painting, so that he could support a family. The decision to teach was an economic one, and Pedro saw how his father wasn't able to develop and fulfill his potential as a painter: "I understand that because of life circumstances well, there was a family, you know, all that type of stuff." Drawing on his father's experience, Pedro studied architecture for his bachelor's degree as way to combine creativity with economic stability. At the time of the interview he was contemplating continuing on to earn a master's in architecture. Pedro's passion for architecture is clear during the interview as he talks about how the process of planning and designing involves a great deal of creativity and how he enjoys the challenge of "giving the best of oneself in that field." His voice reflects excitement and his laughter expresses joy. Yet his choice of work turned to the Jesuits after graduating from college.

Pedro thinks of his experience at Caimito as "an experiment." "Basically, I'm now experimenting the religious life, well, for two years which is the limit that they give you and from here I can have already a decision made I hope that will be for life, no, if I understand that this is not for me, I'll go and continue my life normally with what I had planned and if well, I decide that this is what I'm going to do I'll take the vows, which is like the final commitment." He was drawn to the Jesuits because of the value they place on and the support they give for intellectual life; a master's degree is part of becoming a Jesuit priest. Pedro also enjoys being pushed "to the borders of your abilities, to the limit of your capacities," which is what he expects from the Jesuits. During our conversation he gave extensive responses to my questions, considering out loud the multiple angles from which he contemplated each question, illustrating the approach which was typical of the Jesuit youths I spoke with.

Pedro defines work in these ways:

> Work? Well, an action that you do that you decide to do in accord with your ability, no, or that you or the thing that you

most like to do. I don't know, mostly, that is, it involves something more than, at least for me, my ideal concept of work would be that, no, of course there are other questions that involve also these issues well, the person has to do something to survive and then well decides to utilize their physical abilities as such and does it and that's that. And then there's the other one which to me is the ideal, no, and that is that you get involved not only physically but also emotionally, intellectually, no, everything you do, what you want to do not because you have to do it. Of course there are things that influence, sometimes the society influences your will in such a way that both things join and they function as one single thing. You know, for example, the fact that you love your family or you wish the best for your family well then that is one decision that you make to work and you already want to work and want to do what you have to do but maybe for other things.

Pedro's exploration of what work means is closely connected to his understanding of what love is, underscoring a sense of alignment:

You see love I would say has certain elements of the same things, you know, that is, it combines with everything you feel and think, no, in that way you know I believe that there isn't a kind of separation, you know, love like at the pharmacy that you buy medicine in separate bottles, no, everything is mixed together, like a work of art, then love is that feeling that gives everything I think that gives all of this meaning. Well, for example, if you take the case of that same person that works to support their children and has that necessity that is required by law and all that type of stuff but that person including the quality of the work would be affected to the extent that the person loves their children or loves the things they have . . . It's what glues together all that you are and what you have around you, too, that's to say, the feeling that you give it, no, and then love is that feeling that's like that gives meaning to you going on everyday, no, of course also it involves the affective part above all else, no, like it's the most sensitive part of each one of us and I think that sometimes the most misunderstood but if we're going to talk in general terms I see it that way, no.

Pedro speaks of an "inquietude" which the other Jesuits also discussed, a kind of restlessness with their masculine roles of marrying and supporting a family—a sense of that not being their vocational path. To question that masculine role and choose the priesthood was a process that for all the Jesuit youths involved fear and intense questioning. For Pedro the vision of himself becoming a priest formed when he was three. Pedro discusses how he came to be at the Jesuit Seminary:

> All the vocational process? In the Jesuit seminary? Well, my vocational inquietude goes pretty far back, no, already at three years old I was thinking about being a priest but it was a very idealistic thing, no, you know since that time to me sitting here is a lot and is not a straight line, you know, it's very different to the thinking I had before because I was a child, I don't know, and it was really difficult to precisely know many things. Well, from then on I continued my studies normally, you know, that stayed like in the unconscious but cooking somewhere far away.

Joining the priesthood remained an open question during high school. But when Pedro graduated from high school and found a new independence at the university, the idea of joining the priesthood faded again. Pedro continued "normally," a term he uses to describe living the traditional life of a middle-class Puerto Rican *hombre*:

> And then things went on normally, you know, girlfriend, all that kind of thing, I graduated from high school and everything was fine, you know, well then when I entered the university well, I think that's when the question mostly comes in, no, because I didn't have to depend that much on other people since I acquired independence, you know, and that signified something very important, no, it involved making a series of decisions, you know, since what I had thought of at that time was finishing high school and then beginning with a religious life, I don't know. Maybe I didn't ask myself, you know, there wasn't a kind of consciousness like that of that, no. I did it maybe to try it out and find out, it was that, but also with a little more because it wasn't just me but also I had a friend that was thinking more or less the same thing and a group of youths, there where I was involved and sometimes those kinds of values are very appealing, no, there in the university like one was alone, one didn't have the group of youths, the friend or the friends well, they're not there because they went somewhere else and then like one is left there, one says, and I was already really into architecture, I kept going, and then I met the Jesuits.

Continuing on a journey which began when he was three, Pedro kept moving back and forth between a "religious" life and a "normal" life. These are his two primary places of negotiation. As he became more involved in architecture and gained more independence, Pedro also began to more seriously question what he had been choosing between for so many years:

> Then I was already getting a process which was much more serious, no, making decisions and more significant because in a way well, I was more independent and that means there aren't the things that could influence your decision well, they're not necessarily there. Then already one like sees the obligation to look at things more deeply. Then I continued the process with the Jesuits when I was in the second year of university practically and little by little I started to see.

Recently, I was in touch with Pedro again. He had completed his studies at Caimito and was beginning the required master's program in philosophy at Fordham University. Still questioning his choices, he asked if I could send him a copy of his interview transcript and I said that I would. I asked him why he wasn't studying architecture and he laughed, saying that's why he wanted to read the transcript, to examine what it was that he had wanted when he began his life as a Jesuit.

The work that these youths love to do and want to do as adults can be traced back to childhood play, questions, and passions. This points to a need for revisioning adult work as a continuation of childhood visions, rather than as a choice made during high school or college and a breaking away from childhood fantasy. Carmen, Pedro, Judy, and Carlos each in their own way and through their own particular struggles illustrate the processes of vocation or alignment of skill and desire, of genius and passion.

The support necessary for these young people to get to the place where they are now involved an educative process; it was when they began to formally study that they made the connection that what they were good at could also be their livelihood. This connection was no small matter for Judy and Carlos; it meant going against their families' wishes and expectations and giving up several years of investment in other studies. Pedro also brings up how college gave him the independence he needed to make decisions apart from his family.

Judy, Carlos, and Carmen discuss the importance of self-confidence, of believing in themselves, and how they are gaining this slowly through study. Judy and Carmen wish that no one would have to go through what they went through. Their narratives give clues to where education can meet the psychology of young people. All point to the importance of developing a vocation, talent, and genius that they have had since childhood. Judy, Carlos, Carmen, and Pedro are different ages, but all are coming to terms with finding a place where their talents can finally work for them. They are discovering points of psychological alignment, meeting places for work, love, and identity.

The way things work
is that eventually
something catches.

CHAPTER 9

From Illness and Suicide
to the Work of Art

4.
Every drought-resistant plant has its own story
each had to learn to live
with less and less water, each would have loved

to laze in long soft rains, in the quiet drip
after the thunderstorm
each could do without deprivation

but where drought is the epic then there must be some
who persist, not by species-betrayal
but by changing themselves

minutely, by constant study
of the price of continuity
a steady bargain with the way things are[1]

For other young people the "odyssey" that Judy spoke of in the previous chapter is a journey through serious illness and suicide attempts. William, Jorge, Mirta, and Gloria—all students at the conservatory—spoke openly of their struggle for health, their love of music, and how they came to the realization that these two are bound together. Although illness occupies a different role for each of the four youths, they have in common the fact that illness and, for one youth, suicide occupy a central place in their narrative and that the illness was a catalyst for change.

The relationships between illness, suicide, and art are legendary. Art has always been emotionally turbulent because it *is* emotional, in contrast and often against the dominant rational order. Work, love, and finding one's place within a society that has a love/hate relationship with the arts is a difficult and complex struggle for young people who yearn to be musicians. Music has its own unique place in society; it is the most democratic art, surrounding us wherever we go, made from many different instruments by people from many different backgrounds. But it occupies—just like all the other arts—a peculiarly idealized and at the same time marginalized place. Jorge and William were deeply affected by their parents' fears, born of stereotypes of "the starving artist." Jorge, in addition to being told he would starve, was told that music is for homosexuals and communists. On the other hand, the two young women Mirta and Gloria were given full support.

The narratives profiled here stake out a terrain that is likely shared by many youths even though they are not artists or musicians. It seems likely that the artists would be the ones to freely talk about these feelings; artists have historically been the ones to speak what no one else wants to say. This *frontera* is a crossing place fraught with emotional and physical danger. It is the place of going against the wishes of the father, of the loss of meaning, the difficulty breathing, the inability to talk, the planning to take one's life. These crossings are also coming-of-age stories of finding one's place in the adult world of work (see Figure 9.1).

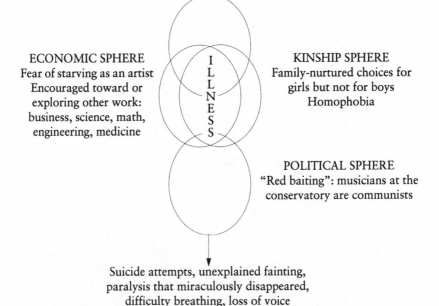

COMMUNITY SPHERE
Conservatory of Music: Critical to a feeling of
belonging and acceptance
Elementary and high schools supported the girls
but not the boys

ECONOMIC SPHERE
Fear of starving as an artist
Encouraged toward or
exploring other work:
business, science, math,
engineering, medicine

ILLNESS

KINSHIP SPHERE
Family-nurtured choices for
girls but not for boys
Homophobia

POLITICAL SPHERE
"Red baiting": musicians at the
conservatory are communists

Suicide attempts, unexplained fainting,
paralysis that miraculously disappeared,
difficulty breathing, loss of voice

Figure 9.1
Moment in Identity: Work, Creativity, and Illness

JORGE

At twenty-five, Jorge is finally studying what he loves, music. When he was sixteen a friend of his gave him a keyboard to play because he had noticed that Jorge had an interest in music. But his family was against his being a musician: "My family didn't want me to have anything to do with musicians, that music stuff, my father said that they were homosexuals and my uncle said that here at the conservatory what there was were a bunch of communists." Jorge is the only young person who brought up homophobia as a reason why he shouldn't pursue a line of work, but not the only one to bring up the use of communist name-calling as a tactic to keep young people away from certain fields; the Jesuits have also been attacked as communists.

Ironically, at the time of the interview Jorge was a successful businessman with his own record store and was also successfully pursuing his studies in music. This combination of interests involved a synthesis of diverse parts of himself as well as a struggle with his family. Jorge points to the business as a place where he is a "productive member of society" and views studying music as a search for a balance between knowledge and working:

> As a productive member I am I consider myself the prototype of the general working man with an academic preparation, um, work, I have my business, and I'm here at the conservatory preparing myself academically because what's the use of having a successful business and not have an education. That is there has to be a balance between knowledge because that helps me integrate myself better in the society. Because, I don't know, that is I'm not very commercial. That is I started the business, yes, to have the business but my orientation isn't totally commercial, no, it's more musical.

Jorge, "the prototype of the general working man," left a school for mostly well-to-do children when he was in tenth grade. The economic and kinship spheres generated for him a sense of disassociation at an early age:

> I was studying at San Antonio Abar in Humacao in a private school and I didn't like it, I didn't like the environment, um, I never had much contact with my friends, that is it was like a thing where I felt disassociated and in tenth grade I definitively said I wasn't returning, and I didn't return. And I finished my

high school through free exams, I took the college board exam and I passed it with good grades and I was accepted in Mayagüez in electrical engineering.

It was at Mayagüez where his health problems began:

> At that time I was eighteen and well my father wanted me to be an engineer because he dreamed that I would be an engineer, he had wanted to be an engineer and so your father like tries to achieve through his children what he didn't achieve himself and it was a disaster. That is when I left Mayagüez because I definitively flunked my second year because it was something that I didn't feel inside. First, I got hypoglycemia because of stress. That is that my blood sugar would go down wherever and I would faint wherever and they would have to take me to medical services and it went on like that. And my father as a matter of fact it was only recently that we could enter into a relationship like that and now he is really happy with his son that I'm a musician. But originally it was an uphill battle but and all my family that is really no one wanted me to be a musician. That is I was going to die of hunger. But one doesn't study for well yes it is one of the functions is to work and gain one's sustenance but one has to do it with something that one likes and if you suffer well you suffer with something that one has proposed to do.

But once he left Mayagüez he never had fainting spells again:

> But I didn't come to realize until I had left. I came to discover it because I was under treatment because that was an experience that was very traumatic and the psychologist told me, "But Jorge don't try to study engineering you really don't want to study that" and he explained to me that I was doing it to please my parents and that I shouldn't do that and that I wasn't the ogre they had painted me out to be because I left Mayagüez but instead that I wanted to do something different and I should do that something different and feel fulfilled in life. And that was how it was, he was right. But after that I tried to get into here in 1986 but I flunked the exam but I continued and I started my business and I tried again and I passed. I got in. This is my second year and I'm going on my third year and I feel very happy. I'm not a great pianist, I don't think I'll ever get to be a great pianist with these hands, they are so ordinary for the piano, usually pianists have fine hands that facilitate lots of things. But the truth is that my inclination is towards composition. I like it a lot. I write songs, popular songs like that, I like them and they give much pleasure.

Jorge felt he was a failure for not living up to his father's dream of what he should be. He was struggling with an image of himself as a working man with ordinary hands with a yearning to compose and play music on the piano. Even though he was losing consciousness—another form of disassociation—and knew he was under a lot of stress, he didn't make the connection between what he was studying and how he was feeling. It was the psychologist who helped him put the two together, gave him a chance to tell his story instead of disconnecting from it, and urged him to reconsider why he was studying engineering instead of music.

The business Jorge started has given him economic stability and allowed him to feel able to study music; he will not starve and "no one can say that I'm irresponsible or anything like that." At the conservatory he finally feels that he is a member of a community. At home people have begun to respect him because "studying at the conservatory is always looked at with a certain status, I don't know why they see it that way but that is the reality." His uncle may still be afraid of conservatory communists but Jorge laughs at his uncle's comments, now.

WILLIAM

Jorge and William are the same age, twenty-five, but whereas Jorge has an outgoing salesman's pitch, William is quiet and describes himself as "a little bit of a philosopher" and as "a little bit of a sad case." He talks a lot about "energy" and how the relationships between people are "like in music there are some notes that go together, that is that sound good in a chord, there are notes that don't sound good in a chord because of the type of vibration, I believe in that." He says he pays careful attention to how this energy feels between himself and others. William has studied theater, which was his first love, and brings this knowledge to music, specifically to playing piano, which is his passion. But what William and Jorge share are the profound changes that they went through to come to terms with their desire to study music:

> I graduated when I was sixteen years old from high school. When I was in high school during the day I was studying eleventh grade and at night I was studying twelfth grade, that is I speeded up high school. I graduated at sixteen years of age and I entered the University of Puerto Rico at seventeen. I always

wanted to study acting, it was what I wanted to study. As a second alternative, well, music, third, science, medicine, and last
computer programming which was beyond what I wanted to do.
And I was more or less two years studying that. I was always in
the middle of the arts because I think it has always been in me
but as a child of sixteen years that was already studying at the
University of Puerto Rico, I was in San Juan and I'm from Ponce,
no, well, all those things influence and at twenty I was all set to
be a computer programmer and be working, with an apartment,
and a car. What society teaches you but I realized that I wasn't
happy. I was suffering, that is, I would go to classes in my second
year, in an emotional state that was anemic, very bad, depressed.
Until one day a friend of mine said, "William let's take music as
an elective, come on!"

It was the experience of taking a course in music and playing the
piano again after many years that helped William make the
change from what was making him depressed—studying computer programming—to what he loved. William's friend was the
only one who supported him in this change, but then she left
music after taking that one class; for her it was an elective, but for
William the piano became his passion. He says he took to music
"like a goldfish to dirty water" that it was his "habitat" and he
took more classes, majoring in the humanities instead of computers. He realized "that this was my thing." But leaving an accepted
and expected path left him alone: "I had to battle against many
things, um, my family because they did not agree with me that I
should study music and professors because there is this myth that
to study piano one has to start at six years old. It's assumed that I
started too late to be what I want to be, it's too late to start at eighteen to study piano." William still feels alone, largely because of
feeling misunderstood by people he studied with at the university
before coming to the conservatory and finding that "I don't think
like all the rest," a statement that is repeated throughout his narrative. He finds that they think of music as a "hobby" and can't
understand why he would go to the conservatory to earn another
bachelor's since he already has one from the university. He says
they "can't see it, for them it's a regression, while, of course I see
it as progress because I'm learning a great many things and I don't
think music has in reality academic degrees or semesters."

William points to his way of thinking about music as what
makes him different from his peers now, but he has felt "differ-

ent" for most of his life. When I ask him to tell me the story of how
it is that he came to music, William responds with:

> Well, let's see, more than just music, a form of expression. I had
> a lot of problems when I was little, it's going to sound very
> strange, I attempted suicide two times when I was little. I was
> about thirteen years old and I didn't feel that school was provid-
> ing what I needed. Everything was geared towards science,
> mathematics, that kind of thing, that field, no? Because what
> they were teaching us was that you have to study to have money,
> you have to study to have money, you have to study that was all,
> that was the *leitmotif*, the theme that since one enters until one
> graduates. That is, it's not to get, not to learn, it's to get "A" so
> that they will accept you in the best universities and from there
> to have the best career to then have the best. But I didn't feel
> good.

William holds school directly responsible for his unhappiness as a
thirteen-year-old because he felt that he was being pushed, and
pushed hard, into a career he didn't want. School was not providing what he needed even though it was providing what society
"needed": math and science. He found the value of education for
money hollow, and no matter how many times the theme of getting an education so that he could earn a good living was blasted
out to him, William didn't want to listen. Eventually he did listen
because there was nothing else to listen to:

> I remember one day there was what they called in good Spanish
> a "career day" and it was well all the professions with their sal-
> aries and I don't know what else. I looked for art, there wasn't
> any and I fought and I but "how can there be no art?" no,
> because it's that it's said that "You can't make good money
> there." And I said "But I'm interested in it." Until well, of
> course, also I was very interested, very interested in science. And
> so I went to the interview for science, and I don't know, but I
> didn't feel in my place.

He found his place when he changed to the humanities and took
acting and music classes after two years of computer science at the
University of Puerto Rico. The earliest memory he tells me about
is when he was six years old:

> I remember when I was six years old, in catechism, the nun was
> teaching us the history of Genesis, that God created man in a
> certain way, in a certain way and I said to her that it was a lie.

That lady opened her eyes and I could see the fire that wanted to come out of her eyes and burn me and she said how dare you say that this is a lie and I said I can't believe in that. Of course a six-year-old thinking these things! and she said look at your hands so that you can see that you are made of dirt and I did and I saw those famous streaks of dirt that come out of the creases and I got scared. I saw my pants burning and then I said wait a minute a little while ago I was playing in the dirt over there and if I go wash my hands well with soap and I look at them again I won't have the creases. The nun gave up on me as incorrigible and hit me on the head and kept on teaching, no? And more or less it was at that age that I stopped believing in God because what they were teaching me wasn't satisfying me and I realized that the error we human beings are making is being preoccupied with knowing something that we aren't going to understand ever because our mind is too small and we are forgetting about ourselves and I had so many problems and then that was what I tried to do was begin getting to know, know who I was. I still don't know what is me, if someone asked me, "William what are you?" well I would have few words. I'm an energy that takes the form of consciousness, that's all. Oh my God! I just got embarrassed!

Although William is embarrassed about how he sounds talking about "energy" and "consciousness" as ways to describe himself, it makes sense that he describes himself this way—not in any bound form, flowing, not contained, evolving. Not unlike music.

William stopped believing in God as a child when he told the teacher that he thought Genesis was a lie, that it couldn't possibly be true that humans were made from clay or dirt and asked for evidence, asked for proof. The scientist in him was hard at work, but he was caught in oppositions. William at six was entering the debate about the origins of human being, but Genesis and science don't mix—they offer opposing explanations. It must have been confusing to be pushed toward science yet not be allowed to be scientific. Recalling the story of Genesis, of the beginnings, he also recalls his own beginnings of not believing in something that didn't make sense to him and his beginning to put the lie to values that left him feeling deeply dissatisfied.

Music, the path not offered, is the only one he wants to follow because for William music is an open question and an evolving answer. Evoking the Eriksonian "sense of knowing where one is going," William tells me, "For me music is not my end, it's my medium to get to my ends, my medium to get to something, to get somewhere."

MIRTA

Mirta is twenty and her plan for the future is to open a voice academy. She began studying music when she was five years old. She views her lifelong dedication to music as a long thank-you to God. Mirta has also endured grave illness and come out with a set of views about what is right for her to do with her life. Like William, she had a crisis, not of faith but of health, when she was six years old. But unlike Jorge and William, Mirta's parents have always given her support:

> My parents always, always to this day have been with me in this and like they would see that I liked it, you know, they never said, "Do this!" they never did. Well they said "Do you like it" and I said "yes" that I did and they always asked me if I wanted to take classes or something. And then I was interested always, always in music, always. Every time I heard a sound I would go find it on the piano, when I was little I was like that, like it really got my attention. And my father would say when I was little that "everyone in this house sings." My father is a baritone and my mother is a soprano and each the majority of people at home sing, and there's only one that doesn't because he doesn't like it. But my mother says that always when I was little they would turn on the radio and put on music and like that and I would always go to the voice and since I was a baby I was about three or two years old and if they pulled me away from the voice I would start to cry. I don't remember that if they pulled me away I would start to cry and that was the thing that since I was born I really liked it.

Mirta also had consistent support from teachers, even from teachers that she says "had little knowledge of music." For example, a science teacher recommended her for an award in the arts even though she would cut science class to sing. Mirta was given the award.

Mirta's support and success in music is a dramatic and extraordinary story of a child that was determined to be a singer because she once found herself without the capacity for movement and expression. Mirta had a rare form of aneurism as a six-year-old, but the exact cause of her illness has never been known. Music for her is a way of giving thanks to life and to God for giving her another chance:

> When I was little, at six years of age, well, that was, well, that was something that can't be explained, it still can't be because the doctors themselves couldn't explain it, that, that, disease. But I suffered symptoms that were very rare in my body and I limped and it was momentary limping that wasn't all the time. And sometimes since I was a little menace as a child they thought I was tricking them and my father would say "Cut it out! Stop doing that!" and I would say "I'm really not making myself limp." Until that same day, it was only days that I had those symptoms, I went to sleep at night and when I got up then when I woke up between the wall and my bed and I woke up and was all twisted, I was completely disfigured and I couldn't move, I couldn't talk, I couldn't do anything, but I was conscious because I could see people around me but I couldn't talk, I couldn't, it was like a shock . . .

That morning transformed her life physically and emotionally:

> They took me to the doctor's office and then the doctor told my parents that they had to do some rare tests some tests with needles and I didn't feel anything. I would see the little pinpricks of the needles in my skin but I felt absolutely nothing. I was numb. Then I was hospitalized for about two months. Six doctors and none of them could find out what I had. I didn't have a tumor. I didn't have a lesion. There wasn't anything. They didn't know where this disease came from. They knew it was from my brain but they didn't know where.

But just as strangely as she had become ill, Mirta's illness went away:

> Those two months passed until one morning I woke up normal, real normal, and in front of the doctors, they were visiting, and they themselves said that it was a miracle because they had told me that I was going to remain a vegetable or if I didn't remain a vegetable I would die because I was very sick, I was in intensive care . . . and up until today I haven't had anything I haven't had to be hospitalized and it's already been more than twelve years. And I got up that day from that bed and my parents at home were very surprised and they accepted it and I accepted it that it was a miracle from God because medicine couldn't cure me. And that was the way from night to morning I got up and even if you

don't believe me this was the major motivation for me to sing, the major motivation. Because I felt very grateful for that for being alive and normal you know and I feel good and very grateful . . . and still today singing isn't sufficient to give thanks to the Lord for everything He did and that is the biggest motivation that I know of that it's a great stimulus for me to sing and always sing.

Mirta began to believe in miracles and to thank God for making her "normal" again. Music is, she believes, her greatest gift to give. The support she has received, no doubt, stems from this experience, too. The adults around her were clearly dumbfounded as to why and how she recovered. Mirta stresses to me that whether I believe it or not what she experienced *was* a miracle.

GLORIA

The earliest memory Gloria has of music is of being two-and-a-half years old and dancing and dancing with a little boy of the same age at a wedding.

Gloria is eighteen years old. Unlike Jorge, William, and Mirta, she has a variety of careers that she is interested in pursuing: social work, "everything that has to do with music," "all work that has to do with art and natural sciences," and teaching. Gloria thinks that music therapy would be a good combination of social work and music, but she still also wants to be a doctor. She describes how she feels when she's working on something she enjoys and how she wants to do a variety of things: "Many times what happens to me is that I want to do many things at once and I can't do them. It's like one expects to know everything in a moment. For example, when I was doing my preregistration now at the university well I wanted to take all the courses, well, that's how I feel that I greatly enjoy what I do, I enjoy it. I would like to do it all the time." Gloria does say that there is an area she most definitely doesn't want to go into, and that is mathematics, and doesn't like work which is "too technical":

I was at one time decided on studying medicine, well, I think it was because I was always, I was raised in a hospital environment because my mother is a nurse . . . I thought that there are kinds of work within the natural sciences that are too technical and well I'm not the kind of person that can adapt to that, that is, I can't, they are routine and are not in direct contact with people. For example, a medical technician which was something that was really recommended to me, "study technology, you'll earn good money, there are many positions," well, I don't like it.

Although Gloria was emphatically told that there are well-paid jobs in medical technology and urged to study for these positions, she is not willing to give up music or "direct contact with people." A paycheck is not enough.

Gloria is caught in wanting to study several kinds of fields that are not traditionally studied together: loving music and also medicine, wanting to sing, and wanting to give therapy. Gloria has not made a final decision, as have the other youths. But Gloria and Jorge have this in common: the bridging of two fields. She has given her career decision much thought:

> I liked medicine at that time because it was dealing with the patient, with nursing, that kind of thing. I was very interested in psychiatry that was what I had decided on studying. Then I entered the university in natural sciences, I applied for natural sciences at the University of Puerto Rico but later I thought that medicine was too long a career. If we consider that psychiatry brings very little satisfaction to the person and then there were other aspects and it was that I wanted to study other things in addition to medicine, see? And it's really complicated, very very difficult to study, for example, music and study medicine because they both require an incredible amount of time . . . So then here I study music and over there I study humanities taking courses in all the departments, philosophy, and all that so then later on I hope to enter into biology to study medicine but not with the rush that I had before, little by little instead.

Where did she get the idea that psychiatry brings little satisfaction to the person who works in that field? I miss another opportunity to ask a question. Gloria at the time of the interview had made a tentative bridge between the university and conservatory and was happy with that, but is not sure which field will become the focal one "since I'm interested in so many things, well, I don't know." She says she still wants to study medicine and says she will but at a slower pace. Part of the reason is that she "has always had delicate health and many times I've put that limitation on myself that I can't do something because of my health but if I like it I make the effort and I try to do it."

Gloria says that since she was little she loved

> everything that had to do with music and I said I was going to
> be a doctor and actress and singer. Those were my three things.
> And then sometimes I thought about being a teacher but I
> thought I couldn't be a teacher if I was all those other things
> since I saw the work of professors as very sacrificed all the time
> and then I always said that I wanted to study those. And my par-
> ents well, always had a great fondness for music, they couldn't
> because their economic situation since they were little well
> didn't permit them to do anything with music but they always
> wanted to. Then when I came I was about nine years old when I
> started studying piano.

Gloria explores a range of work options that she's interested in.
All of them are in the arts or health and in Gloria's own combination of these two, music therapy. This reminds me of the youths
from ADT who, lacking economic and educational resources, also
give a range of work they would like to do which often is beyond
their reach. Gloria's parents wanted to study music but couldn't
because they didn't have the financial resources but Gloria has
made it to the conservatory. It's as if now that she's there she
wants to fulfill both her parents' dream and her own; she speaks
of work as if it is a buffet at a banquet that she is enjoying choosing from. Later, she adds "writer" to her options.

But unlike the youths at ADT who share Gloria's economic
background and dreams of working, Gloria has been able to move
toward her goals through a process of education beginning at the
age of nine and continuing now at two well-respected and good
schools, the University of Puerto Rico and the Conservatory of
Music:

> Well, since I was little I was always interested in music. I always
> said I was going to be a singer and a doctor. I always sang in
> church activities, in family activities, and sometimes they would
> call me for, well, activities for example of the Council of Nurses,
> that type of activities to sing. I always participated in drama at
> school in everything that was in the artistic environment well
> that's where I enjoyed being. Then when I was around nine years
> old I began to take classes in piano and later when I was going
> into middle school one of the professors of music from elemen-
> tary school brought a group to take the entrance exam to the
> Free School of Music and that's when I got on the road to study
> music formally. Later when I passed all of middle school and

high school and decided to take the entrance exam for here and here I am.

Gloria's gift for singing was nurtured by a professor of music that took an interest in her and took her, as part of a group, to take the entrance exam to the only public school in Puerto Rico that specializes in music. Her mother, who is a nurse, brought her to sing at nursing activities, and Gloria would also sing at her church's activities. For Gloria the critical sources of support were her mother, her boyfriend, her teachers, and church. Gloria was and is surrounded by people urging her on, helping her to sing, giving her opportunities to express her talent. Gloria's experience points to the kind of support that young people need to be able to move forward in their dreams.

But Gloria's health remains delicate. Our interview had to be divided up in two parts. The first time we met had to be cut short because she was picked up every day by her mother at noon sharp and then we didn't meet again for a week because she caught a cold and had an asthmatic attack. Gloria has already experienced the anguish of the possibility of not being able to sing, but if Gloria can't sing she will study medicine and heal others through music therapy:

> About three months ago they did a study on lung function and then well, I have a problem in my lungs that is that they are getting smaller each time, but it's because of my condition, that is that I have a deviation and like that and then right there I thought I can't keep going and that was a tremendous depression that I went through. I had one or two months that I said well I won't be able to sing anymore because to sing that is the main thing. I said well I can start as a teacher, well, I don't know another kind of work within the same area of art but as a singer well, but now well, I've realized that I can do it, music therapy and all that but it would be very frustrating, very depressing if I couldn't sing. It's that it's like it's a part of my life, music. It's not like anything else that one can say, that I could say well if I can't be a writer then I, I've always wanted to be a writer, well maybe it wouldn't hurt me as much as not being able to work in music.

Jorge, William, Mirta, and Gloria are crossing the *frontera* of illness, depression, paralysis, and loss of consciousness to get to the work they love. It's interesting how each connects with psychology in one way or another. Jorge talks about losing consciousness.

He was losing an awareness of what he was doing, and it wasn't until a psychologist pointed out to him that he was studying engineering to please his parents that he became aware of that. He never lost consciousness again.

William describes himself as "energy" that has a consciousness. His suicide attempts were at the age of thirteen, the beginnings of adolescence, but his attempts to understand life began with his questioning of Genesis at the age of six. His crisis of faith brought with it an awareness that the world could not be taken just on beliefs but had to be accountable to rules of logic and evidence, subject to proof. At thirteen, his own consciousness rearranging itself into the capacity for abstract reasoning, he was thrown into a crisis of meaning. Money meant nothing to him, and a good career for good money left him feeling bad. His place was not in the Catholicism he was schooled in, not in the capitalism he was thrown into. William was alone, aware that he didn't fit in, and, looking around at a career day fair, chose computer programming, a field of study that follows rigid rules of logic, the "if x, then y" where everything is ordered and flows according to its predetermined structure. Ordering his own chaos through a field of study was not satisfying after several years, but I wonder if the ordering and structuring of computer logic didn't help, at least for those years.

Mirta describes her experience of being able to look out at her family and doctors but not being able to move and talk. Her experience of disconnection, of being conscious but unable to respond, left her with an awareness of the need to express herself; it gave her the awareness of just how much she needed to sing. She has never forgotten that.

Gloria is considering blending her two passions, music and medicine, into work as a music therapist. Her difficulty breathing and her love of singing are combined. Her depression and frustration getting a chance at being worked out through a therapeutic process.

These youths all share a self-reflection and knowledge of what they are going through, what they have gone through, and the connections between that and music. Rather than deny physical ills, as Rosa does (she can't take the chance of giving the impression she is ill for she may lose any chance of getting work, even though she too has difficulty breathing and wants to be a nurse), these young men and women have been able to integrate their illness into their life choices. Indeed, they've taken their illness as an opportunity to search, reflect, and acquire an awareness of what it is they want to do.

Socioeconomic class plays a critical role in the choices these youths have been able to make. But class by itself doesn't explain everything. Gloria says she is from a family with limited economic resources. It was through the support she received from teachers and her family that she was able to study music. Both Jorge and William went to private Catholic schools, but even with their resources they felt ill, depressed, and unable to do what they felt they cared about. Mirta suffered a rare form of stroke but was able to "miraculously" recover; although the doctors didn't know what she had, she had doctors. For each, class and economic resources, love of music, and a catastrophic event in their lives set them on a path of recovering what they loved.

It's worth noting that only the young women were given the emotional support they needed to pursue music. For the young men the trampling of gender wore a path through their childhood: Jorge was told that music is for homosexuals, and William was told he must make good money. Jorge and William had the economic resources to change from what they were expected to do to what they loved to do but had to find within themselves the psychological and social resources.

Their narratives put the lie to simplistic "career days." Yet they support the idea that one teacher can make a difference, as can one psychologist, one friend, a parent. Of crucial importance to the process of development for these youths has been the self-realization that they had a genius to share, a gift to give, a thank you to sing. Unlike their counterparts at the conservatory who have always wanted to be musicians and were able to pursue that, with struggles too but without illness, these youths have gained a self-awareness of their identities through a particular process of reflection that accompanied their illness and crisis of meaning.

Wheel, kinetic flow,
rising and falling water,
ingots, levers and keys,
I believe in you,
cylinder lock, pully,
lifting tackle and
Crane lift your small head—

I believe in you—
your head is the horizon to
my hand. I believe
forever in the hooks.

CHAPTER 10

In Uniform:
Seguridad as Symbol and Work

Almost twenty years ago, I came across one of my high school teachers lying on Flamenco Beach on the island of Culebra, which is a small island of Puerto Rico. Flamenco has white soft sand and curves around like a half-moon with brilliant blue waves and sea grape trees along the shore. She, a fair-skinned North American in her forties, was trying to get a tan and was there alone. I was alone, too, having managed to get away from my family to have some time to think my teenage thoughts. I remember feeling extremely insecure and timid about even saying a simple "Hello, how are you?" But there she was and there I was on a beautiful and empty beach except for the two of us and a huge sign warning people to go no further: WARNING BOMBING ZONE.

She recognized me, so what could I do? I said "Hello," and to my surprise and, then, horror she asked me a question about how it felt to be young or something to that effect. "How does it feel to be young?" I wondered to myself, "Well, it feels like you're always insecure and not sure of what's going to happen next." I told her something like that.

She seemed to think that feeling insecure was not at all about being young but about the fear of nuclear war, uncertain times, and general turmoil in the world. In other words, she didn't think insecurity was unique to youth. I remember feeling as if once more the world had proven that it was quite useless to talk with adults because they always somehow said in one way or another, "Oh, you'll get over thinking that it's just your problem and realize that it's the human condition."

Looking back at this experience, I really did mean that I felt insecure. I know that my friends also felt this in uniquely youthful ways. I wish I could call her up and tell her, "Sure, I feel insecure on occasion, especially when I'm trying to do something new, but not in the way I used to feel, not in that what will tomorrow bring? way, that is, if tomorrow comes at all." And I wonder if she was asking me something she had been mulling over in her mind as she lay on that beautiful beach with the WARNING BOMBING ZONE sign. Or was she remembering when she was young? Was she trying to understand her own children better? Or was she trying to get to know me? I'll never know, but I remember what started it all—the question about being young and the insecure answer and that beautiful beach with the warning sign.

Today, I understand what she meant about war and it's impossible to tell that Flamenco Beach was once ground zero for U.S. military bombing practice. The beach is as beautiful as ever, the military has stopped bombing after years of protest by the local fishing community, and the sign has been taken down. If you go snorkeling, however, you'll see enormous fragments of the coral reef, dead and bleached white, strewn along the bottom, and your heart will probably ache, as mine did years later, for all that is senselessly destroyed in the name of security.

Reading and reflecting on the narratives of young people who told me they wanted to wear uniforms, I remembered that beach and that high school teacher. What is it about a uniform that calls to attention the many feelings about security? The word itself says there is one form, one way to do things, one place. And then there are the other words around this place: *unify, unity, unit, unique, union, universal.* All these wonderful words are derived from Latin, from a concept that is problematic in a social world: *unus*, meaning one, meeting another one and another one and . . . to make up a whole. The collection and assemblage of individuals into a universe, a uniquely united unit, is called society. Uniforms simplify this tangle of individuality that erupts from the complexities of having more than one way to do things, more than one form.

Uniforms serve as identity markers that clearly signal where youths place themselves in the cultural spaces they can inhabit. Uniforms have the power of expression, whether it's street fashion—the baggy pants, the baseball cap, the expensive sneakers, the dark blue parka—or school uniforms, skinheads, tattoos, and so on. Uniforms mark the spot. What to wear on one's body, how to represent oneself to the world, how to fit in and yet remain unique and individual—this is a *frontera*, a borderland where youths stake out their connections and disconnections with the adult world, with the society they are in the process of entering and with each other, with who they are and who they are not.

Covering and uncovering the body is about taking up space, claiming a territory; this is who I am and this is where I belong. Clothes when used as a deliberate method of claiming space are about conquest and reclaiming turf, putting up borders and warning signs, as well as about bridges, invitations, promises, commonality, and safety. Just as in any taking of land, there are some who are allowed in and others who are not; clothes are passports, ID cards, licenses. Military uniforms have their own gravitational pull that is related to power and enforcement of the law of the land.

The narratives of the youths who want to have a uniformed future illustrate a *frontera* where the symbolic relationship between individual psychological security and the public *seguridad* is negotiated. This symbolic relationship—in addition to the critical economic one, since most people in the military and police are from poor or working-class backgrounds—points to possible reasons why youths want to wear the uniform. Security, discipline, laws, order: which one of these youths hasn't yearned for these in chaotic and uncertain times?

The symbolism of the use of the word *seguridad*, which means security, is striking because the youths who want to enter the military or the police are at the Volunteer Corps largely because they have, and have had, little security in their lives. In addition, the Volunteer Corps is structured on a military model. The executive director was the head of the Federal Emergency Management Agency (FEMA) in Puerto Rico and also a military man. MRT is required therapy for the first thirty days, and the youths in the security workshop wear green military uniforms.

Even though all the *recintos* have a security workshop, the *recinto* of Ensenada has a security workshop that has been recognized for its discipline and neatness in Volunteer Corps and military activities. Ensenada gives youths the opportunity to enter the military or police by providing a foundation through its security workshop. A diploma from the Volunteer Corps in security is a solid step in the recruitment door. This is a clear goal of the workshop as expressed by the two young men and one young woman. There were other youths who wanted to enter the security workshop but weren't able to because there are two basic requirements: a high school diploma or GED—one of the youths I interviewed was waiting for her results—and eighteen years of age.

This means that in addition to having the status of enforcing rules and regulations, the youths who can enter the workshop are the relatively few who have met the two basic requirements. The security workshop is elite because it's the only workshop that has these requirements and because few of the youths who enter the Volunteer Corps have *cuarto año*. The workshop is also unique in generating hostility. One of the youths spoke of the resentment that he has felt coming from youths not in security because the youths in security are supposed to enforce the rules and tell on anyone that breaks them.

The youths in the Volunteer Corps were the only ones that talked about their desire and ambition to be part of the army, marines, national guard, or police. Four youths were in the *recinto* at Ensenada and participating in the security workshop. Three youths who were in the *recinto* in Aguadilla expressed an interest in joining the army but were not in a security workshop. The youths profiled here were at Ensenada (see Figure 10.1).

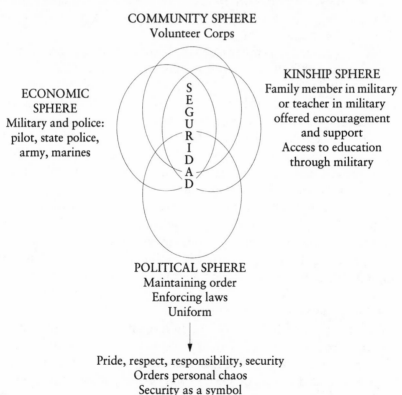

COMMUNITY SPHERE
Volunteer Corps

ECONOMIC
SPHERE
Military and police:
pilot, state police,
army, marines

SEGURIDAD

KINSHIP SPHERE
Family member in military
or teacher in military
offered encouragement
and support
Access to education
through military

POLITICAL SPHERE
Maintaining order
Enforcing laws
Uniform

Pride, respect, responsibility, security
Orders personal chaos
Security as a symbol

Figure 10.1
Moment in Identity: Work and *Seguridad*

JULIA

Julia is sixteen. Before entering the Volunteer Corps she had worked in the cafeteria of a tourist center. She had recently left school because she "didn't like the idea of being in high school," and since she was sixteen she could legally leave. Looking for something to do the week she left school, Julia saw on television an ad for the Volunteer Corps. Julia and her sister both agreed to join. (Her sister then left to get married.)

When Julia entered the Volunteer Corps, she wanted to go into the *nautica* workshop, which specializes in the construction and navigation of boats. But at that time there wasn't a teacher and there weren't any assistants either. Julia then decided on entering the *seguridad* workshop, but she didn't have the required *cuarto año* and was not eighteen. Interestingly, Julia chose two fields which are traditionally occupied by men. But after her attempts at these two interests fell through, she chose the *hostelería* workshop, which focuses on food preparation and serving in restaurants, cafeterias, and hotels: an area that is mostly occupied by women. This has gone well for her, as is clear from her responses, which she gives with wide-eyed excitement:

> Well, for me work is a help like for one to be able to be clear about oneself, help and develop oneself . . . An example of that well, would be me being able to help myself, working for myself. What I'm studying . . . *hostelería*.

> *For what work do you feel love?*

> For the kitchen! Because since I was little well, my family always, that is, we have leaned towards the kitchen and I since I was little well, I always liked being in the middle of the kitchen and I got into the habit and now I like it a lot and I feel love for the kitchen. In my home I am the one that makes the menus . . . I feel good because one of the things that I feel good about being there because being there cooking for other people or for ourselves I am demonstrating what I know and I am giving what I feel for the kitchen.

Julia and the other youths in the *hostelería* workshop prepare meals and snacks for all the youths at the *recinto*. This workshop is intensive, and the youths get a hands-on experience of food preparation and serving on a daily basis. After the interview Julia went back to the kitchen to prepare vanilla cup cakes for that evening's snack.

But even though Julia loves the kitchen, cooking, and demonstrating what she knows, continuing with this depends on how quickly she can find work. When I ask her about her plans, Julia switches from the kitchen to the army and explains why:

> Well, being here I want to finish this and when I leave if I don't find work right away in a cafeteria or restaurant or something well, I want to go into the army . . . Because since I was little I had an uncle that was in the army and they killed him a year and a half ago in a fight, he left the army and since I was little I liked to look at pictures of how he jumped out with a parachute and I fell in love with that. When he left the army he said to me, "I want you to follow in my footsteps" and I always have wanted to do it, I've felt, in addition to the kitchen, I have felt a great affection for the army. Everything that has to do with the army, *me encanta.*[1]

Julia is not yet in uniform but is still drawn to follow in the footsteps of an uncle. Had she met the requirements of the security workshop perhaps she would have been in the green uniform worn by the following three youths profiled.

LUZ

Luz is twenty-three and in the security workshop, which she tells me she feels love for. She left school before completing her *cuarto año* and recently took her GED. At the time of the interview she was waiting for the results. Luz came to the Volunteer Corps to get her GED and participate in the security workshop so that she could then enter the police academy or the army. She describes the Volunteer Corps as "a door" to get to where she wants to go. It was through a cousin that she heard about the program, and then she came, filled out the forms, and began.

But our interview began with a great deal of reluctance. When I ask Luz what work means to her, what her definition is, she answers with a brief, "I don't know." When I ask her what she thinks about when she thinks about work, again her answer is brief: "There are so many things that I don't know how to say a single one." I persist with "Whichever one, you can pick one, whichever is fine." Luz responds with "I don't know." I stumble on to the next questions, and slowly Luz begins to open up a bit, but throughout remains guarded.

When I ask her if she could tell me the story of how she came to think that she wanted to be a state policewoman, Luz tells of how she has always wanted to be in a uniform, and even though she is clear that she wants to wear a uniform, it's just as clear that she isn't sure why:

> I don't know, I think that since I was little, I don't know, in real-
> ity I don't know why it was but always, well, I would see those
> people dressed like that with those uniforms and it would really
> get my attention, I don't know why. I was growing up like that,
> I was about seven or eight years old, well, since then I always
> grew up with that idea always and well, I would see them and
> that would give me enthusiasm, I don't know, until I arrived
> here and I still think that, I haven't gotten that out of my head,
> and so I've kept going forward.

Luz remembers feeling enthusiastic about people in uniforms. When she would see them she would feel good and want to be one of them. She regrets leaving school because it has kept her from what she wants:

> I left school and after that I regretted it so much because I
> always, well, I would see people like that all dressed up and I
> would say *contra*, no, and after that I was out of school for four
> years, and then I went to *afuera* and began to study again. Then
> I came back to here and definitively started to study again to get
> my *cuarto año* so I could go to the police academy. But I don't
> know, that's what I've got thought out now, I've always liked
> that and I'm going to do it, but I want to go for two years to the
> army then come back to enter the academy because the last thing
> I'm going to do is that. I'll be two years out there and then return
> and I'll get into the police academy and I'll stay there until God
> says.

OVIDIO

Fresh out of high school, Ovidio is planning his route to the armed forces, to be what he most wants to be, a marine pilot. Ovidio is eighteen. Like Luz, Ovidio says that security is the work that he loves. But even though he had his high school diploma when he began in the Volunteer Corps, he was only seventeen and couldn't enter the security workshop. He first began taking workshops in maintenance, electricity, and *hostelería* but kept an eye on what was going on in security.

Ovidio finally went to talk with the lieutenant in charge and explained that he would be eighteen in a few months, and that he wanted to join the marines when he finished the Volunteer Corps. The lieutenant was supportive and made arrangements to get Ovidio into security. Ovidio describes why he chose security and what the process has been like for him so far:

> I like this workshop because I have plans to go into the marines in the future, well, like the discipline and all that comes with the workshop is more like the military level, I was interested because of that point . . . When I entered into the course itself, that is, when I saw how people were dealing with it, exercises, the classes, the discipline, everything, everything in the course in reality I liked it. I said, *contra* I made a good choice. Thank God I got here not knowing anything and I've learned and risen up to what I am now, a sergeant. They promoted me for discipline, courtesy, and labor and well, later I took the physical and oral exams on certain activities that were presented in the course. I passed and was promoted to sergeant. I've stayed here because I consider that the work I'm doing doesn't go above what I have, but doesn't go below the level that I have. I like it, I like the rank I have and for the moment I'll stay at this level.

Ovidio made a lot of progress in a short time. He has every military book he can get because he is determined to get into the marines. The support of the lieutenant has been critical to him, both because he allowed him to enter slightly early and because of the material support he gave him:

> The lieutenant helped me a lot. I got in quickly and he began to motivate me, "Look the course is this and that. There are always problems but we're going to teach you how to confront them and everything." He got me a uniform right away, all the uniforms, the dressy ones, with the shoes, good, all the equipment without my being officially in the course yet so that when I was I get fully into it right away. Well, when I got in I was very happy because always in reality always I had liked this using the green military uniform but I had never had the opportunity to use it. And when I entered here and they gave me the opportunity to use the uniform and when I put it on for the first time, I felt good. And I felt like finally I had made a step forward towards

what I wanted. If I don't achieve what I want at least I feel good because I put on a uniform and I'm doing it.

Initially it was his stepfather who suggested the Volunteer Corps and gave him support:

My stepfather was the one who told me, "Look, in Ensenada they're offering these courses. They give you an incentive, a payment for being there, whatever you want, we'll work it out. We'll take you there for you to get oriented and if you like it you can stay, that's fine." Well, I started to talk with Rafi, the recruiter, I would call him and he would explain on the telephone more or less what it was and a cousin of mine that had been here filled out the papers for me. I got all the documents, and well, I entered here four days after I graduated from *cuarto año*, I entered.

Over the time that he has been in security Ovidio has participated in various activities, as well as the day-to-day maintenance of order in the *recinto*. This experience has made him feel proud and confident that he can carry out orders and also give them. The director of the *recinto*, during their daily morning formation, thanks the youths who provide security for Ensenada. On occasion, the director says, "It's thanks to the youths in security that the *recinto* is doing so well." There was one experience that Ovidio described that made him feel particularly proud and that filled him with joy :

We went to an activity at a military base where the teacher who had been here was and I had to carry out my work at the gates registering signatures of captains, officials, from cadets from the National Guard to people of high rank. And when he saw all the work I had done, well, he congratulated me. And he told me, "Thank you, everything was well done. You did a better job than sometimes even the guards who work here do," the National Guard and I was filled with joy because I said, *contra* well what I learned wasn't in vain and I can go anywhere to work and well, my labor will be satisfactory.

The end of this interview is one of the more memorable ones to me because of how formal it was. After I said that we had come to the end of the interview, Ovidio responded with: "It has been a pleasure to share with you this morning and whatever little thing, whatever doubt you have, well, we are at your *ordenes*." The word *orden* literally means order, and so he was saying they were at my orders, ready to receive orders. But it is also a common expression, a way of saying "You're welcome," to say "I'm at your service." The literal meaning had never really occurred to me before Ovidio said it, a youth who dreams of being a military man.

ALVARO

Alvaro is twenty-three. He is in his second year at the Volunteer Corps and has been promoted to a teaching assistant in the security workshop. The training he is receiving in the Volunteer Corps gives him satisfaction and makes him feel proud of what he has been able to accomplish. Like Ovidio, he tells me about how their security team has been recognized for their discipline; they have won first place at military activities. The rewards and satisfaction of being recognized for the good work he does keeping order, helping others, teaching the youths who are younger, and making friends are important to him. Beyond the program itself he sees himself as helping to bring down "criminality" in society and believes that he could make security into a profession, even though his "ambition is to be a doctor and a pilot."

Before joining the Volunteer Corps Alvaro was working with the marines as a youth recruiter. He would go to schools and give talks about the marines and encourage young men to join. Alvaro recalls that when he would recruit three youths to enroll and swear allegiance to the flag he would obtain another stripe, which would give him more money and other benefits. Alvaro was a "first lieutenant" and would give new recruits orientation and classes. He was also involved in civil defense.

Alvaro joined the Volunteer Corps because it was a way for him to get experience that he could use toward his goal of becoming an "MP," military police. It was a sergeant in the marines who told him about this program. He is clear in his decision to pursue this path, but at a point during his initial orientation at the Volunteer Corps he wasn't this certain yet. Alvaro tells of the process he went through, what he calls an "experiment":

> I thought that I could see the different workshops for a certain time during the day, observe the workshop, see what the orientation is, observe to decide what was the workshop I wanted to take. I went through that experiment and it was difficult for me

to decide because I came into the program with one condition, that I could take security because I'm going into the marines. I'm going to the military police, I'm going to MP and I need for MP an experience in security. If I'm going to be in the marines and take MP I have to be serving four or five years in security, taking the course over there, but here they told me that I could take one or two years of security and well it would be valid for MP over there and then I would save all those years and totally, here, well here well I would work with experience, just like over there but it was difficult for me because I thought totally if I was going to take it or not because there were a few workshops that teach things you can really learn. They're all good. Actually there are some where you make more money than others, for example, electricity is a workshop that you make a lot of money, totally, and it's a basic and essential part of life, because without money you can't maintain a family, you can't get dressed, transportation and all that in life. Until finally, at the end I decided when I thought that part of the workshop was one that was related to my future and I had to decide on security, that in the future I'm going to the marines and it'll be valid the diploma in security.

Alvaro went through a process of trying out different workshops, keeping in mind what kind of future each workshop would facilitate. He was clearly interested in electricity because of the income. Later, in the same response, he adds that he was also interested in *hostelería* and in medicine. Alvaro did participate in the health workshop because, he says, "It was related in something I liked, medicine and the biology of the human body." When I ask him about what work he would like to be doing in the future, the pull of medicine is still strong but gets overrun by the military. The meeting place for both fields follows a logic of "giv[ing] protection and security to human life":

> In my future I have, well three decisions. To get to be a doctor and what I have left is 60 credits to obtain my bachelor's in biology and keep going forward to obtain my master's, pilot, and at the same time that I'm getting my bachelor's and finish ROTC well I'll be able to be promoted to lieutenant and then when I'm promoted to lieutenant at the same time I'll be able to be a pilot too. Well, after all security is very important to me because I've seen how it is that criminality is increasing in society. Everyone has to see, every citizen has to do their part to give protection

and security to human life and so I would like to work in security most of all.

Unlike Gloria, who is considering combining her two great interests—medicine and music, into music therapy—Alvaro doesn't. Medicine and the military run on parallel lines, although there are military doctors. Alvaro views his future as containing three big decisions made up of many areas: finishing his bachelor's, then a master's, ROTC, MP, pilot, marines, medical doctor.

Alvaro's experiences have been both studying biology and participating in the military as a recruiter. The military may well be a way that he can pay for his studies. In this way, the military is part of an educational strategy that gives him access to training he would not otherwise have. It is not uncommon for young poor and working-class people in colleges around the island to also be part of ROTC as a way of financing their studies.

Ovidio and Alvaro both want to be military pilots. Luz wants to be a state policewoman. Julia is considering the army. It's clear that for Luz, Ovidio, and Alvaro the Volunteer Corps' security training has been instrumental in providing support for pursuing their interests. From the uniform which gives them pleasure and pride to the awards they've received at military activities, the training is hands-on and is close to a real-life simulation. The workshop is both a dress rehearsal and an affirmation. The adults who provide material and emotional support—uniforms and counseling—are in the military; one is a captain, the other a sergeant, and another was an uncle.

The Volunteer Corps' security workshop works on two levels; the youths in it provide security for the residential program and they prepare for a life in uniform. This combination is good for the program because the youths in security take on the responsibility of keeping order and providing help: Ovidio and Alvaro both talked about how they felt responsible for teaching the other youths, helping when needed, and making sure the rules are followed. The youths feel that the workshop is good because it gives them pride, respect, satisfaction, and confidence as well as a foundation on which to build their interest in the military.

Pointing to the role the youths play in keeping order, Luz said, "I'm not the same here as I am at home. Here, well, I'm very strict but out there, well, I'm normal." Her dual roles or living by two different rules—"strict" and "normal"—highlight the distinction between those who wear a uniform and those who don't. In uniform one enforces rules; out of uniform one leads a "normal" life within the rules. It's interesting to note that when one inverts the name *state police* to *police state*, there is no distinction between "here" and "out there," no distinction between the places of enforcement; the whole state or country becomes a place where rules have to be enforced and order has to be kept. Luz's strong desire to be part of the state police, to be a *policia estatal*, can be viewed as a blending of the two roles she now plays.

Like Flamenco Beach with its abundance of color and texture, beautiful on the surface while scarred by military destruction underneath, the dream of uniformed life holds a promise of paradise which covers the historical work of the military, that is, the work of war. Expressing what the Volunteer Corps has provided for the youths who want to wear the uniform, Alvaro says, "It's a paradise for me and not only for me but for other youths. It has everything, everything, everything."

MAKING PEACE

A voice from the dark called out,
      "The poets must give us
imagination of peace, to oust the intense, familiar
imagination of disaster. Peace, not only
the absence of war."
                  But peace, like a poem,
is not there ahead of itself,
can't be imagined before it is made,
can't be known except
in the words of its making,
grammar of justice,
syntax of mutual aid.
             A feeling towards it,
dimly sensing a rhythm, is all we have
until we begin to utter its metaphors,
learning them as we speak.
             A line of peace might appear
if we restructured the sentence our lives are making,
revoked its reaffirmation of profit and power,
questioned our needs, allowed
long pauses . . .
             A cadence of peace might balance its weight
on that different fulcrum; peace, a presence,
an energy field more intense than war,
might pulse then,
stanza by stanza into the world,
each act of living
one of its words, each word
a vibration of light—facets
of the forming crystal.

CHAPTER 11

Peace, Justice, Development: The Complex Workings of Social Change

Passion, commitment, focus, persistence—these are the words that come to mind when I think about the youths who talked about their work specifically as a place and process of psychological and social change.[1] Work for these youths is inseparably linked to making what Mel King (1981) calls "a chain of change." These young men and women do not make a separation—there is no commuting—between what they do for work and how they view the world; the work they do is interwoven with their visions of what the world ought to be but is not. In this chapter, the narratives of four youths are included as illustrative of this complicated process: Renzo from the Jesuit Seminary, Sandra from ADT, and Migna and Rana from PECES.

For the Jesuits, the process of coming to terms with what they call their "calling"—*el llamado*—involved a complex movement toward uniting their hearts and minds with the work of helping the hearts and minds of poor and struggling people. This was a slow and deliberate process, no bolt of lightning and a promise to become a priest, and was filled with intense self-questioning and reflection. But once the decision was made they all expressed a combination of good feelings; they felt "calm," "joyous," "like a *fiesta* inside myself," "complete security," and they all said that they felt "at peace." They expressed how peace, tranquility, freedom, and liberation are central elements of their work. They all spoke of how when one works on something one loves there is a process of growth and of liberation.

These young men spend much of their time thinking and talking about, reflecting on, and studying issues of community, work, and love. Their narratives show their deep process of engagement with these issues. Work and love are their bread and butter. Like

COMMUNITY SPHERE
Punta Santiago
Afro-Panameños
Marginalized people

KINSHIP SPHERE
Family members killed
Family involved in
same work
Community
experienced as family
Education seen as
central to changing
conditions
Women and men
participate as agents of
social change
Participants did not
have children

ECONOMIC
SPHERE
Educators,
cultural workers,
community-based
leaders, *jovenes
creadores, lideres,
coordinadores,
Jesuita,* lawyers,
senators

POLITICAL SPHERE
Liberation theology
Legal system favors the privileged
Belief that political structures can be changed
Political transformation linked with personal changes
and development

Internal liberation
Social justice
Helping those in need
Individual responsibility for change on many levels
Decisions about work made with awareness of political and
community interactions as well as individual consequences

Figure 11.1
Moment in Identity: Work and Individual and Social Change

Martin Luther, in his time, the young men are making a reforma-
tion in the Catholic church; they are within the revolutionary
Christianity that takes place in Latin America in the form of liberation theology. Luther's formulation of *opera manum dei* is
clearly elaborated in their narratives. In their own lives they are in
the process of formation in the *noviciado,* the novitiate.

PECES is also a Catholic organization which is grounded in
the social justice perspective of liberation theology where *comunidades de base,* or community-based action, is a critical focal

point. For the youths working in PECES, the concept of community is a central one that is both a guiding principle—an ideal—and a geographic place made up of the relationships between people working toward social change. Community for these youths is local and national, and their work is situated at the borders where their community meets society, where a neighbor meets another, where a teacher works with children, where people get together to better their lives, where love meets injustice.

All these youths share a *frontera* where ideals meet with the realities of oppression and are struggled with in ways that benefit the community; this is the daily work of development. Their *frontera* is a place of psychological and political struggles, a place where political, economic, kinship, and community relations are interlocking and engaged with intensively for the purpose of individual and collective change (see Figure 11.1).

Sandra wants to study law and become a judge or legislator. A knowledge of the rules governing the democracy is critical to being able to change what is not right. From her own perspective of moving through the world physically challenged and the *barreras* that she has encountered, she has gained a view of what has to be removed to gain access to justice.

RENZO

Renzo is twenty-five. He is of African descent and from a large family in Colon, Panama. Colon is a city in northern Panama where many Afro-Panamanians live. In a conversation after the interview, Renzo told me that he lost two brothers in the U.S. invasion of Panama, not because they were in the military but because "the bullets were flying in every direction." They were two of the hundreds of innocent Panamanian civilians killed by crossfire. He was serene when telling about his loss but said that it was traumatic for his whole family at the time. They were young, too. One was a teacher. After expressing my sympathies for his family and feeling enraged inside, I said to him that the killing of civilians wasn't highlighted on the news or in the newspapers. Renzo responded that this is part of the silence, invisibility, and marginalization he wants to work against. We talked about the invasions of our countries by the U.S. military, what it means to us and to the future of our *pueblos.*

Renzo, at the time of the interview, was beginning his studies and work at the seminary:

> Well, we, as you know, we are right now in a period of formation, the novitiate for now is a period of formation, that is, we are preparing for that concrete work that initially attracted us. It's something that I felt passionately about not only to accompany people which is the case in this religious work but also to accompany people in their needs, internal and spiritual or those needs that are a little profound that well maybe they are not too material if I can say it that way on the one hand, but on the other hand to accompany people also in their material needs, like at two levels. Last year I obtained my associate license in economics in Panama and then what had motivated me because I'm fascinated by economics, what had motivated me to study economics was the environment of poverty that is lived within my city, in the city of Colon that is located in the northern side of Panama. It was an environment where there is much unemployment, much violence, much delinquency, and then I felt like one feels like *caramba* one has to do something and it's partly that one was born there and that one sees that there are so many people that don't have hope, that are losing like an option of a good life. We saw that the economic structures themselves that are part of the whole country made many of the problematics of Colon were based on economics. And so my option was well to study economics to see if at least the field of economics had the kinds of concrete elements at the theoretical or practical levels that I could as a professional make a contribution.

Renzo's passion for investigating the structural ways that economics breaks hope and destroys the option of a good life was a response to his own conditions. As with the youths at ADT and the Volunteer Corps who gave examples of work that they would like to do that are clearly related to their own immediate needs, physical and emotional, Renzo's decision to study economics was based on the economic "problematics" that he grew up with. But unlike the youths at ADT and the Volunteer Corps, Renzo clearly articulates the connections between his own experiences of poverty and his fascination with economics. Renzo engages the connections between his material conditions and their relation to the economic system, his own psychology, and his choice of work: by doing this he exposes the politics which generate and sustain poverty and racism.

Making these connections enables Renzo to feel that he has the capacity to change the structures that oppress him and gives him an awareness of himself as someone who is able to make changes both within and outside himself. This awareness was empowering and a source of transformation which he wants to share with others through his religious work:

> If I tell you right now what is concretely and passionately a part of me now besides economics it's trying to learn deeply how to help someone, concretely and in general, like in that place that internal liberation that sometimes we are missing. I say that sometimes it's an internal liberation that sometimes like it gets shaped from outside at the educational level and at the level of our religious thoughts, like we sometimes feel and then we have to work to liberate ourselves to then be able to be the people we want to be. It's an internal liberation through transmitting a little of my experience to them. My personal experience that I have lived and felt like something that has helped me, sharing with others. Also sharing the reality of another person, their life experience too, that is working to know people, knowing how they live, how they suffer, what their joys are like, and through this it's like a mutual exchange that brings out something new that is useful.

Renzo has been through this process of getting to know himself and others as a way to "internal liberation." When he was studying economics he felt that he was finding a way to directly contribute to the welfare of his society and to improve the quality of his own life. Renzo felt that this was a good combination, although looking back he also says that it was "egocentric" in the way that he was preparing to "be an economist, have a good job, have a good house, and a life living quietly" but "it didn't give me the complete internal peace, the internal security that I was doing what I really felt called to be and it began to come out, all of that vocation and all."

Even after Renzo came to an awareness of what he wanted to do and why, he still had doubts. He began to feel the call of religious life. Part of this was his participation in a youth group that concentrated on learning more about their African roots. For Renzo this process of historical and personal investigation put him in touch with another kind of passion, the passion to directly help people of African descent. He felt that as an economist he wouldn't get close enough to people he wanted to help and finally realized that economics, although fascinating and a field of study that held a key to understanding structural violence, didn't "touch" him. Renzo describes his experience of learning about his African roots:

> Since I'm black, then we have, sometimes there are certain prejudices that are in society in terms of people of color, then, concretely there I felt a very strong impulse to work for the specific problematics of Afros, it was like a passion that absorbs you, that you want to learn, that you want to study the roots of the problem, that you want to give alternatives but that everything is focused and that you see that this serves you as north, it serves you as a light, it serves you as a guide, a magnet, no, and then for a moment well, there was like that an interest a curiosity but then when I saw what touched me, what touched so many people living in Panama. I say I only can describe it as a passion that leads you to canalize everything, all your efforts.

In finding this "passion that absorbs," Renzo was brought to another level in his search for work that he could feel sure was what he was called to do. This is the historical one: the place where he joined with, not only those alive with him, but also those who had died before him and their particular place in the story of human being. Renzo, throughout his narrative, talks about "levels" and the interrelationships between his personal experiences and his work. Through his investigation of Afro-Panamanian history he came upon his own historical moment, his own place in history.

Renzo is on the cover of the *National Catholic Reporter* (June 15, 1990), and an article about him and another young Jesuit novice, "Latin American novices link faith, justice," is inside. The reporter describes Renzo and his journey this way:

> Martin Renzo Rosales, a thin, shiny-eyed, black youth, intended to marry and have a family. He was socially conscious, had grown up poor with 11 brothers and sisters in urban Colon, Panama, and discovered rural poverty on a youth trip sponsored by Salesians . . . In addition to the rural experience the desperation of the Colon slums kept prodding Rosales. His meeting after Mass one day with Jesuit Father Fidel Sancho moved him on to his present path. (p. 30)

Renzo expresses that he had an "inquietude," a restlessness, and "spiritual agitation" that he describes as "the process of the calling of religious life" that didn't subside until he joined the Jesuits. The experience of the "slums" and poverty more than "kept prodding" Renzo. It kept him in a profound process of reflection, lasting over the course of three intense years, on where to put his passion to work. Upon entering the novitiate, he began to feel that he had finally come to the place where it all came together, the place where something caught. But at first he was frightened:

> Then at the beginning I was scared, but the curious thing was and for me it was the clearest external thing to know that I had done the right thing was the moment I made the decision, "Yes, I'm going to try it," I had an authentic sensation of internal peace and it was like completely in tune then what it was that I was going to do. I didn't feel that what's called, that inquietude for my future, for example that I felt when I was studying economics, no, or when I made the decision to study economics, when by the fact of my uncertainty about my future like I made myself a lot of plans. I'd say, "Well, if I don't find a scholarship then I'll go to work, if I don't get this then I'll keep going to the university," that is, always looking for something to tie myself to because of the insecurity. In turn, now I'm not sure how I'm going to do this, maybe I'll die before I begin to feel fulfilled but I feel that right now, after making the decision I feel calm, like at peace with myself and I feel like it's through here that everything is canalized that throughout my life and my history, things that consciously and unconsciously have begun to unite and that now are fulfilled, yes, it's this way, and I felt that all my being is going that way.

For Renzo, the Jesuit novitiate was the place where his personal history—the economist from Colon—could join his passion for justice and internal liberation, and in turn this could join the historical moment through his work with those whom he loves, Afro-Panamanians who live in poverty.

I recently received a long letter from Renzo, who is now in El Salvador where the death squads continue to do their work. Renzo is studying for his master's degree, continuing his journey toward becoming a Jesuit priest and teaching mathematics to seventh graders. He writes:

> This year a little while after finishing the school year the father of one of my students was assassinated at the time he was taking his other child to another school in this city. As I understand it, this means that my student is now a complete orphan because

her mother was assassinated several years ago . . . But in spite of all this, I like the spirit of struggle, work, and hope of so many of the people here in El Salvador. Here in spite of all the pain, people maintain a sense of humor and the will to not be beaten down.

SANDRA

Sandra walked in supporting herself with a cane and I noticed that she had trouble walking. Sandra is seventeen years old. At the time of the interview she was working at ADT as her summer job. She made this clear to me before we started the interview, and at first I wasn't sure why she went out of her way to tell me this. But as the interview went on I could see that she had wanted to underline that her long-range plans are different, that she doesn't see herself as part of an agency. On the contrary, she sees herself as an agent of change.

Sandra is in her junior year of high school and planning upon graduation to enter college. Sandra says she is "very motivated to study law, to be a lawyer." Sandra views work this way: "Work for me is a way that human beings have, a person has, to contribute with their abilities to society, and also, well, try to not become a useless person, but instead help oneself and other people through work because if one doesn't work, well, one becomes a person, well, that doesn't value herself and it's a way to increase one's self-esteem when one sees that one is truly useful." Sandra uses the word *util* (useful) to describe what she would like to be through her work. She wants to be of use, to not be *inutil* (useless), which, in Puerto Rico, is often used to describe people who are not able to care for themselves because of, for example, illness, disability, or age. *Inutil* is also a word that conveys a lack of hope and giving up. Without work a person becomes "useless," but through work one can have "self-esteem" because one sees that "one is truly useful." I wonder about this use of vocabulary to describe what work means for her, how she has picked up these words, and why. Sandra's view gives a glimpse of the psychological process that accompanies loss of work because of the heavy social burden of having to be of use primarily through working. I wonder if she has feared this for herself and what battles she has fought.

When I ask her what work she feels love for, Sandra responds: "I feel much love for my studies and well, because I have several goals and I know that it's that way that I'll be able to reach them and I like when I see that my efforts are rewarded and I like it." Both her parents are lawyers but Sandra says that they have never pressured her or in any way made her feel that she had to study law. She says that they have always let her "be free" in her choices for the future. When I asked her who had supported her in her interest in law, Sandra responded with:

> Well, my parents are lawyers and obviously I was raised in that environment all the time but that I have realized that, for example, my abilities are not in the areas of mathematics, for example, it's not that I don't understand them or anything like that it's just that I've always excelled more in the areas of literature, of languages, in letters, and well, I have a lot of ability in talking and expressing myself, that's what a variety of people have told me and well, that was what like what put me on the path towards that.

Sandra also said that she has "always had many social preoccupations." This has meant that she needed to find the best way that she could contribute to solving the problems that she sees in Puerto Rico:

> I'm attracted to law because I believe that the person who knows the laws can contribute a great deal to change a lot of things and avoid being pushed and run over and much oppression for many people. I see it as a good way to contribute a little to society . . . I'm very concerned with the state of the country, the conditions of life of people, the social inequalities and it seems to me, it seemed to me that for me to be able to help, to contribute something with respect to that well, I had to know the system and to know the system, well, it seems to me that knowing the law and the ways it is implemented well, that it's the best way that I can contribute in some way, and well, really I haven't had any experience even though my parents are lawyers, I've never had the opportunity to go to the court, for example, I've never seen a trial but I think that I could do good work in that area.

Like Renzo, Sandra feels that a central step on the path to helping people achieve social justice is to learn how the inequalities are systemically structured: "to know the system." For both of them this takes the form of a formal educative process—degree programs. For Renzo it was an associate's degree and license in economics; for Sandra, a law degree after studying her bachelor's. Neither one ever expresses that the difficulties they have encountered in their individual ways are their own fault; by accurately identifying the structures of social injustice they feel they will be able to change what is at fault, the socioeconomic system.

Sandra feels that she's strongly connected to her community in San Juan and to her country. And although she has not been in court or witnessed a trial, she already has, over the last three summers, been contributing to making life more equal for young people. Sandra talked about her physical challenges in relation to how she participates in her community: teaching children with "physical impediments to swim and develop a kind of manual ability that I well, already have learned."

As to her work at ADT during the summer, Sandra connects what she's doing with the community. In her narrative there is a class-based bias which illustrates a moment when two social categories meet—physical challenge and economic class:

> Well, the work here is well, I know that I'm at a government agency, I know it's important, it's very important, this agency is part of the state, it's the base of the rest of the community and above all else in the area in which I'm working, the disbursement of payments, it's something that's very important to keep motivating the employees so they will make a real effort to serve the community and I see that as important.

Sandra believes that being paid is very important to motivate "employees" to work in a community and, clearly, it is important to young people to make money for *sustento* and to *sobrevivir*. But there's more to what she is saying. Underlying this view of work is a stereotype about young people who are employed through ADT, that they only get motivated for a paycheck. Sandra sees the agency as "the base of the rest of the community." Her view is grounded in the agency's role as a funding source for community employment—giving a picture of funding as the central motivation for community development. Yet the youths at PECES, who are actively involved in community development and who do receive funding from ADT, express a different reason for working: improving their quality of life in social, psychological, and economic ways.

This is also what Sandra wants to do, but class is getting in the way. Even though Sandra shares a similar commitment to social change with the youths at PECES and has similar questions about where to put her energies to work, she reduces the importance of work for people who work in communities to a paycheck. As a youth employed for the summer, in high school, and with plans and the resources for college and a profession, Sandra is in a more privileged position than the other youths at ADT. Her experience of oppression and "being run over" is based on her physical challenges but not on economic class. Yet the phrase *more privileged position* is problematic when brought to Sandra's difficulty in walking, pointing to the complexity of social categories.

Sandra is caught in a complicated place. The work she wants to do, is similar to the work that many people working in community-based projects want to do and she has experienced *barreras*. Yet, perhaps because she doesn't have the personal experience of class oppression, she holds a stereotypical view of why youths who are poor work in communities. At this *frontera* is an opportunity to critically question how Sandra came to this view and how this is linked with a capitalist ideology.

Sandra has also considered being a psychiatrist "because it seems to me that it's very interesting to analyze the human mind, the reasons why people have certain attitudes, and all that." Her interest in understanding "certain attitudes" points to the personal dimension of change that is as necessary as the structural one: the ability to focus on the system as the source of injustice and then how this connects with individual problems runs throughout Sandra's narrative. Both Sandra and Renzo identify these two levels of social change, the personal and the structural, but in different ways. Sandra views analyzing attitudes as a process where she could learn about other people, and Renzo views it as an internal process where he learned about himself.

When she was a child, Sandra's "dream" was to be a doctor, later a psychiatrist, and finally a lawyer:

> My dream when I was little was to become a doctor of medicine but then, well, suddenly I found that I began to find out that the areas of study that were included in medicine well, were the areas of study that I was really less interested in, that is to say, that medicine well, is like a world that is very apart in terms of that one is not in contact with the social problems of people that there are and I, well, felt inclined towards that kind of problem and I real-

ized that was not my path and that there had to be an area that could get into those problems and I realized that it could be law, just like it could be many other field because psychology deals with a lot with that type of problem, the individual problems of a person that can be general social problems of a whole community but that's why those two careers attracted me.

Although medicine also lends itself to what you want to do.

Hmm, yes, there are always ways that one can contribute in any kind of field.

Sandra makes connections between psychological and social problems. She links the two together, realizing that one is affected by the other. But for Sandra, the study of medicine is not connected to social problems: she views medicine as disconnected to the daily struggles of people. Yet young people who are ill and poor could definitely be helped by a doctor. On the other hand, Sandra sees how the law touches everyone and how it clearly presses harder on oppressed people. At the end, she agrees that actually there are many ways to participate in social change through work in any field. The challenge seems to be making the complex connections between one's work and change.

Sandra sees herself as being able to change things by knowing how the system works and then using her skills and knowledge as a lawyer to change what is unfair. Pointing to her awareness of the importance of politics in how the social structure is formed and reformed, Sandra also sees herself as "pursuing some kind of political career, or getting to be a judge, or legislator, or in whatever branch of that area."

RANA

Rana is one of several young people who are called *jovenes creadores*—creative youths—at PECES. The creative youths are young leaders within the community-based project and are responsible for organizing and carrying out a variety of activities, for example, sports and recreation, literacy and math, cheerleading, and community events. Their work involves outreach to parents, collection of information on community needs and problems, working with each other to coordinate the different services available through PECES, and working closely with Sister Nancy, who is the project director, Migna, who is the community coordinator, and José, who is the program coordinator. Everyone who works within PECES is a community member, even Sister Nancy: she lives on the second floor of a small house that also has offices and is a meeting place.

Rana is twenty years old and has been working in PECES since he was fifteen. His name literally translated means "frog" and is a nickname. Several times during the interview he would refer to himself as Rana and then remind me that this is his nickname, but how could I forget? When I asked him what work means to him, his answer was directly linked to his work at PECES. Indeed, all the young people at PECES responded to the first interview question in his way; they explained the meaning of work through a concrete description of what they do at PECES. In this way they revealed an alignment between "the real" and "the ideal" which was absent from the youths' definitions at ADT and the Volunteer Corps:

> Well, work for me in the PECES project is to develop other leaders, well, so that in the future, well, there will be good leaders in the community and that they'll know how to deal and that they'll know about from the beginning, since they are children, the problems that exist in the community and that they'll be able to involve themselves, that is, in the problems and know the problems and be able to work to solve them.

When I ask Rana about which work he feels love for, his response is also directly connected with his work at PECES:

> For what work do I feel love? Okay, well, for this one, and especially for the *muchachos*, in this work I especially direct myself towards the *muchachos*, the little children, who are the future, well, because I see all the needs and all the problems that there are in this community and I have, you know, I have cousins, nephews and nieces and I wouldn't like that they take the bad path, you know, same as the others and especially I direct myself towards the children. Work with the *muchachos* so that, you know, they'll be at least, I'm coordinating the recreation and my work is primarily my work is in sports, you know, with the *muchachos* keeping them busy after their studies and tutoring to maintain them busy so that they don't go down another path.

Rana's primary responsibility is coordinating the recreation component of PECES. He sees sports as a critical part of community development because of how a game can bring parents together with their children when other activities haven't been able to. Games also keep children "busy" and off the wrong path. Rana discovered that there was a need for organized recreation when a group from PECES did an assessment of community needs. It was through this process of asking people what the problems were and what was needed that he found the place where he could go to work:

> At the beginning, well, we did some interviews to see what were the needs of the community and one of the greatest needs what well, recreation, you know, there wasn't a recreation area and then there was a lot of dropping out of school, a lot of vandalism, you know, a lot of drugs and alcohol, you know, little children were already in that dynamic and then we saw this and thought, look, well, that is one of the most important needs to attract children and their parents, you know, to unite the community so that there can be more unity and more cooperation in the community. Then I said well, I'll take the recreation area, it's an area I know a lot about, you know, an area that I have a good handle on, you know, because I played, I play and I like sports and I know a little about sports and well, I directed myself towards that and I said well, I'm going to deal, you know, mainly with that, you know, deal with what I think is one of the most important needs. And I directed myself towards that and to the *muchachos* with the same love that they give me, you know, love that they have given me has made me keep falling in love, you know, with these things and I keep struggling and dealing with it and so far I've been here four years and I think I'll keep on dealing.

Through an organized process of investigating the community needs, Rana was able to connect his talents with what was needed to solve the problems. He easily connected with the need for recreation and took this up with a steady focus, which he describes as a process of "falling in love."

Rana has found that sports are the best way of getting parents to come and watch their kids and in this way get them interested in becoming more involved in their education and the community. He organized a baseball team made up of children between the ages of nine and twelve. For him winning is not the point of the games, and he specifically organized the team around a philosophy that did not stress winning but, rather, recreation as a good way for children to travel to communities and make friends in other *barrios*. The kids, however, want to win. At the time of the interview they hadn't lost a game; they were 16 to 0. Rana was concerned that when they lose he's going to have to be patient and cheer them up because they will "feel down when they lose." In some ways he looks forward to them losing so that they will know what that feels like, "that all the time is not winning."

Rana is fully engaged in his work at PECES. When I ask him about alternatives he has considered, his response is not about personal choices for himself but what kinds of things he can get for the project:

> In terms of my work? Okay, as a matter of fact I've thought about a bunch of things, you know, because in terms of the area in which I work well, I've thought about that the *muchachos* ought to have a park for, you know, a recreation park, a park. And we've talked about that to try and form that so that the *muchachos* will be occupied because I see that sports is one of the most important things to *muchachos* and it's a way to unite the parents in this community because there isn't unity in terms of the parents, unity is needed to make a school for the *muchachos* and it's very few parents that, you know, they stay watching the soap opera or they go only three or four times, you know, and I see that one of the ways of uniting parents is sports because when I invite parents to a meeting about the baseball team fifteen parents come, you know, that is something and I say *contra* well, sports are a medium, I think a facilitator to unite the community.

Rana became involved in PECES when he was fifteen years old and in tenth grade. After working a summer job through ADT cleaning up vacation cabins, he was unemployed but wanted to continue working summers. A friend of his told him about the project and said that Sister Nancy was conducting interviews. He felt timid about going to the interview because he didn't know her personally even though he did know about her, for example, that she came from the United States and that she had established herself in the community. But Rana went and interviewed and says, "Luckily, they took me."

He started that summer, and through a series of *charlas*—talks—he received orientation in PECES with other youths who came in as "young leaders." Rana was the youngest in the group and felt unable to participate because he felt "blocked" by his own "shyness." Over the course of the summer, though, he gained confidence and went out into the community to do a survey, and it was then that he was caught:

> I fell in love with the community because I saw because I saw that there were problems in the community and you know, I had a consciousness of what was going on there, I had thought that there were only a few little things going on but I didn't know that so much was going on.

For example?

> For example in this community that is so small the number of businesses that sell alcoholic beverages, you know, the amount of alcoholism came out, the amount of drug addiction that came out, the amount of school dropouts, the amount of vandalism, you know, one sees all this and says *contra*, you know, with all of us here and so we went to deal with these situations and we were stuck, you know, the youths themselves and I see this group of youths and they want to deal with those problems and well, that makes you fall in love, you know, that was the point where one says, *contra* I'm going to work, you know, and one goes little by little, little by little, and the affection that one receives well, one keeps falling in love with the problems themselves and makes a bigger effort, one sacrifices because sometimes I come in at 9 in the morning and leave and at 10 at night . . . When I started I didn't have, I didn't know how to stand up in a group or express myself, I was even afraid, you know, my own shyness blocked me and I put a lid on my growth, you know, and that's why that I thank the PECES project because it has itself helped me as a person and it's helped me to develop other people.

Throughout Rana's narrative the phrase "falling in love" appears as an explanation of how he feels about his work. But he also expressed that to work with young people one has to be "patient" and that it's "not at all easy." One has to have "certain self-control" and "have certain values" and be "an example." All those add up to a lot of hard work.

Rana points to how change is risky and invites feelings of vulnerability. Like Renzo, Rana felt afraid of beginning something new; he was the youngest, and feeling blocked by his own shyness was unable to express himself. But Rana remained within the group and over time began to change. Pointing to the role of courage as critical in making changes, both Renzo and Rana expressed that feelings of fear were part of their process of coming to the work they love.

Rana feels that he has developed through his work and has helped other youths in the community to develop. Rana's growth includes confidence, which gave him the security to speak out and the ability to be a leader to other youths. He achieved this through an interactive process that began with assessing the needs of his community, which gave him a clearer view of his own needs, of where he felt "blocked" and unable to grow, where he was "stuck." The survey revealed the extent of the problems of alcoholism and drug addiction in the community and made the excessive amount of liquor stores abundantly clear.

In the future, Rana sees himself continuing to work for the community as a recreational leader, which is what gives him the most satisfaction. Rana says that he enjoys having everyone in the community know who he is, that everywhere he goes kids will say, "Hey, Rana! Look, Rana!" and that his girlfriend is impressed and has said to him, "But it looks like you're a governor or a mayor!" This echoes Sandra's knowledge that politicians have power to make change and her desire to be a legislator, perhaps a senator. Sometimes kids will go to the school windows and shout "Hello!," and the teachers ask, "Who is Rana?" The teachers don't know what the kids know; there's someone in the community that loves them and has dreams of making a park that is green, open, growing, with space to move. And Rana's name reminds me of another prince that loved transformation.

MIGNA

Downstairs, on the front yard of the house where Sister Nancy lives and which is also a center, the *muchachas* are practicing moves, the tape is blaring disco funk, I can feel the base line vibrating, and there's a lot of shouting that sounds like numbers being counted and words being spelled. I walk out onto the roof, which doubles as a porch, and look down. The young women are moving to the music, waving pom-poms and shouting: I see the PECES cheerleaders. These are some of the young women Migna has been working with over the last several years.

Migna is the community coordinator and previously had been an intercessor in PECES. As the community coordinator Migna is in charge of maintaining "contact with the parents of the *mucha-chos*, meetings in the community with the groups that have orga-nized in the community." Migna is also one of several intercessors who are a central part of PECES. An "intercessor" is a young per-son who is a resource person and works as a kind of liaison between teachers, parents, and youths to facilitate communica-tion. An intercessor also gives support to youths who, for exam-ple, need help getting out of drugs or alcohol. The intercessor helps by linking them with available services. At the time of the interview, Migna, who is twenty-five years old, had been working in PECES for five years.

Migna became involved with PECES when she left college after two years of studying business administration. The reasons she gives for leaving college are "personal problems and well, I couldn't continue my studies." I didn't pursue the details and Migna didn't say anything further about this. After leaving her studies, she began to look for work. Like Rana, Migna heard that interviews were being held for positions in PECES. Migna was interested in PECES because she had been part of a "society of youths" in her church where there was one young man who was active in his community. He would bring the "society of youths" to see the community work he was doing. This was "key" for Migna:

> There was a *muchacho* that was always involved in the dynam-ics of community and always would bring us to the communi-ties, to see how poor communities could develop, how they got organized and all that and that was really key for me because that was when I began to be interested in everything about poor communities, about the base community development and that motivated me, you know.

Already having an interest in community development, Migna went to be interviewed and was offered a job as a tutor. After one year of working as a tutor she was then given more responsibility as the supervisor of the youth leaders, but left PECES after six months of being the supervisor for work at a bank. She later returned to PECES and worked as an intercessor for four young women between the ages of eleven and sixteen. Migna outlines her process of involvement in PECES:

> I felt that this work reached inside of me and I began to work with them as a tutor, giving them support in school, well, having

a relationship of friendship with them , and well, you know, try-ing to integrate myself more with their families. And after that I wasn't an intercessor anymore because the position of commu-nity coordinator came up and well, I went on to be the commu-nity coordinator that is more about dealing with the preadoles-cents, too but then also dealing with the intercessors that also youths have their problems, they study, and they also have jobs, they have their pressures, sometimes they come and come frus-trated because the *muchachos* are not responding, well, and you have to deal with that and well, I feel that I'm a double interces-sor because I have to intercede with the younger ones, they inter-cede with the younger ones but we then have to make a positive effort for them and well, try that they not get frustrated because the *muchachos* are learning now and maybe it won't be for three or four years that the results will be seen because the results are not going to be immediate.

Like Sandra, Migna also speaks of civil rights and views her work as related to reclaiming them. Just like what Rana felt he went through as a process of growth, Migna expresses her thinking about her work and community development and describes it as a process of gaining a "voice" and the ability to "stand up" and say "Enough!"

The best work that I can do is in my community, is in the place where I was born, is teaching the people that they can develop, that they can get an education, that they can, well, organize themselves to resolve the problems that are here and there are many, that they can stand up and say "Enough!" and reclaim their rights, that their civil rights are not stepped on and educate the people so that they have a voice, you know, of theirs that they can and that they can decide the way they want to live.

Migna herself has had to stand up and say "Enough." When she was working at a bank, which is what her education was prepar-ing her for, she found herself overwhelmed by the pressure to be someone she was not:

In the bank I felt suffocated, well, with a lot of pressure, demanding more and more and more and like that my personal life, my, what is human about me wasn't any good, what was good was the machine part, the person who produces, the per-son that does the work well, if you didn't do it well then you were reprimanded, but that Migna as a human being, wasn't any good, she was nothing in that bank . . . When I would get home

I didn't feel any satisfaction, I felt frustrated, and I lived through moments that were very disillusioning. It was a very negative experience for me and I still have it, you know, I feel it.

How long did you work there?

Eight months, almost a whole year living that very frustrating experience.

And what was that got you out of it? Was it a day you said "okay, that's it?"

Well, I resigned, you know, well, I didn't feel comfortable, it was a decision that I made really to please my father and my mother that they wanted me to leave PECES because of reasons of that they thought that, you know, that working in a small community group that it was I don't know, that one isn't going to progress, that one isn't going to learn anything else, and that one doesn't grow, and that was the pressure, "You have to find better work. You have to make more money. You have to" and then I even told my father that I couldn't handle the job any longer and he said "no" that I had to continue and that I should keep trying even though he supported me, you know, like that yes I could do it, but he didn't understand that it wasn't for me, that it wasn't, that I wasn't developing in that way. And well, you know, until I said "Enough, I can't anymore!" you know, it was like a routine life, that you, that they would get there and it wasn't with any kind of joy, or anything, they would get there with long heavy faces, and I got that face too, you know, and I started getting there like that too. I got to feeling like a robot.

The feelings of being pushed to the edge to "produce" erupted one afternoon when Migna's accounts didn't add up and she was accused of stealing the money. She felt at the "edge of her nerves and of crying" and had problems with other people who worked at the bank because she says, "They treat you like a machine, you know, like a machine and it's produce and produce and produce and produce and nothing else." This was her moment of crisis:

One explodes, you know, a moment comes when there are many people that can't get out because they have children, because they think about how else are they going to support them, that's a secure job. I didn't have any of those pressures, I'm single and I don't know, well, I said "Enough, I can find other work and I can progress in something else" and I was looking for work for eight months and I found that job and I thought so I'll stay here for eight months but I couldn't deal with it. It doesn't satisfy me as a person.

Migna felt terrible after she resigned because she felt that she had wasted her education and all the effort she made to get the work at the bank. She said to herself, "Look, I'm no good, what I studied isn't worth anything" and she felt bad and frustrated. But she continued her ties to PECES through being on the executive board, which was central to her feeling better because she became fully involved with community work again. Lately, Migna says that she has been "thinking a lot" about going back to school to study what she feels brings out the best in her, social work. She says that she has the "practice" and now feels that it would be helpful to learn "theory" and "technique."

No longer feeling treated like a "machine," Migna feels that she is useful and good in the work she does to help young women to develop:

> Well, I feel that, here well, I give of my life experiences, you know, I've had problems just like all the preadolescents who are downstairs right now, I had *lagunas* in my development too just like them. I was able to overcome them by way of the church, by way of PECES when I came here, and all that I learned and like I developed myself during the years when I was in PECES and the church, in the group dynamics, the leader development, leadership, community development and all that, well, it has brought me to discover that I have a lot to give, you know, I have a lot to offer them, I have a lot to teach them, that can take them to the goals that they define for themselves in life, even though problems will come up, that drugs and alcohol are not an escape because well, I in my situation in my family well, my parents are divorced and I was I had to take charge of my family at a certain time and I didn't opt for drugs, I didn't opt for alcohol, I didn't opt for running away with my boyfriend, that is, and it's knowing to be with your life to make with your life a work so that they well, can see that your life even though you had all these problems, goes on and goes on positively.

The relationships that Migna has formed with the younger women are clearly important to her. She feels able to help them in their development because she feels that she has experienced what they are going through. Migna connects her own life experiences with the larger social one. Just as she thinks that poor communities have to say "Enough!" Migna, too, said "Enough" to the institution that was oppressing her by making her work as if she were a machine, leaving her feeling like a robot.

Numb and depressed, Migna resigned only to find herself again depressed and questioning her ability to not waste her life. This was a time of both resignation and standing up for herself. As she stood up for herself and gave voice to her frustration, she "exploded," and this voicing gave rise to her courage to leave. Migna then had to negotiate the difficult terrain of leaving what her parents thought was good work and confronting the disappointing reality that her studies in business administration were not valued at the bank. Migna left behind not only a "secure job" but also a way of being: a place where people are not valued beyond what they can produce. For Migna, this created a crisis of meaning through which she navigated by staying connected to PECES.

All the young people included in this chapter had several commonalities which point to the *fronteras* of where things caught for them. Renzo, Rana, and Migna, expressed that they were single and without children, and that this was related to their ability to do their work because they didn't have that "responsibility." They each faced *barreras* which they are working to break down. For each, to a greater or lesser extent, their decisions about work are also political decisions which connect them as individuals to the broader social structures. These youths articulate the reasons for their choice of work through making the connections between what they feel inside themselves and what is happening in the outside world.

The *frontera* where something catches for Renzo, Sandra, Rana, and Migna is a place where genius not only survives but is a source of psychological and social transformation. For three of the youths, work is also a religious *frontera* where spiritual and material needs meet. Involved in liberation theology and community-based action for justice, their Catholicism is bordered by activism for social change. Aware of how their own psychological development and social lives have brought them to this place, they have the passionate work of leading others to an awareness of how changes—both psychological and social—can be made.

CHAPTER 12

Working Together:
Plotting the Coordinates of Work,
Love, and Identity

When young men and women work on what they love, care deeply about, or just simply like, they feel confident and competent, gain security and independence, and feel satisfied, happy, and needed for what they are able to give to themselves and others. These feelings provide youths, even young people who have been abused, neglected, and victimized, with peace and calmness: *paz y tranquilidad*.

Working out feelings through mixing cement or playing a cello to say what needs to be said: these young people tell stories of a wide range of human experience within the process of finding work that they care about. Gilberto began working when he was nine years old cleaning basements in New York City and is "fascinated" by hard physical labor because he enjoys feeling the "sweat on his forehead" and that he has to "make the effort" and put his body and mind to work. Melania, who is twenty-three years old, studies music, and often feels like an outsider for speaking up and voicing her politics, tells of how playing the cello is a way she can speak out:

> I can scream out and no one tells me to shut up. I play and no one tells me to shut up. On the contrary when you go to talk and everyone starts to stare at you or you go to say a word, I can say anything, I can scream at the world that I'm against them, playing. It doesn't matter where I am, if I'm in Fine Arts, or in a park, or if I'm at home.

For youths who are poor and have children to support, are just getting out of drug violence, have left school in the elementary grades or were told they were not intelligent, or are sick with illnesses that they can't afford to cure, work is a critical support that is needed to face the constant stream of challenges and provide

247

them with *sustento* (sustenance) so they can *sobrevivir* (survive): work is a basic economic necessity.

The difference between the youths who have found what they love and are able to pursue it and those who are searching out work and not yet able to find it can be a good teacher, a supportive family member, a friend, or an illness. But finding work is also a complex meeting of class, race, and gender. The intersections often take the form of institutionalized *barreras* which are so pervasive that the daily struggle of moving through them becomes itself a part of identity development.

Often I was left feeling overwhelmed by the struggles of young people, especially the daily battles of youths who are poor. The chapter on work as a path out of abuse, neglect, and violence was particularly difficult to write. Trauma and its relation to work, love, and identity as experienced by youths is an area that needs further study, more detailed questioning, an attentive ear for clues to violence, further attention to how young people can be helped, and educational processes that support reflection on choices and the reasons why youths choose the work they do.

The chapter on work and gender illustrates the daily makings of tragedy as well as of strength and survival. Identity at this *frontera* is a journey which is difficult to navigate. For these youths, work, love, and identity are a negotiation between "the real"— being poor, getting a GED, having no health care, institutional *barreras*—and "the ideal"—being middle class, educated, and professional, with open access to privilege—within a relentless context of systemic limits. The process of how idealized cultural scripts of femininity and masculinity push both young *hombres* and *mujeres* into roles and particular work is also an area that needs further study, specifically the ways in which constructions of gender both limit and support the identities of young people who are poor.

There is courage and strength evident in all the narratives. Perhaps this is because I interviewed young people who had made it to organizations, youths who were determined to make life better for themselves and their families. Yet I believe that each story speaks for more than just the particular youth. The narratives are bittersweet, painful, and difficult to take in. The cost of becoming an adult was also made clear. The themes map ways out of childhood that provide *sustento* to *sobrevivir*. The themes also map the difficult and sometimes violent terrain from childhood to adulthood, to love and work. These identity crossings mark the *fronteras* where we need to work together.

Nelida, in her "permission for publication" form in the section for "comments," wrote in Spanish: "If the book reaches P.R. and if it's in Spanish because I speak it more than English I would be very happy that there is a book with interviews of youths and then see if the adults understand the youths a little more and don't blame us for everything that happens on the streets etc . . ."

UNSETTLED AND UNSETTLING JUNCTURES

The themes stake out junctures of identity: a kind of psychological terrain where the psyche meets social and historical conditions, where schooling and dreams meet, where genius confronts parental fears, where socioeconomic class collides with gender, where a yearning to be important, useful and needed borders with bureaucratic indifference. These junctures are places where crossings are often made without crossing signs, where there are accidental meetings that move a young person just a little bit further toward that particular work because he or she entered this school and not that one, or a letter from ADT arrived a day late, the happenstance of timing, healing that cannot be explained, a miracle! And she is singing now.

The youths' narratives render a portrait of *las fronteras* as often chaotic and arrived at by accident, by willful determination, by the will to live. The direction each youth takes is influenced by community, family, friends, partners, teachers, priests, and even strangers in the right place at the right time. Each *frontera* is entangled in concrete and imagined *barreras* which constrain explorations of identities. These *fronteras* and the moments in identity point to where and when the deals were struck, the decisions were made, the borders crossed, the alternative routes considered, taken, regretted or not, but taken, who was there to help, and who wasn't. They support a view of identity that is not static or essential but, instead, responsive, forming, and with the capacity to develop and transform—radically, traumatically, incrementally—over time.

There *are* places where something catches, where work and love meet, during youth. Youths do grasp for adult work, and for many something catches. Yet these places are, for the most part, not what Erikson means by "that particular combination." Like young Martin Luther, the youths consider a variety of occupational roles and experiment with alternatives before committing themselves to one occupational identity. But this commitment is precarious; occupational identities are constantly unsettled and changed by the historical and economic conditions within which the youths live. "A sense of knowing where one is going," Erikson's (1959, p. 118) statement of what identity is, emerges out of the negotiations that take place where these interlocking conditions meet. For Latino/a, Puertorriqueña and Puertorriqueño youths these are the border struggles occurring at the margins of the Eriksonian "empty boxes" (Erikson, 1963, p. 272).[1]

Although the schematic diagrams are simplified renditions of complex processes, they do show how within the different narratives there are a variety of identity interactions. For example, the two moments in identity with the most overlap are the ones illustrating narratives of security (military, police) and activism (community, religious, legal). Both moments illustrate an intensive engagement with all the spheres of social life but with different approaches; these youths want to improve the lives of those they care about and to improve their own lives by maintaining the laws already existing or changing the laws and social conditions. Yet political relations are more explicitly engaged by the youths who see themselves as activists for change, whereas the political sphere is not explicitly engaged by the youths who see themselves in a uniform. Illustrating the feelings of isolation that typically follow traumatic events, the moment with the least overlap is "work and trauma." In addition, I think of the schematic diagram of "work and gender" as one that overlies all the others to a greater or lesser extent because all the narratives had within them gender negotiations.

When in these moments in identity and where on these developmental borders can youths and adults meet to create spaces that nourish and support identity? Following is a summary of the *fronteras* that the themes pointed to; all of these are critical meeting places.

The Frontera *of Masculinity and Femininity*

This is where gender roles create enormous pressure for young *mujeres* and *hombres* to envision and follow routes to work based on traditional gender scripts rather than on a wide range of human being. This is a place where educators can provide alternatives, not just in choices of work, but also in views and expressions of gender. As Maxine Greene (1988, p. 3) argues, freedom "is the capacity to surpass the given and look at things as if they could be otherwise." Here, at this intersection of work and gender, is a critical opportunity to open questions about gender and consider new possibilities.

The Frontera *of Independence and Vulnerability*

This is the place where work is a road to physical and emotional survival and independence for youths who have suffered from abuse and neglect. But basing their emotional independence on economic independence still leaves them vulnerable. This is a fragile and precarious place as well as a location of strength built on struggling for survival. The balance between these two is tentative. The wounds of violence still ache, and the losses suffered are interspersed throughout the narratives. This is a place of putting back together what was broken apart and left fragmented by traumatic events.

The Frontera *of Childhood Genius and Adult Work*

This *frontera* illustrates how important it is to listen and take children seriously when they express "what they want to be when they grow up." This is a place that cannot be negotiated at "career days" or by infrequent and brief "guidance counseling." Educators can meet youths here by exploring their own struggles with vocational decisions and their own fears—not tell youths what to do but seriously engage with their own processes and support youths in exploring their genius.

The Frontera *of Creativity and Illness*

This transition is fraught with doubt as well as filled with joy. At this *frontera* is a dangerous crossing of experiences of illness, suicide attempts, parental pressures, and studying for many years in a field that leaves youths on the verge of exploding, feeling like they've wasted time. This is also a place where adult fears meet with childhood dreams and youths' creativity. This place was described vividly by the young musicians with surprising frequency. As artists they have often felt that studying music was a risky decision even though their passion and genius were apparent since childhood.

Community-based activists also struggled at this crossing. Just as there is a lack of economic support for the arts, so too, community-based education is seen as economically marginal. When Migna decided to leave the site of economic wealth (a bank) and return to working with her community, her parents, who had made sacrifices to send her to school, at first did not support her decision and were angry and hurt that she had quit her job as a teller. Whether community-based action or music, the lack of family support was based on a fear of not being able to survive economically. In particular, in music, for at least one youth there was homophobia and the fear that the arts are for political radicals.

The Frontera of Symbolic Work

This is where particular work meets the symbolic and associative logic of the psyche: where work is both a practice—something one does—and a symbol—something that represents what one needs emotionally and physically. Although this was made clearest to me by the young man who doesn't have a place to go and wants the security of a uniform, there were other examples as well: the young man who studied a branch of engineering called instrumentation, until he realized that what he really loved was playing a musical (not mechanical) instrument; the young woman who is ill with a severe cough and suffered an accident that made her have to leave school and who wants to be a nurse; the young woman who has been told that she is slow but would like to be a teacher; and the young woman who was abused and neglected as a child and would like to fly away as a flight attendant.

The Frontera of Individual and Social Change

This is where the individual meets with society for the purpose of transformation, in both psychological and social ways. Perhaps it is this *frontera*, where there is a complex layering of self-reflection on the psychological and social dimensions of human being and civil rights and, then, on how this knowledge can be put to work for the individual and social good, that most closely matches Erikson's interpretation of *opera manum dei*.

This is a place where youths studying or planning to study in a variety of areas (religion, law, community activism) navigate the intersections of individual and social change. These youths see society as a system that needs to be transformed: like young man Luther, they identify systemic injustice and corruption and then position themselves for making social change.

CONSTRUCTING IDENTITIES

> The problem of self-identity is not just a problem for the young. It is a problem all the time. Perhaps the problem. It should haunt old age, and when it no longer does it should tell you that you are dead. (p. vii)
> From *Young Men and Fire*, Norman Maclean, 1992

Norman Maclean was haunted by his search for identity. This is what joins him to this work. Maclean was searching until the very moment he died in 1990, at the age of eighty-seven, fourteen years after he began to write the tragedy of the Mann Gulch fire—the story that would finally tell him about himself as a once young and, then, old man. His manuscript remained unfinished, and the press prepared the book for publication. The publisher writes: "*Young Men and Fire* had become a story in search of itself as a story, following where Maclean's compassion led it. As long as the manuscript sustained itself and its author in this process of discovery, it had to remain in some sense unfinished" (p. vii). Maclean's search for "the story" of the Mann Gulch fire, which killed thirteen young "smoke jumpers," was a recovery of the psychological and physical details of the lives that were devoured by that "blowup": a fire so intense that it knocked the watches off the wrists of the young men. Yet the youths were found kneeling, as if in prayer. Maclean, who lived nearby and had been a forest ranger himself, went to see what had happened. Looking at trees that were still smoldering days later, he was overwhelmed by feelings of loss and was determined to not let the lives of these young forest rangers slip into statistical summaries or into the confusion of the controversy that followed.

Determined to tell the story of the last minutes of their lives, Maclean went back to the gulch twenty-seven years later at the age of seventy-three, because he felt that it was only in the telling that he could honor the young men and turn catastrophe into tragedy: for Maclean felt acutely that the young men knew, in those last horrible minutes when they could no longer fight the fire, that they were going to die young and that, surely, they felt alone and betrayed. Maclean, an old man climbing and reclimbing the steep and rocky gulch, attempts to accompany them by telling their story, as if to insist that they did not die alone, betrayed by the dreams and promises of youth, devoured by fire.

As Maclean searches out the mystery of Mann Gulch he finds his own story of youth; as he comes closer to seeing what the last horrible minutes must have felt like, he moves closer to his own death. Thus the novel is not just a story of a fire that was deadly; it is also the story of Maclean's life and his relentless search to discover a story that could tell him who he had been and who he had become. Maclean's novel is a brilliant illustration of what he himself says: "The nearest anyone can come to finding himself at any given age is to find a story that somehow tells him about himself" (p. 145). Because Maclean has a profound compassion for the young men—which he feels is a form of love—he is able to join with their story and make it his own. Maclean's search for "finding himself" through his attempt to "find a story" illustrates how identity is a "problem all the time," that identity is ongoing. The search for who we were and have become leads to new reflections on who we are, joining us with new stories.

Toward the end of the book, Maclean tells the reader that as he stood on Mann Gulch he could see where the ashes of his wife had been, at her request, scattered. Jesse Maclean died of cancer of the esophagus, he tells us, and said it felt like having her "head under water" (p. 297). Maclean also tells us that a doctor had told him that to die in a "blowup" feels like drowning. This is the way Maclean brings us to another story that he was in search of and perhaps could not tell directly because it was too painful: the story of his beloved companion's death not far from Mann Gulch. He ends by writing:

> I, an old man, have written this fire report. Among other things, it was important to me, as an exercise for old age, to enlarge my knowledge and spirit so I could accompany young men whose lives I might have lived on their way to death. I have climbed where they climbed, and in my time I have fought fire and inquired into its nature. In addition, I have lived to get a better understanding of myself and those close to me, many of them now dead. Perhaps it is not odd, at the end of this tragedy where nothing much was left of the elite who came from the sky but courage struggling for oxygen, that I have often found myself thinking of my wife on her brave and lonely way to death. (p. 301)

Maclean's story is thus many stories in one which meet in the search for the reality of what happened at Mann Gulch. The story of identity for him is many stories of searching, accounting, reckoning, mourning, climbing; the problem of identity is that it leads us in many directions. Perhaps it is also a yearning that in old age all our stories can be told as one. For Maclean, Mann Gulch is the place where something caught.

I caught the youths at a moment in time through interviews and photographs, and they, in turn, told me their story of what had caught them at the time. If Maclean is right, then, I ought to have learned something, not just about the youths but also about myself.

Looking back over my "Postcards from Memory," I can see my struggles with coming to "see" what I saw in new ways: photography was not just a technical process but also a symbolic one. It provided a view of the world that I could hold still, that wouldn't change, as I felt my body changing in mysterious ways. I could turn the plot this way or that way, stitch it together, like Carmen at the sewing machine making up stories as she makes clothes. Taking pictures was a way I could, like Melania, scream and no one could tell me to shut up. It gave me a way to grasp what I needed badly: visibility and stability. When I picked up a camera the world was made visible, and since I was part of the world, I was also visible, especially through self-portraits. I knew at an early age that I was a lesbian and I knew just as clearly that this was not something to tell my family and high school friends. Even now, I still feel the pull of silence and the push toward invisibility; I struggled with the decision to include this part of my story.

I ask myself today, What if at the time someone had asked me why I love photography? What would I have answered? Would I have said that taking pictures helped me make sense of the world? That taking pictures felt like it was saving my life? Would telling the story of photography have helped me to see its symbolic meaning? Who might I have told this to? At what place? Would it have made any difference in the choices I made? The answers to all these questions would be guesses now, but I can't help but wonder what I would have said to a Boricua researcher getting her doctorate from Harvard. What I do know is that at the time the "alternatives" that I am engaged with now (writing this book and including photographs, teaching psychology, working with youths) had never crossed my mind as possibilities.

In identity, the plural *we* as well as the singular *I* is mediated through race, gender, class, and sexuality and constantly interacting with spheres of social life. The specifics of the story are told through this experience: there is no single story of identity. For Latinas/os the negotiation of identity under colonialism is a political process not only of external action but also of internal decolonization, what Paulo Freire (1970, 1973, 1985) calls "critical consciousness." But this process is fraught with ambivalence, especially during youth. The coordinates for traditional alignments are deceptively simple; the gender stories are readily available; the ideology of working harder and harder is in place—have a family, provide, nurture; the military extends its long arm to provide its uniformed security. It is the artists and community activists who refuse these stories.

Constructing identities at *fronteras* of development has critical implications for those of us who are committed to working for educational change with youths. We—and here I mean educators, psychologists, counselors, and anyone who works with educating youths—are also changing and developing. We, too, tell our stories not just to be heard but also to know who we are. Constructing an identity is an ongoing process of knowing and negotiating who we are, of asking ourselves and others new questions. What if those who work with youths critically questioned their own constructions of identity? Their own reasons for doing the work they do? Their own processes of making the work they do meaningful and important?

It would be useful to ask ourselves: What would it mean for the process of educating youth to understand development as *fronteras*—to explore identity as a location of possibility between individual desires and prescriptive norms? The answering of these questions could help us explore the multiple relationships youths and adults have with our work, how these are negotiated, changed, and maintained—always with an eye to how individual visions and institutionalized norms interact to affect our actions, limit or expand the possible, liberate or oppress.

The challenge for us is not simple. The challenge for me is not simple. Working together implies that there is a group and that this group has common interests. Who is this "us"? What are the multiple identities included and excluded in "we" and "us"? Yet, as the youths' narratives illustrate, these groupings are overlapping and also at times conflicting. Making places for dialogue about these overlapping and conflicting relationships (family, school, workplace, community, society) would perhaps uncover places of solidarity where, although agreement may not be possible, critical dialogue about work and love is. Educational places could be sites for questioning and participating in building community, generating new liberating cultural stories, interrogating our needs and wants, taking action against institutionalized *barreras*, opening up questions of identity where each person's genius can be nourished.

Constructing identities is a process of change: developmental, social, and political. The challenge to work together is a challenge to each one's willingness to change, to engage with her or his struggle to tell and listen to the stories of work and love—familiar and strange—and to retrace where she or he has been and gather up where she or he is going. Working together means taking on the risks and vulnerabilities of exploring the places where something catches: the unsettled and unsettling *fronteras* where the unfinished stories of identity are lived.

APPENDIX A:
INTERVIEW QUESTIONS

PART I

1. *For you, what is work? How do you define it? What meaning does it have for you? Please give an example.*
   ¿Para ti , que es el trabajo? ¿Como lo defines? ¿Como tu lo entiendes?Por favor dar un ejemplo.

2. *For you, what is love? How do you define it? What meaning does it have for you? Please give an example.*
   ¿Para ti, que es el amor? ¿Como tu lo defines? ¿Como tu lo entiendes? Por favor dar un ejemplo.

3. *What work do you feel love for? Why?*
   ¿Por cual trabajo tu sientes amor? ¿Por que?

4. *How do you know that you are working on something that you care about?*
   ¿Como tu sabes que estas trabajando en algo que realmente te importa?

5. *How do you feel when you work on something that is important to you or that you love?*
   ¿Como te sientes cuando trabajas en algo que te importa o algo que amas?

PART II

6. *What were the alternatives you considered?*
   ¿Cuales fueron las alternativas que consideraste?

7. *Who helped you find this work? Who gave you support?*
   ¿Quienes te ayudaron encontrar este trabajo? ¿Quien te dio apoyo?

8. *What work would you like to do in the future?*
   ¿Que trabajo deseas hacer en el futuro?

9. *Do you feel that you are a part of a community? Which one? In what ways?*
¿Sientes que eres parte de una comunidad? ¿Cual? ¿De que maneras?

10. *Do you feel that you are a part of a society? Which one? In what ways?*
¿Sientes que eres parte de una sociedad? ¿Cual? ¿De que maneras?

PART III

11. *Could you tell me the story of how you arrived at this work? or here?*
¿Me puedes hacer el cuento de como fue que tu llegaste a este trabajo? o aqui?

APPENDIX B:
INTRODUCTION TO THE VOLUNTEER CORPS AT THE SERVICE OF PUERTO RICO ACT

The youths of Puerto Rico are a source of creative energy in the country and are therefore a fountain of hope for generating the massive effort that Puerto Rico needs to confront crucial problems and make into reality the desires and aspirations of our people.

The problems of Puerto Rican youth, by their nature, magnitude, and complexity, constitute one of the foremost challenges confronting Puerto Rican society, as is evidenced by the following considerations:

1. The high percentage of youths that form the total of the demographics of the country.

2. The increasing index of lack of occupations and unemployment that the country is suffering in general, but that youths find themselves singularly the greatest affected by.

3. The high dropout rate and low levels of school achievement that are generally recorded in the public schools.

4. The limitation of the public school system to provide to youths skills or minimum labor capacities that can facilitate a real opportunity to find employment.

5. The constant lurking of vice and crime that confronts those that suffer from unproductive idleness.

6. The resulting despair and weak motivation for personal excellence, self-help, and community action which is concerted and in solidarity.

These and other problems affect almost all or many of the diverse social groups of our youth, in particular families who are less fortunate, from both the urban and rural areas of the country. Their legitimate claim to opportunities to participate in the welfare of the country and to contribute their love, their creativity, and their work is a painful outcry that our country, through our government, cannot ignore. (pp. 1–2)

Note: The act is in Spanish and English. I only have the Spanish version. This translation is mine.

NOTES

CHAPTER 1. THE CATCH

1. Robert Coles (1964) was one of the first to speak out against the profound limitations of normative labels. Coles gives a moving account of how his training as a psychiatrist failed him in *Children of Crisis*. Boston: Little and Brown. Although much has changed over the last thirty years, I would argue that the ideology which Coles challenges remains firmly in place and thus, Coles' critique is as valid today as it was in 1964.

2. These lines from "Visons of Mexico While at a Writing Symposium in Port Townsend" are reprinted from EMPLUMADA, by Lorna Dee Cervantes, by permission of the University of Pittsburgh Press. © 1981 by Lorna Dee Cervantes.

CHAPTER 2. RETURNING TO A QUESTION

1. I am grateful to Dr. Florence Ladd for kindly sharing a copy of a lecture she gave as part of the Annual Erikson Lectures, Cambridge, MA, 1989. "War as Child's Play" has helped me think more deeply about the transformation of child play into adult work within an Eriksonian framework. Through a case study of her eighteen-year-old son, Ladd retraces Erikson's stages and observes the following developmental modes: builder stage with construction vs. destruction as the conflict; warrior with peace vs. war; historian with the past vs. the future; musician with harmony vs. cacophony; sportsman with enthusiast vs. athlete; collector with objet d'art vs. junk.

2. I wrote up this research study in a paper called "A Dialectic of Change: The Importance of Love and Work in Adolescence," January 1986.

CHAPTER 3. CONCEPTUAL STRATEGIES

1. Mel King, "On Transformation: From a Conversation with Mel King," *Harvard Eductional Review*, 59:4, pp. 504–519. Copyright ©

2. From Chrystos, "Table Manners," in *Not Vanishing* (Vancouver: Press Gang Publishers, 1988), p. 73. Used with permission.

3. From Chrystos, *Not Vanishing* (Vancouver: Press Gang Publishers, 1988), frontispage. Used with permission.

4. Alberto Sandoval Sánchez, "Song of a New York Boy From East 81st.," in *Nueva York Tras Bastidores/New York Backstage* (Santiago, Chile: Editorial Cuarto Proprio, 1993), p. 4. Used with permission.

5. The body of work by liberation theologians in Latin America is large and diverse. For example, private journals of revolutionary Christians and analytical works by theologians have been published under the heading of liberation theology. Some critical works are *Teologia de la liberación: Perspectiva verdad e imagen* (1987) and *We Drink from Our Own Wells: The Spiritual Journey of a People* (1985) by Gustavo Gutierrez, the foremost writer in this field; the life and homilies of Saint Oscar Romero, murdered in El Salvador in 1980; the work of Bishop Pedro Casaldaliga, *Prophets in Combat* (1987); and *Guerrillas of Peace: Liberation Theology and Central American Revolution* (1985) by Blase Bonpane.

6. The youths I interviewed at the Casa Jesuita, who are studying to be Jesuit priests, discussed these and other dangers.

7. By "drenched" here I mean being embedded within a structure completely but with a struggling awareness of being thoroughly within this: what Adrienne Rich (1978) brings forth in her poem "Origins and History of Consciousness."

CHAPTER 4. METHODS

1. The married couple told me that they did not want to be interviewed separately and wanted, instead, to be interviewed at the same time, together. I also conducted a group interview because of time constraints; the six youths (five boys and one girl) were there to apply for a job training program and the individual interviews before them were taking a long time and this was holding them up. Rather than have each one wait for an individual interview or have them all leave, I decided to interview them together. Unfortunately, the text from this group interview differs from the individual interviews in its lack of detail and depth. Therefore, I did not include the six youths in this study. The actual number of youths I spoke with was sixty-two.

2. At one site, several youths thought I was interviewing them for a job placement. I felt terrible when I realized that the interviews had been linked to finding jobs. This occurred both through my not telling the

youths what the interviews were for when they were all sitting at the job training meeting and the director telling them not to leave after the meeting. At this site, I had to additionally say that the interview had no direct relationship with the agency and that the interview would not facilitate or hinder a job placement.

3. In one instance, a youth who had always wanted to be a photographer, but couldn't afford a camera, seemed eager to use the camera equipment I had put down on the table. I asked him if he wanted to take pictures. He said "yes," but that he didn't know how. I put the camera strap over his head, pointed to where the shutter was, showed him the focus ring, and then continued the group interview while he took pictures.

4. See Trinh T. Minh-Ha (1992), *Framer Framed*; Tessa Boffin and Jean Fraser (Eds.). (1991), *Stolen Glances: Lesbians Take Photographs*; Rosa Linda Fregoso (1993), *The Bronze Screen: Chicana and Chicano Film Culture*.

5. From Alberto Sandoval Sánchez, "Una lectura puertorriqueña de la América de West Side Story," *Cupey*, 7 (1, 2) (Jan.–Dec. 1990): 30–31. Used with permission. In this passage Sandoval analyzes the stereotypes made by Hollywood through *West Side Story* by exposing the film as a racist ideological representation. He points to how this movie was made after the immigration of millions of Puerto Ricans to the U.S. in the forties and fifties in search of work in the factories. *West Side Story*, Sandoval argues, is a projection of the racist fears of Anglo-Americans which casts Puerto Ricans in New York as a "threat to the supposed coherent identity, monolithic and absolute of the anglo-american subject" (p. 31).

6. Unfortunately, Sandra Harding does not include the work of "women of color other than black Americans" (p. 14) in her edited collection *Feminism and Methodology* (1987). Harding, in footnote 20 (p. 14), implies that writings by women of color—Latinas, Native Americans, Asian Americans—were dropped. She does not, however, make her criteria regarding women of color clear, aside from stating that black Americans were included. She does say that writing by two men, an anthropologist, and several others were also dropped. As a Latina, I am excluded from feminist methodology in a vague footnote.

CHAPTER 5. THE YOUTHS

1. Gloria Anzaldúa (1990), in *Making Face, Making Soul: Haciendo Caras*, uses this term to describe the purposeful absence of critical aspects of the lives of people of color from theory and research. She understands the process by which white people "blank out" as a form of racism. She understands the process by which people of color "blank

out" as a form of internalized oppression. Anzaldúa argues that to transform racism and internalized oppression whites and people of color need to confront and work through "blank-outness."

2. A front page article, "Trade Pact Threatens Puerto Rico's Economic Rise," L. Rohter, *New York Times*, Sunday, January 3, 1993, pp. 1 and 21) had a chart that accompanied it entitled "Puerto Rico at a Crossroads" that displayed the economic trends of Puerto Rico alongside the United States. It was striking to see how the metaphor of a national crossroads joined with the psychological one facing young people moving into the adult world of work. But as a country, this is by no means the first time Puerto Ricans have been caught between turbulent shifts in political and economic policies. Our history is an ongoing story of crossroads.

3. The following historical composite of Puerto Rico is drawn from a variety of historians and political economists, local newspapers (*El Nuevo Dia, The San Juan Star, El Mundo*), and my own Boricua experiences. The texts used as sources are: *Panorama de la Cultura Puertorriqueña*, M. T. Babin, 1958; *Descubrimiento, Conquista, y Colonización de Puerto Rico*, R. Alegría, 1975; *Breve Enciclopedia de la Cultura Puertorriqueña*, Rosario, Diaz, and Masdeu, 1976; *Factories and Foodstamps: The Puerto Rico Model of Development*, R. Weisskoff, 1985; *Historia General de Puerto Rico*, F. Picó, 1986; *Economic History of Puerto Rico: Institutional Change and Capitalist Development*, J. L. Dietz, 1986.

4. In Cambridge, Massachusetts, near Harvard Square where Concord Avenue and Garden Street split, there is a bronze statue of a soldier which honors the men who gave their lives to defeat the Spanish in the Philippines, Cuba, and Puerto Rico. Passing this every day on my way to school I felt that I was in enemy territory; the statue celebrates our defeat, does not mourn our dead.

5. This is a condensed translation of a story she would tell. Roger Baldwin was the founder of the American Civil Liberties Union.

6. *Cuarto año* means "fourth year" literally and is the way Puerto Ricans refer to having graduated from high school or obtained the GED.

7. G. L. Little and K. D. Robinson, both psychologists who focus on correctional settings, in an article entitled "Moral Reconation Therapy: A Systematic Step-by-Step Treatment System for Treatment of Resistant Clients" published in *Psychological Reports* (1988, 62: 135–151), give the following summary: "Moral Reconation Therapy is a systematic treatment strategy designed to enhance ego, social, moral, and positive behavioral growth in a progressive, step-by-step fashion. It is based upon the assumption that fully functioning, reasonably content, happy persons have a strong sense of identity and that their behavior and relationships are based upon relatively high moral judgment levels. The therapist strives to reeducate clients socially, morally, and behaviorally and instill appro-

priate goals, motivation, and values. Moral Reconation Therapy has slowly evolved in response to the unique needs of particular client populations who are considered resistant to treatment. The therapy is an adaptable and utilitarian treatment system" (p. 135). This article, and several others, were given to me to read by the executive director of CVSPR, Salvador Padilla. In addition to MRT, the two head psychologists of CVSPR, Dr. Isabel Alonso and Dr. Pedro Muñoz Amato, integrate Erikson's stages of development into their work with youths in the program.

8. A *recinto* is similar to a campus of a state university.

9. With the change in government in 1992, many of the administrative directors have been replaced by the new governor with people of his own party. Unfortunately, this is a common occurrence in Puerto Rican politics at all levels of employment within the government: a new party in power leads to massive firings and hirings. This makes for a highly discontinuous experience for the youths within the programs.

10. *Municipio* means district or county, and the *municipio* is often used as a geographical reference point.

11. "We're late!" is what I said. But the saying *"Ay, bendito"* is a typical Puerto Rican phrase that I can't translate except to say that it means something like "I'm sorry."

12. José de Diego was a Puerto Rican educator and *patriota* from Aguadilla.

13. The literal translation is "This is something that is pretty," but in Puerto Rico this saying means "This is something that is good."

14. These are suburban developments of identical cement houses constructed for working- and low-middle-class families.

15. Reprinted with permission, National Catholic Reporter, P.O. Box 419281, Kansas City, MO 64141.

CHAPTER 6. BECOMING *HOMBRES* AND *MUJERES*: WORK, LOVE, AND CONSTRUCTIONS OF GENDER

1. See, for example, J. Dietz, *Economic History of Puerto Rico: Institutional Change and Capitalist Development*, 1986, and R. Weisskoff, *Factories and Foodstamps: The Puerto Rico Model of Development*, 1985.

2. The word *afuera* literally means "outside." In Puerto Rico, *afuera* is colloquially used to describe the United States. When Puerto Ricans on the island say *afuera* it means somewhere in the United States. This expression is symbolic of the complex relationship between the two countries and how Puerto Ricans experience it: the United States as a distinctly different place but in direct relation, somehow bound, to the island.

3. *"Chacho"* is a shortening of *"muchacho,"* which is a common expression that means something like saying the phrase "That's right" but carries with it a tone of struggle, difficulty, strife.

4. *"Chévere"* is a colloquial expression which means that something is good.

5. Being called *rubia* is in contrast to another term used to describe skin color, *trigüeña,* which means dark skinned. But *rubia* is not to be confused with *blanquita/o* (little whites), which has negative class connotations and is a word that is mostly used for wealthy light-skinned Puerto Ricans. But *trigüenos/as* who are wealthy can be called *blanquitos/as* since the term connotes class privilege as well as skin color. All of this illustrates the importance of color and its relation to socioeconomic class.

CHAPTER 7. GETTING OUT OF TROUBLE OR GETTING WHAT YOU WANT: WORK AS INDEPENDENCE AND SURVIVAL FOR YOUNG *MUJERES*

1. The narratives included in this chapter illustrate traumatic events at home and at work, yet these were not the only youths who expressed having lived through violence and abuse. This chapter, therefore, is interconnected with the other narratives, especially with psychological and social processes noted in the previous chapter on the construction of gender. For more on how negotiating gender can be traumatic for girls' development, see, for example, Lyn Mikel Brown and Carol Gilligan (1992), *Meeting at the Crossroads: Women's Psychology and Girls' Development.*

2. See also Susan Griffin (1993), *A Chorus of Stones: The Private Life of War.*

CHAPTER 9. FROM ILLNESS AND SUICIDE TO THE WORK OF ART

1. The lines from "The Desert as Garden of Paradise" are reprinted from TIME'S POWER, Poems 1985–1988, by Adrienne Rich, by permission of the author and W. W. Norton & Company, Inc. Copyright © 1989 by Adrienne Rich.

CHAPTER 10. IN UNIFORM: *SEGURIDAD* AS SYMBOL AND WORK

1. *"Me encanta"* is a common expression that means one really likes and enjoys something, is delighted.

CHAPTER 11. PEACE, JUSTICE, DEVELOPMENT: THE COMPLEX WORKINGS OF SOCIAL CHANGE

1. Mel King teaches a seminar called "Peace, Justice, and Development," which I participated in at MIT. I want to acknowledge that the title of this chapter is borrowed from that seminar.

CHAPTER 12. WORKING TOGETHER: PLOTTING THE COORDINATES OF WORK, LOVE, AND IDENTITY

1. In *Childhood and Society*, Erikson ([1950], 1963) writes of his illustration of his developmental model: "An epigenetic diagram thus lists a system of stages dependent on each other; and while individual stages may have been explored more or less thoroughly or named more or less fittingly, the diagram suggests that their study be pursued always with the total configuration of stages in mind. The diagram invites, then, a thinking through of all its empty boxes . . . All this should make it clear that a chart of epigenesis suggests a global form of thinking and rethinking which leaves details of methodology and terminology to further study" (pp. 272–273).

BIBLIOGRAPHY

Agosín, M., with photographs by D'Amico, A., and Sanguinetti, A. *Circles of madness: Mothers of the Plaza de Mayo*. 1992. Fredonia, NY: White Pine Press.

Albert, M., Cagan, L., Chomsky, N., Hahnel, R., King, M., Sargent, L., Sklar, H. *Liberating theory*. 1986. Boston: South End Press.

Alegría, R. E. *Descubrimiento, conquista y colonización de Puerto Rico 1493–1599*. 1975. San Juan, PR: Coleccion de Estudios Puertorriqueños.

Anzaldúa, G. *Borderlands/La frontera*. 1987. San Francisco: Spinsters/Aunt Lute.

——— (Ed.). *Making face, making soul: Haciendo caras—Creative and critical perspectives by women of color*. 1990. San Francisco: Spinsters/Aunt Lute.

Babín, M. T. *Panorama de la cultura Puertorriqueña*. 1958. New York: Las Americas Publishing Co.

Berger, J., and Mohr, J. *Another way of telling*. 1982. New York: Pantheon Books.

———. *Ways of seeing*. 1981. London: British Broadcasting Corp. and Penguin Books.

Boffin, T., and Fraser, J. (Eds.). *Stolen glances: Lesbians take photographs*. 1991. London: Pandora.

Bonpane, B. *Guerrillas of peace: Liberation theology and the Central American revolution*. 1985. Boston: South End Press.

Braden, S. *Committing photography*. 1983. London: Pluto Press.

Brown, L. M., and Gilligan, C. *Meeting at the crossroads: Women's psychology and girls' development*. 1992. Cambridge, MA: Harvard University Press.

Casaldáliga, P. *Prophets in combat: The Nicaraguan Journal*. 1987. Oak Park, IL: Meyer Stone Books.

Cervantes, L.D. *Emplumada*. 1981. Pittsburgh: University of Pittsburgh Press.

Chrystos. *Not Vanishing*. 1988. Vancouver: Press Gang Publishers.

Delano, J. *Puerto Rico mio: Four decades of change/Cuatro decadas de cambio*. 1990. Washington, DC: Smithsonian Institution Press.

Del Rosario, R., Melon de Diaz, E., and Martinez Masdeu, E. *Breve enciclopedia de la cultura puertorriqueña.* 1976. Hato Rey, PR: Editorial Cordillera, Inc.

Dietz, J. L. *Economic history of Puerto Rico: Institutional change and capitalist development.* 1986. Princeton: Princeton University Press.

Dostoyevsky, F. *The brothers Karamazov.* (1958). 1988. London: Penguin Books.

Easter, E., Cheers, D. M., and Brooks, D. M. (Eds.). *Songs of my people: A self-portrait.* 1992. Boston: Little, Brown.

Erikson, E. *Childhood and society.* (1950). 1963. New York: W. W. Norton.

———. *Insight and responsibility.* 1964. New York: W. W. Norton.

———. *Identity, youth and crisis.* 1968. New York: W. W. Norton.

———. *Life history and the historical moment.* 1975. New York: W. W. Norton.

———. "The problem of ego identity." 1959. In *Psychological Issues* 1 (1): 101–164.

———. *Young man Luther.* (1958). 1962. New York: W. W. Norton.

Fregoso, R. L. *The bronze screen: Chicana and Chicano film culture.* 1993. Minneapolis: University of Minnesota Press.

Freire, P. *Education for critical consciousness.* 1973. New York: The Seabury Press.

———. *Pedagogy of the city.* 1993. Translated by Donaldo Macedo. New York: Continuum.

———. *Pedagogy of the oppressed.* 1970. New York: The Seabury Press.

———. *The politics of education: Culture, power, and liberation.* 1985. Hadley, MA: Bergin and Garvey.

Freud, S. *New introductory lectures on psycho-analysis.* (1933). Vol. XXII, p. 59. In *The standard edition of the psychological works of Sigmund Freud.* London: The Hogarth Press.

Geertz, C. *Local knowledge: Further essays in interpretive anthropology.* 1983. New York: Basic Books.

Gilligan, C. "Clinical interviewing as a method of inquiry." 1987. Harvard Graduate School of Education, course notes.

———. *In a different voice.* 1982. Cambridge, MA: Harvard University Press.

Goldberg, N. *Wild mind: Living the writer's life.* 1990. New York: Bantam Books.

Graham, J. *Hybrids of plants and of ghosts.* 1980. Princeton: Princeton University Press.

Greene, M. *The dialectic of freedom.* 1988. New York: Teachers College Press.

Griffin, S. *A chorus of stones: The private life of war.* 1993. New York: Anchor Books Doubleday.

Gutiérrez, G. *Teologia de la liberación: Perspectivas verdad e imagen.* 1987. Salamanca, Spain: Ediciones Sigueme.

———. *We drink from our own wells: The spiritual journey of a people.*1985. New York: Orbis Books.

Hall, S. "Ethnicity: Identity and difference." 1991. In *Radical America* 23 (4): 9–20.

Harding, S. (Ed.). *Feminism and methodology.* 1987. Bloomington: Indiana University Press.

Harjo, J. *In mad love and war.* 1990. Hanover, NH: Wesleyan University Press.

Heider, K. G. *Ethnographic film.* 1976. Austin: University of Texas Press.

Herman, J. L. *Trauma and recovery: The aftermath of violence—from domestic abuse to political terror.* 1992. New York: Basic Books.

Heyward, I. C. *The redemption of God: A theology of mutual relation.* 1982. Lanham, MD: University Press of America.

———. *When boundaries betray us: Beyond illusions of what is ethical in therapy and life.* 1993. New York: HarperCollins/HarperSanFrancisco.

hooks, b. *Yearning: Race, gender, and cultural politics.* 1990. Boston: South End Press.

King, M. *Chain of change: Struggles for black community development.* 1981. Boston: South End Press.

Klepfisz, I. *Keeper of accounts.* 1982. Watertown, MA: Persephone Press.

Lanker, B., *I dream a world: Portraits of black women who changed America.* 1989. New York: Steward, Tabori, & Chang.

Levertov, D. *Breathing the water.* 1984. New York: New Directions Books.

———. *The freeing of the dust.* 1975. New York: New Directions Book.

Levins Morales, A. ". . . And even Fidel can't change that!" 1981. In *This bridge called my back: Writing by radical women of color.* Moraga, C. and Anzaldúa, G. (Eds.). Watertown, MA: Persephone Press, Inc.

Lightfoot, S. L. *The good high school: Portraits of character and culture.* 1983. New York: Basic Books.

———. *Journey of a healer.* 1988. Reading, MA: Addison-Wesley.

———. *Worlds apart.* 1978. New York: Basic Books.

Lorde, A. *Sister outsider.* 1984. Trumansburg, NY: The Crossing Press.

Maclean, N. *Young men and fire.* 1992. Chicago: The University of Chicago Press.

Mapplethorpe, R. *The perfect moment.* 1990. Philadelphia: Institute of Contemporary Art, University of Pennsylvania.

Mishler, E. G. "Meaning in context: Is there any other kind?" 1979. In *Harvard Educational Review* 49 (1): 1–19.

———. *Research interviewing: Context and narrative*. 1986. Cambridge, MA: Harvard University Press.

———. "Validation in inquiry-guided research: The role of exemplars in narrative studies." 1990. In *Harvard Educational Review* 60 (4): 415–442. November 1990.

Moraga, C., and Anzaldúa, G. (Eds.). *This bridge called my back: Writings by radical women of color*. 1982. Watertown, MA: Persephone Press.

Morrison, T. *Beloved*. 1987. New York: Plume Books, New American Library.

———. *Playing in the dark: Whiteness and the literary imagination*. 1992. Cambridge, MA: Harvard University Press.

Oliver, M. *Dream work*. 1986. New York: Atlantic Monthly Press.

Ortiz Cofer, J. *The Latin deli: Prose & poetry*. 1993. Athens, GA: The University of Georgia Press.

———. *Silent dancing: A partial remembrance of a Puerto Rican childhood*. 1990. Houston, TX: Arte Público Press.

Osuña, J. J. *A history of education in Puerto Rico*. (1923). 1949. Rio Piedras, PR: Editorial De La Universidad De Puerto Rico.

Parks, G. "Introduction." 1992. In *Songs of my people African-Americans: A self-portrait*. Easter, E., Cheers, M. D., and Brooks D. M. (Eds.). Boston: Little, Brown.

Picó, F. *Historia general de Puerto Rico*. 1986. Puerto Rico: Ediciones Huracan, Inc.

———. *Vivir en Caimito*. 1989. Puerto Rico: Ediciones Huracan, Inc.

Rich, A. *The dream of a common language: Poems 1974–1977*. 1978. New York: W. W. Norton.

———. *Time's power*. 1989. New York: W. W. Norton.

———. *What is found there: Notebooks on poetry and politics*. 1993. New York: W. W. Norton.

Sandoval Sánchez, A. "Una lectura Puertorriqueña de la América de *West Side Story*." 1990. In *Cupey* 8 (1, 2).

———. *Nueva York tras bastidores/New York backstage*. 1993. Santiago, Chile: Editorial Cuarto Proprio.

Shahn, B. *The shape of content*. (1957). 1980. Cambridge, MA: Harvard University Press.

Silko, L. M. "Narratives of survival: Linda Niemann interviews Leslie Marmon Silko." 1992. In *The Women's Review of Books* 9 (10, 11): 10.

Trinh, T. Minh-Ha. *Framer framed*. 1992. New York: Routledge.

Walker, A. "Duties of the black revolutionary artist." 1983. In *In search of our mother's garden*. New York: Harcourt, Brace, Janovich.

————. "How long shall they torture our mothers? The trials of Winnie Mandela." 1991. In *Ms.* 1 (6): 22–25.

Weisskoff, R. *Factories and foodstamps: The Puerto Rico model of development.* 1985. Baltimore: The Johns Hopkins University Press.

Welch, S. D. *Communities of resistance and solidarity: A feminist theology of liberation.* 1985. Maryknoll, NY: Orbis Books.

INDEX